Julia Mergner
Translating Student Diversity Within the
German Higher Education System

Julia Mergner

Translating Student Diversity Within the German Higher Education System

How Universities Respond to the
Political Discourse on Widening Participation

Budrich Academic Press
Opladen • Berlin • Toronto 2025

The dissertation was written as part of the junior research StuFHe at the University of Hamburg, which was funded within the BMBF funding program "Accompanying Research Regarding the Teaching Quality Pact" from 2014-2018 (FKZ: 01PB14005).

I would like to thank the Society for Higher Education Research (GfHf), which generously supported the publication with a printing subsidy thanks to the Ulrich Teichler Prize.

All rights reserved. No part of this publication may be reproduced, stored in or introduced into a retrieval system, or transmitted, in any form, or by any means (electronic, mechanical, photocopying, recording or otherwise) without the prior written permission of Verlag Barbara Budrich. Any person who does any unauthorized act in relation to this publication may be liable to criminal prosecution and civil claims for damages.

You must not circulate this book in any other binding or cover and you must impose this same condition on any acquirer.

A CIP catalogue record for this book is available from
Die Deutsche Nationalbibliothek (The German National Library):
https://portal.dnb.de.

© 2025 by Budrich Academic Press GmbH, Opladen, Berlin & Toronto
www.budrich.eu

    ISBN   978-3-96665-089-2 (Paperback)
    eISBN 978-3-96665-909-3 (PDF)
    DOI   10.3224/96665089

Budrich Academic Press
Stauffenbergstr. 7. D-51379 Leverkusen Opladen, Germany
www.budrich-academic-press.de

86 Delma Drive. Toronto, ON M8W 4P6 Canada
www.budrich.eu

Cover design by Bettina Lehfeldt, Kleinmachnow – www.lehfeldtgraphic.de

Acknowledgments

This work would not have been possible without the help of so many people. My sincere gratitude goes to my research team StuFHe and particularly Dr. Elke Bosse from whom I have learned so much during the four years of working together. Her encouragement, guidance and motivation were so important in the process of thesis writing. I also wish to thank Prof. Dr. Miriam Barnat who pushed me into the direction of Scandinavian Institutionalism when I was lost in theories. My warmest thanks go to Vanessa Jänsch for being a perfect PhD (and mother) role model and office mate.

Moreover, I would like to extend my high appreciation to my supervisor Prof. Dr. Liudvika Leisyte who guided me through the whole process in the most structured way and tried to get me back on the right track when I got lost in details. She taught me the high standards of qualitative research and I am very thankful for her critique. I also wish to thank the members of my PhD committee, Prof. Dr. Uwe Wilkesmann and Prof. Dr. Bernhard Kreße, for generously offering their time and guidance throughout the preparation and review of the thesis. Special thanks also go to my PhD family at the *Zentrum für Hochschulbildung* at the University of Dortmund: Anna-Lena, Sude, and Benjamin: it was great having you all by my side over the years.

For the final stage, I received valuable assistance from Nina Jürgens who did not only proofread this thesis but who was also a great sparring partner to discuss my findings, thank you so much for your work.

In general, my special thanks are extended to the partner universities and the people who helped me with my data collection and were willing to participate in interviews and group discussions.

I dedicate this thesis to

> my wonderful parents who paved the way to let me experience something they never had the chance to,
> my patient husband Gregor who always did his best to support me during this exhausting ride
> and my lovely daughter Leni who pushed this thesis to come to an end.

Table of Contents

1	**Frame of Study**	13
1.1	Motivation	13
1.2	Problem Statement	15
1.3	Research Questions and Study Objectives	17
1.4	Approach	21
1.5	Structure of the Thesis	22
2	**Widening Participation in the Context of German Higher Education**	23
2.1	Definitions of Student Diversity, Heterogeneity and Widening Participation	24
2.2	Student Diversity in the German Higher Education Context	26
2.2.1	Access Routes to Higher Education	28
2.2.2	Socio-Demographic Characteristics	30
2.2.3	Living Situations	32
2.2.4	Individual Competences	33
2.3	The German Widening Participation Agenda: Policies to Deal with Student Diversity	35
2.3.1	Legal Framework for Widening Participation and Central Political Stakeholders	36
2.3.2	Policy Programs and Initiatives Aimed at Student Diversity	40
2.4	The German Widening Participation Agenda: Discourses on Widening Participation	44
2.4.1	Prior Research on Political Discourses on Widening Participation in Higher Education	45
2.4.2	Analysis of the German Political Discourse on Widening Participation	48
2.5	Summary	52
3	**Theoretical Framework and Literature Review**	55
3.1	Ontological and Epistemological Assumptions	55
3.2	Universities as a 'Special' Form of Organization	58
3.2.1	The 'Special' Structure(s) of Universities	59
3.2.2	The 'Special' Culture(s) of Universities	61

3.3	Explaining Universities' Responses: Choosing an Institutional Perspective	65
3.4	Scandinavian Institutionalism	70
3.4.1	Translation and the Travel of Ideas	71
3.4.2	Editing Rules and the Role of Agency	73
3.4.3	Loose Coupling and Decoupling	75
3.4.4	Scandinavian Institutionalism in Higher Education Research	76
3.5	Research on Organizational Responses of Universities to Widening Participation	78
3.5.1	Organizational Responses to Widening Participation: The Strategy Level	79
3.5.2	Organizational Responses to Widening Participation: The Structure Level	81
3.5.3	Organizational Responses to Widening Participation: The Action Level	87
3.6	Explaining Local Variations in Organizational Responses to Student Diversity	91
3.6.1	Institutional Characteristics of (German) Universities	91
3.6.2	Diversity Paradigms and Ways of Dealing with Student Diversity	94
3.7	Conceptualization of the Idea of Student Diversity	101
3.8	Summary	104
4	**Research Design and Methodology**	**107**
4.1	Research Design	108
4.2	Case Study Design	109
4.3	Selection of Cases	111
4.4	Operationalization	112
4.5	Methods of Data Collection	113
4.6	Data Analysis	118
4.7	Quality Criteria in Interpretive Qualitative Research	125
4.7.1	Inter-Subject Comprehensibility	126
4.7.2	Triangulation	128
4.7.3	Reflection on the Role of the Researcher	129
4.8	Summary	131
5	**Case studies**	**133**
5.1	Case 1: The University of Hamburg	133

5.1.1	Student profile	133
5.1.2	QPL Initiative	137
5.1.3	Summary	139
5.2	Case 2: The University of Kassel	142
5.2.1	Student profile	142
5.2.2	QPL Initiative	146
5.2.3	Summary	148
5.3	Case 3: The HAW Hamburg	149
5.3.1	Student profile	150
5.3.2	QPL Initiative	153
5.3.3	Summary	155
6	**Cross-case Findings: Organizational Responses of German Universities to Student Diversity**	**159**
6.1	Editing Rules	160
6.1.1	Editing Rules of Context	160
6.1.2	Editing Rules of Formulation	164
6.1.3	Editing Rules of Logic	169
6.1.4	Summary	171
6.2	Retelling the Narrative of Student Diversity — The Importance of the Local Context	172
6.2.1	University of Hamburg	174
6.2.2	University of Kassel	179
6.2.3	HAW Hamburg	184
6.2.4	Summary	188
6.3	Definitions and Organizational Practices to Deal with Student Diversity	189
6.3.1	Prior Knowledge: Deficit Compensation	190
6.3.2	Individual Learner Personality: Learning Community	193
6.3.3	Special Target Groups: Starting Aid	195
6.3.4	Learner, Writer and Student Types: Practice Space	197
6.3.5	Individual Problems and Needs: Individual Assistance	201
6.3.6	Mismatch Between Student and Study Program: Orientation and Guidance	204
6.3.7	Performance of Students: Alternative Paths of Studying and Learning	205

6.3.8	Summary	209
7	**Conclusion and Discussion**	**215**
7.1	Answers to Research Questions	215
7.2	Main Contribution of the Study	226
7.3	Limitations	228
7.4	Avenues for Future Research	231
7.5	Implications for Policy and Practice	235

For further information, see the online appendix:
https://doi.org/10.3224/96665089A

List of Tables

Table 3.1	Diversity Paradigms in the Context of Higher Education	100
Table 5.1	Student Profile at the University of Hamburg	135
Table 5.2	Student Profile at the University of Kassel	144
Table 5.3	Student Profile of the HAW Hamburg	151
Table 6.1	Summarized Findings: Editing Rules Identified at the Three Levels of Strategy, Structure and Action	171
Table 6.2	Summarized Findings: Definitions of Student Diversity and Organizational Practices	212

List of Figures

Figure 2.1	Summarized Findings: Analysis of the German Political Discourse on Widening Participation	52
Figure 3.1	Theoretical Framework for Analyzing the Travel of the Idea of Student Diversity	103
Figure 4.1	Categorical System for the Analysis of Organizational Responses to Student Diversity	122
Figure 4.2	The Coding Paradigm According to Corbin/Strauss (1990)	124
Figure 5.1	Structure of the QPL Initiative at the University of Hamburg (First Round)	138
Figure 5.2	Structure of the QPL Initiative at the University of Hamburg (Second Round)	139
Figure 5.3	Structure of the QPL Initiative at the University of Kassel (First and Second Round)	147
Figure 5.4	Structure of the QPL Initiative at the HAW Hamburg (First Round)	154
Figure 5.5	Structure of the QPL Initiative at the HAW Hamburg (First Round)	154
Figure 6.1	The Story of Student Diversity in the Context of the QPL Initiative at the University of Hamburg	179
Figure 6.2	The Story of Student Diversity in the Context of the QPL Initiative at the University of Kassel	184
Figure 6.3	The Story of Student Diversity in the Context of the QPL Initiative at the HAW Hamburg	188

List of Abbreviations

ASD	Arbeitsstelle Studium und Didaktik an der HAW Hamburg (Office for Degree Courses and Teaching at the HAW Hamburg)
BAföG	Bundesausbildungsförderungsgesetz (Germany's Federal Training Assistance Act for students)
BMBF	Bundesministerium für Bildung und Forschung (Federal Ministry for Education and Research)
DFG	Deutsche Forschungsgemeinschaft (German Research Foundation)
EQA	Betriebseinheit für Evaluation, Qualitätsmanagement und Akkreditierung der HAW Hamburg (Evaluation, Quality Management and Accreditation Unit at the HAW Hamburg)
FTE	Full-time equivalent employment
FYE	First-year experience
GT	Grounded Theory
HAW	Hochschule für angewandte Wissenschaften (university of applied sciences)
HRK	Hochschulrektorenkonferenz (German Rectors' Conference)
IELTS	International English Language Testing System
KMK	Kultusministerkonferenz (Standing Conference of the Ministers of Education and Cultural Affairs)
MBA	Master of Business Administration
MIN	Mathematik, Informatik und Naturwissenschaften (Mathematics, Informatics and Natural Sciences)
OSA	Online self-assessment
QPL	Qualitätspakt Lehre (Teaching Quality Pact)
PDCA	Plan, do, check and act
STEM	Science, Technology, Engineering and Mathematics
StuFHe	'Studierfähigkeit – institutionelle Förderung und studienrelevante Heterogenität', Nachwuchsgruppe im BMBF-Förderschwerpunkt 'Hochschulforschung/Begleitforschung zum Qualitätspakt Lehre' ('Academic Competence – the Role of Institutional Support and Student Diversity', junior research group within the funding program 'Accompanying Research Regarding the Teaching Quality Pact')

1 Frame of Study

1.1 Motivation

The inspiration for researching how German universities deal with student diversity was inspired by several personal and pragmatic reasons. During my studies, I became interested in the inequalities with respect to the access to and participation in education. At the University of Twente (Enschede, NL), I completed the minor program 'Education in Developing Countries' which would subsequently inspire my career substantially and fundamentally. Not only did I then decide to change my study subject after graduating with a Bachelor of Science in Psychology to study Public Administration with a focus on higher education. It also provided the starting point for my sustained involvement in higher education research.

When I started to work at the German Centre for Higher Education Research and Science Studies in Hanover, I was involved in a research project that investigated the introduction of flexible study formats at German universities to meet the demands of an increasingly diverse student population. What interested me in this research project was the observation that universities had fundamentally different understandings of student diversity. Some universities emphasized the diverse levels of the prior mathematical knowledge of students entering higher education, thus introducing extended introductory phases of study and arguing that students could use these longer time periods to fill gaps in their knowledge. Others focused on the diverse interests and motivations that students brought with them and which could not be satisfied within the strict and predefined study plans of Bachelor's and Master's study programs. Therefore, they developed free time slots for students to be filled with lectures or activities they were interested in. Interestingly enough, definitions of heterogeneity or diversity seemed to somehow correspond to certain structural or cultural characteristics of the universities, depending on their profile, history, size or student composition. However, this observation seemed to contradict the assumptions of organizational theories that I had studied during my Master's. Those commonly describe universities as 'organized anarchies' (Cohen/March/Olsen 1972) or 'loosely coupled systems' (Weick 1976), their core activities characterized by unclear objectives, goal ambiguities and inconsistent preferences. When confronted with external demands, they only adopt these as 'rational myths' (Meyer/Rowan 1977) in order to preserve legitimacy and, thereby, secure their survival, while their organizational practice remains unaffected. But what I observed was that there was a clear and well-fitting agenda with a common understanding that resulted in actual measures! That was when I decided to spend more time on this topic and turn it into a PhD thesis. Luckily, I received the opportunity to work in the junior research group called *Studierfähigkeit – institutionelle Förderung und studienrelevante Heterogenität* (academic abilities, institutional support and student diversity, in the following abbreviated as StuFHe)[1] at the University of Hamburg under the leadership of Dr. Elke Bosse. As a research project accompanying the *Qualitätspakt Lehre* (Teaching Quality Pact, in the following abbreviated as QPL[2]), StuFHe[3] was concerned with the individual and institutional conditions allowing a successful completion of studies. Special attention was given to the institutional offers of support that had been developed at the participating universities in the context of the QPL initiative. This focus was particularly exciting for my research interest because it allowed me to look at specific universities and their responses to the demands of dealing with student diversity within their traditional structures of teaching and studying. Within the research project, I worked very closely with the partner universities: I organized regular cooperative workshops and visited the partner universities to hold workshops where I presented and discussed our findings in cooperation with different organizational actors. This allowed me to get a very detailed and comprehensive picture of the situation and processes at the universities over a period of four years.

I hope this study makes an interesting contribution to a more complex understanding of German universities and their responses to the external demand of student diversity. With this thesis, I want to emphasize how important a closer look at the organizational level is in order to understand how universities differ considerably in the ways they approach the topic of student diversity and the extent to which they make it relevant for themselves.

---

[1] In order to ensure readability, German titles of programs, government institutions, university units etc. appear in abbreviated form throughout the text except for where they appear first. There, full titles or names in German are followed by the English translation and the German abbreviation in parentheses. A list of abbreviations used in this work is to be found on page 12.

[2] The QPL funding program was a support program funded by the BMBF which aimed to improve the framework conditions for studying and teaching at German universities. The funding program ran from 2010 to 2020. More detailed information about the QPL funding program will be provided in Chapter 2.3.2.. For further information on the QPL funding program, see BMBF (2020b).

[3] The junior research group StuFHe at the University of Hamburg was funded within the BMBF funding program 'Accompanying Research Regarding the Teaching Quality Pact' from 2014-2018. For further information on the junior research group, see Bosse et al. (2019). For further information on the accompanying research funded by the BMBF, see BMBF (2020a).

1.2 Problem Statement

The change from an elite to a mass system of higher education has resulted in a quantitative expansion of participation rates. This, however, does not necessarily entail wider access for groups that have traditionally been underrepresented in HE systems (Osborne 2003a; Schuetze/Slowey 2002). According to the European policy agenda, widening access to and allowing for participation in those systems while also making them more representative of national populations is a clearly stated political goal (Orr/Hovdhaugen 2014). The same is true for Germany and its widening participation agenda. Here, the German government has initiated a number of soft regulation policy instruments incentivizing universities[4] to "become more accessible for all population and age groups and develop strategies to improve the individual study success since the student body has become much more diverse" (Wissenschaftsrat 2013: 9). This quote shows how political discourse urges universities to respond to student diversity. Germany is an interesting example in this policy area: on the one hand, it provides free higher education, yet on the other hand, it still faces serious issues with regard to reducing dropout rates and providing equal access (Mergner/Leisyte/Bosse 2018). So far only a small number of studies have investigated the role of 'softer' forms of steering instruments that aim at stimulating organizational change and development within a particular area of interest, like the widening participation agenda (Eurydice 2011; Osborne 2003a). Here, soft regulation instruments provide an opportunity to gain valuable insights into the way universities legitimize their practices (Boch Waldorff 2013).

However, there is no clear or consistent definition for the concept of widening participation. The German political discourse calls on varying notions of student diversity without concretizing the kind of rationales, purposes and target groups it comprises. At the same time, the concept of widening participation is used in a normative way to transport value-laden expectations about the role of 'good' universities in general and, more specifically, about how universities should respond to student diversity (Pasternack/Kehm 2000).

In addition to the varying meanings given to the notion of widening participation, research findings on German universities' responses to the political demand to deal with student diversity as well as the way these can be explained theoretically show inconsistencies. According to neo-institutional theory, it is expected that universities comply with this demand at least on a

---

[4] The present study uses the term 'university' as referring to institutions of higher education that have the right to award academic degrees in several academic disciplines. Where this study refers to the term 'university' in the German context it includes universities and universities of applied sciences.

rhetorical level to secure their legitimacy. This is based on the neo-institutional assumption that organizations incorporate widespread social expectations about what is deemed 'rational', which provides survival benefits to the organization (Meyer/Rowan 1977; Scott 2004). In this context, scholars argue that universities are more vulnerable to institutional pressures due to their special characteristics, described as 'organized anarchies' (Cohen/March/Olsen 1972), 'professional bureaucracies' (Mintzberg 1979) or 'loosely coupled systems' (Weick 1976). As research suggests, this vulnerability increases the probability of decoupling (Brunsson 1986) or universities' resistance to change (Kezar 2014; Kezar/Eckel 2002; Manning 2013; Pasternack/Kehm 2000). Indeed, literature within the German higher education context suggests that German universities meet these demands on a plain rhetorical basis to fulfill the normatively appropriate behavior while the organizational practice remains unaffected (Hanft 2015; Kehm 2000). Other studies claim that universities tackle this problem by developing multiple measures without a coherent underlying strategy. These measures are often criticized for their haphazardness instead of following a more holistic approach that promises to bring a new consciousness into the university about how to deal with student diversity (Leicht-Scholten 2011).

Contrary to these findings and theoretical assumptions, a closer look at the organizational level reveals that German universities differ considerably in the way they approach the call for dealing with student diversity and the extent to which they turn it into a relevant topic for their own agenda (Hanft 2012; Kehm 2012). This study argues that it requires richer, qualitative approaches that can cope with the institutional complexity of universities and develop an in-depth understanding of their dynamics at the organizational level. Additional research could help find answers to questions such as what happens with the political impetus at an organizational level, its interpretation and translation in the organizational context and how variations can be explained. This study introduces Scandinavian institutionalism (Czarniawska/Joerges 1996) as an interesting complementary theoretical lens because it helps to understand how institutional pressures lead to local variations. More concretely, this strand of theory is concerned with the question of how institutional pressures are interpreted by organizations and how these interpretations affect everyday organizational practices (Boxenbaum/Strandgaard Pedersen 2009). One of the most prominent concepts from Scandinavian institutionalism is that of translation or the travel of ideas (Czarniawska/Joerges 1996), which acknowledges that an idea or practice undergoes modifications when it is implemented in a new local context. Such a perspective is particularly suitable for studying the phenomenon at hand (i.e., student diversity) at both the macro-level of the political discourse and the organizational level of organizational responses. The study regards Scandinavian institutionalism and the concept of translation (ibid.) as useful accounts for the complexity of universities in their treatment of student diversity which, despite their explanatory power, have received to date little attention in the field of German higher education research.

1.3 Research Questions and Study Objectives

Deriving from the problem statement, the major research question of the study is:

How do German universities respond to student diversity in the context of the widening participation policy agenda? How can variations in the organizational responses of German universities be explained?

In order to address the overall research problem, four sub-questions will guide the research and data analysis. As a first step, this study seeks to put the implications of student diversity in concrete terms to analyze organizational responses to student diversity. It pays close attention to how student diversity is conceptualized in the German political discourse since the state represents the most significant stakeholder for German public universities (Hüther/Krücken 2018). Particularly the identification of the political discourse underlying the widening participation agenda plays a crucial role in this context (Archer 2007; Boch Waldorff 2013) as it transports certain perspectives on student diversity and how universities should respond to this demand. The German widening participation agenda is characterized by its extensive use of soft steering instruments like funding programs that support widening projects at universities financially, while these projects leave the universities considerable room for interpretation concerning definitions of student diversity and derived actions (Hanft/Zawacki-Richter/Gierke 2015; Mooraj/Wiese 2013; Buß/Erbsland/Rahn 2018). Central political stakeholders construct the political discourse by producing texts that determine appropriate ways of talking about the topic of student diversity (Fairclough 1993; Phillips/Lawrence/Hardy 2004). Thus, these produced texts, like statements, reforms and program initiatives, give a shape to perspectives on student diversity, while they simultaneously legitimize certain organizational practices over others (Boch Waldorff 2013). Consequently, an analysis of the political discourse that underlies the German widening participation policy agenda serves as a frame of reference for the analysis of organizational responses, i.e., how German universities interpret the demand of student diversity. Therefore, the first sub-question is:

Research Question 1:

What perspectives on student diversity can be identified in the political discourse on widening participation?

According to a translation perspective, the present study conceptualizes student diversity "as a story of ideas turning into actions in ever new localities" (Czarniawska/Joerges 1996: 13). In other words, the idea of student diversity travels around on the macro-level of the (academic) organizations' environment and is manifested within the national political discourse on widening participation. To investigate how the idea of student diversity is translated from the macro-level of the political discourse on the organizational level within German universities, the present study chooses a concrete example for the political demand to deal with student diversity in the context of soft steering instruments. Consequently, this research investigates organizational responses in the context of the QPL funding program[5], as one of the funding programs within the German widening participation agenda. This nation-wide funding program funded by the *Bundesministerium für Bildung und Forschung* (Federal Ministry of Education and Research, in the following abbreviated as BMBF) is one of the most extensive programs in terms of financing and outreach. This program aims to contribute to a more general improvement of the quality of teaching and learning, while simultaneously supporting initiatives that focus on first-year study programs to "acknowledge the heterogeneous student composition" (BMBF 2010: 2). The comparatively open character of the funding program's guidelines provides universities with a high degree of autonomy in choosing to what extent they link their QPL initiatives[6] to the topic of student diversity.

The concept of translation helps here to understand how an abstract idea from a broad national context like student diversity travels around in the field of (academic) organizations and is adopted in a local context, whereas "involved actors infuse the idea with meanings so it makes sense in the local context" (Boch Waldorff 2013: 284). In this context, the present study investigates how German universities translate the idea of student diversity within their QPL initiatives, resulting in the following second sub-question:

---

[5] The study refers to the term 'QPL funding program' when references are made to the overall funding program that was initiated and funded by the BMBF.
[6] The study refers to the term 'QPL initiative' when references are made to the general QPL initiatives that were developed by the participating universities and funded within the overall BMBF funding program. In most cases, universities' QPL initiatives subsume a varying number of single projects. The study refers to these single projects with the term 'single QPL projects'.

Research Question 2:

How do German universities respond to student diversity in the context of the QPL initiative?

In line with Scandinavian institutionalism, the present study assumes that ideas and practices undergo changes every time they are applied in a new local setting (Czarniawska/Joerges 1996; Sahlin-Andersson 1996). Thus, during the travel, the idea of student diversity is subject to modifications which result in local variations of the idea (Wæraas/Sataøen 2014). The present study builds on research findings that indicate how these variations are the result of edited narratives in which ideas tend to be framed in a way that is familiar and commonly accepted in the specific local context (Sahlin-Andersson 1996; Sahlin/Wedlin 2017). The process of translation might not always be conscious and strategic, it is rather steered by institutional beliefs and norms that derive from the local context (Boxenbaum/Jonsson 2008). According to previous studies, structural and cultural characteristics of the university provide the background for how actors tell and retell narratives about the idea of student diversity (Kirkpatrick et al. 2013). Besides such institutional characteristics, studies from the field of diversity management suggest that local variations can also be influenced by dominant diversity paradigms (Gaisch/Aichinger/Preymann 2017) apparent at the respective university. These diversity paradigms impact the definition of student diversity at those universities and their perception of which organizational responses are deemed appropriate. The present study aims to identify the aspects that have influenced the translation of the idea of student diversity in the context of the QPL initiative and, thus, have led to variations in organizational responses to student diversity in the local context of German universities. Consequently, the third sub-question is:

Research Question 3:

How can variations in organizational responses to student diversity be explained?

From an institutional perspective, universities are suspected to use window dressing strategies in order to deal with institutional demands without setting processes of change in motion (Meyer/Rowan 1977). This criticism relates to the mechanisms of decoupling that are described by Brunsson (1989) in his classic distinction of talk, decision and action. In other words, classical neo-institutional theory suggests that organizations follow the institutional demand only rhetorically (i.e., on the strategy level) or make ceremonial decisions (i.e., on the structure level) to preserve legitimacy, while their daily routines and activities (i.e., the action level) remain unchanged (Hasse/Krücken 1999; March/Olsen 1984; Brunsson 1989). However, Scandinavian research has shown how over time ideas have long-lasting effects by being adopted into organizational practice, for example by introducing new terminology and models (Sahlin/Wedlin 2008).

The present study follows the Scandinavian argumentation and states that in the long run – despite some degree of decoupling – a diffused idea does indeed trigger institutional change in organizational performance. Previous research tends to focus more on rhetorical practices, that is, how verbal accounts of organizational responses are constructed to manage perceptions of organizational legitimacy (Vaara/Tienari 2008; Wæraas/Sataøen 2014; Mueller/Whittle 2011). This study, however, argues that special attention should be paid to identifying how organizational practices dealing with student diversity actually look like. As contributions from the field of university didactics suggest, German universities have developed numerous measures and support offers to deal with student diversity over the last couple of years (Buß/Erbsland/Rahn 2018; Wildt 1985; Hanft 2015; Kift/Nelson/Clarke 2010). These organizational practices differ greatly in their understanding of student diversity, the main obstacles associated with student diversity as well as in their suggestions to deal with student diversity. To gain a better understanding of different organizational practices that deal with student diversity, the fourth sub-question asks:

Research Question 4:

Which organizational practices dealing with student diversity can be identified?

In order to answer these research questions, this study follows four main objectives:

- To identify dominant perspectives on student diversity in the German political discourse on widening participation.
- To retell the narrative of how the idea of student diversity is translated at German universities in the context of the QPL initiative.
- To indicate how these translations relate to institutional characteristics and dominant diversity paradigms deriving from the local context of German universities.
- To identify organizational practices to deal with student diversity at German universities.

1.4 Approach

Arguing from a constructivist-interpretive perspective (Denzin/Lincoln 2011), this study focuses on the process of reality construction which provides the basis for collective forms of action (Berger/Luckmann 1966). Consequently, this study uses qualitative inquiry to examine the phenomenon and relies on 'thick' descriptions of organizational reality. Following the Scandinavian institutionalist tradition, this research is based on a narrative research design (Czarniawska 2000, 2010). The study aims to identify organizational narratives as a main mode of communication. These narratives are basic instruments to make sense of organizational life and exchange understanding among organizational members (Czarniawska 2010; Weick 1995). They contain actors' understandings of specific 'recipes' for dealing with student diversity (Feldman et al. 2004).

To provide an answer to the first research question, a document analysis of the German political discourse on widening participation was executed, which draws on policy documents, statements and program descriptions from central stakeholders. This includes the BMBF, the *Kultusministerkonferenz* (Standing Conference of the Ministers of Education and Cultural Affairs, in the following abbreviated as KMK) and the German Science Council (*Wissenschaftsrat*), which all produce the political discourse on widening participation through funding programs, decisions and recommendations. In total, 37 documents were collected and analyzed thematically (Schreier 2014), supported by the QDA software MAXQDA. The coding of the data was informed by a literature review on policy implementation and widening participation research in both the international and German context.

Regarding the research questions 2 to 4, organizational responses were analyzed within a qualitative case study design. In order to examine local variations in universities' responses to the demand of student diversity in the context of the QPL funding program, this study builds on a multiple case study design (Yin 2003). The multiple case study includes the University of Hamburg, the University of Kassel and the *Hochschule für Angewandte Wissenschaften* Hamburg (University of Applied Science, in the following abbreviated as HAW), all three of which were received funding by the QPL funding program. They differ in the type of institution, location and institutional profile. The University of Hamburg is located in a metropolitan region and strongly research-oriented, the University of Kassel is located in a peripheral region and has a regional orientation and the HAW Hamburg, again, located in a metropolitan region, is teaching-oriented.

Data sources from the three universities used as case studies include publicly accessible text materials concerning widening participation (e.g., mission statements, websites, project presentations and annual reports), thirteen semi-structured interviews with persons involved in the QPL initiatives (e.g., persons involved in QPL management, persons working in single QPL projects and lecturers involved in single QPL projects), three group discussions with persons working in single QPL projects and eleven protocols gained from participatory observation (e.g., joint workshops with persons involved in the QPL initiatives from all three universities, QPL workshops at the universities).

The processes of data collection and analysis were guided by strategies of grounded theory (Glaser/Strauss 1967), including theoretical sampling, open coding, writing memos, axial coding and selective coding. Quality criteria that were regarded as appropriate for the present research design, like inter-subject comprehensibility, triangulation and reflection on the role of the researchers, were met.

1.5 Structure of the Thesis

The thesis is structured as follows: As a first step, relevant background information on widening participation in the German higher education context is presented. This is followed by an analysis of the political discourse on widening participation (Chapter 2). The next, theoretically informed, part of this study presents the theoretical framework of Scandinavian institutionalism and literature reviews on previous research on organizational responses of universities to student diversity (Chapter 3). Following this theoretical part, the next chapter is concerned with the qualitative research methodology (Chapter 4). The next chapter introduces the three cases, including background information about the universities, their QPL initiatives and a short summary of the main findings of the case-specific analyses (Chapter 5). This is followed by a chapter introducing the cross-case findings concerning organizational responses to student diversity (Chapter 6). These findings include 1) editing rules that have been used at the three universities, 2) the narrative of student diversity at the three universities and 3) organizational practices to deal with student diversity that have been identified at the three universities. The study concludes with a discussion of theoretical contributions, limitations and avenues for further research (Chapter 7).

2 Widening Participation in the Context of German Higher Education

Student diversity, heterogeneity and widening participation have received much scholarly attention over the last decades. Although the interrelated phenomena have been widely discussed, interpretations of these three concepts differ substantially. Thus a conceptual clarification of how student diversity, heterogeneity and widening participation are used in the context of this study, as well as a review of these concepts in the context of German higher education, should precede any further discussion. This is followed by a description of central policies to deal with student diversity in German higher education, including the legal framework for widening participation, central stakeholders as well as policy programs and initiatives aimed at student diversity. This information provides the necessary background for a document analysis of the German political discourse on widening participation. This analysis serves the aim to identify dominant perspectives on student diversity embedded in the discourse and, thereby, answers the first research question of this study.

The terms 'diversity', 'heterogeneity' and 'widening participation' can be interpreted in a number of different ways. This chapter seeks to provide insights into historical and recent discourses and debates related to these terms in order to arrive at definitions that provide the necessary background for this study. It should be acknowledged, however, that discourses can vary according to the disciplinary lenses applied. The present research is influenced by an interdisciplinary perspective that combines concepts from organizational sociology and university didactics. Therefore, there are no strict lines to be drawn between perspectives from economics, pedagogics, psychology, sociology or similar disciplines. However, the present study concentrates on recent literature with a specific focus on higher education research (Auferkorte-Michaelis/Linde/Großi 2018). Higher education research is often situated at disciplinary interfaces that include for example pedagogical and psychological learning/teaching research or sociological or economic-oriented organizational research. It is not obligated to specific disciplinary orientation and neither defined in terms of theories, nor methods (Hüther/Krücken 2016). In the discussion on indicators for study success and the postulated growing heterogeneity and widening participation within the student body, questions of diversity have become an important topic for higher education research and its institutions. The study follows Walgenbach (2014) who predicts that the interdisciplinary character of higher education research will allow researchers to cope with the complexity of the object of investigation by considering the variety of theoretical approaches, co-operations and interdisciplinary research designs available.

2.1 Definitions of Student Diversity, Heterogeneity and Widening Participation

In the political discourse about the diversity and heterogeneity of student populations, these terms are often used synonymously. They emphasize the changing nature of the student body and ask universities to develop initiatives to improve widening participation. Problems associated with this are the different positive or negative connotations underlying those concepts: Heterogeneity tends to be evaluated as negative, associated with contradictions and conflicts. Diversity, in turn, is more often used in a positive way to emphasize commonalities and variety (Buß 2010; Seidel/Wielepp 2014). However, it can be useful to make distinctions between these terms more transparent.

The term 'heterogeneous' (*heterogen*[7]) derives from the Greek word for "uneven" or "not alike" (Wielepp 2013; Duden 2019b). Heterogeneity in its original sense describes the neutral result of a comparison of certain characteristics among group members (Bosse 2018; Wolter 2013b). In the field of higher education research, this term serves to differentiate persons by means of selected categories. In this context, the task of higher education research is, for example, to empirically analyze the postulated (social) differentiation among the student population (Middendorff 2015). Thus, 'heterogeneity' is an empirical term that refers to changing participation patterns within higher education. It is used to refer to differences in descriptive terms with regard to characteristics of groups without any judgment (Wild/Esdar 2014; Wolter et al. 2014).

The term 'diversity' (*Diversität*) has its origin in biology and refers to a richness in species or biodiversity (Buß 2010). Thus, in its original sense, the term refers to the variety or wealth of different species or forms in which something can exist or occur (Duden 2019a). However, diversity is also a sociological concept to recognize and differentiate between the characteristics of groups or individuals. In this regard diversity often relates to demands for equal opportunities for discriminated or disadvantaged groups (Wild/Esdar 2014). Accordingly, the term can be understood in a programmatic sense which combines the consideration of people's affiliations, living situations or orientations with certain policy guidelines (Bosse 2018). This linkage between the term 'diversity' and certain normative demands has its origin in history:

---

[7] As the present research takes place in the context of German higher education, it is important to distinguish between these German concepts and how they are treated differently within German literature on higher education. This might be quite different to an understanding of these concepts in other language contexts. Thus, although the present study is written in English, the author refers to these concepts and their use of language from a German discursive perspective.

The concept is closely related to the anti-discriminatory agenda of the United States Civil Rights Movement that took place in the 1960s and 1970s. It conceptually overlaps with related concepts such as inclusion, exclusion, inequality and intersectionality (Wielepp 2013; Wild/Esdar 2014; Wolter 2013b). In this context, diversity is based on the differentiation between majorities and minorities. The term 'majority' describes dominant groups with similar characteristics that – due to their superiority in numbers – control decisions and positions within organizations. The term 'minority', in turn, refers to several subgroups that share some similarities and differ from the dominant group by certain characteristics (Schulz 2009).

The demand for 'widening participation' (*Hochschulöffnung*[8]) refers to an increase in participation rates of certain student groups that were traditionally excluded or underrepresented within the higher education system (Wolter 2011). In Germany, higher education participation rates among the general population have increased substantially. While in 1900, the percentage of first-year students in Germany within one age cohort was one percent, it has increased to 33 percent in 2000 and even to 57 percent in 2016 (Autorengruppe Bildungsberichterstattung 2018). The massive expansion of the tertiary education sector in terms of access, participation and number of universities is one of the most defining features for the second half of the 20th century in German higher education. This trend aligns with the worldwide trend in the transformation from elite to mass to universal higher education (Clancy/Goastellec 2007; Wolter 2013b; Trow 2005). A controversial question often discussed in this context (in Germany as well as in other countries) is whether this educational expansion has resulted in more social inequality concerning participation in higher education (Wolter 2011). International comparative studies indicate that higher education expansion has not significantly reduced inequalities in access to higher education with regard to social class (Clancy/Goastellec 2007). On the contrary, some researchers even assume that the massification of education has resulted in a deterioration of social inequalities (Jones/Thomas 2005; Middendorff et al. 2013). For example, research conducted in a German context assumes that educational expansion has primarily resulted in higher degrees of qualification among higher social milieus, while the members of lower social milieus have benefitted from the expansion to a much lesser extent (Middendorff et al. 2013). Furthermore, findings from international comparative studies suggest that international expansion entails an increasingly stratified system of higher education (Hauschildt/Vögtle/Gwosc 2018; Marginson 2016). Within such a system, disadvantaged students might have better access to higher education. Still, these are mostly to be found among lower-ranking institutions, a fact which carries severe consequences in terms of career prospects, financial

---

[8] *Hochschulöffnung* is literally translated as the 'opening up of the university'.

security and social status (McCowan 2016; Riddell/Weedon/Holford 2014). Moreover, a student's socio-economic status and academic family background determine the choice of institutional type of higher education institution or the field of study, varying according to academic and economic prestige, retention rates and labor market value (Marginson 2016). Such a development contributes substantially to the reproduction of social inequalities.

As it can be noticed here, underrepresented student groups can be defined along various diversity dimensions. Here it is important to consider that the concepts of student diversity and widening participation are always embedded in the wider national (education) system. Therefore, it is important to look at the national context and to examine the existing systems of access to higher education whose criteria, in turn, determine who can or cannot participate. In addition, the present study acknowledges that widening participation not only means ensuring underrepresented student groups access to higher education, but also enables them to successfully participate in higher education, resulting in a university degree. Therefore, this study goes beyond international research that mostly concentrates on examining changes with regard to access criteria and admission procedures (Clancy/Goastellec 2007). Instead, it investigates widening participation policies and organizational practices that concentrate on the whole student-life-cycle, including access to, participation in and successful completion of studies.

Such a broad definition of widening participation means, in turn, to expand the definition of student diversity as well because the present study does not restrict itself to underrepresented student groups whose transition to higher education is hampered. Rather, the study wishes to look at student groups who face barriers during their studies, either with regard to students' learning and teaching in higher education or students' academic success (Gorard/Smith 2006). These groups are commonly defined as 'non-traditional students' (Teichler/Wolter 2004). The following part will introduce how the present study defines student diversity in the context of German higher education.

2.2 Student Diversity in the German Higher Education Context

Due to the wide range of different characteristics that describe the dominant student group, the definition of student diversity is complicated. Overall, there is no "completed catalogue of characteristics" (Wielepp 2013: 365) that can be used to describe the diversity of students as there is an endless variety of possibilities in comparing students. Thus, diversity is no objective feature or characteristic. Diversity is rather always linked to the respective person or group under observation that can be diverse in several respects, depending on the respective features that are used for comparison. Consequently, diversity is alterable and always highly context-related (Seidel 2014).

According to Wilkesmann et al. (2012), how to define non-traditional students depends on the respective national context, the spirit of the time and certain demographic characteristics. Many German higher education studies build on the definition of non-traditional students provided by Teichler/Wolter (2004). They characterize non-traditional students as (1) students who do not enter the higher education system on the traditional 'direct way', (2) students who do not fulfill the regular educational requirements for access to higher education and (3) students who do not study in the general full-time format. This resembles a differentiation on the basis of entry routes to higher education, educational biography and the mode of study (Schuetze/Slowey 2002). This definition focuses on the specific German higher education system in which students mostly enter higher education as full-time students directly after attaining the school-based university entrance qualification. Such a definition might help in determining what non-traditional students are not in comparison to the 'normal' student, but it leaves a relatively large scope for interpretation. For example, this definition does not include any references to socio-demographic characteristics, although research findings show that these characteristics have a huge impact on the probability of students' access to and participation in German higher education (Middendorff 2015). Further, longitudinal studies indicate that there is an increasingly large proportion of students who study full-time, although they have other obligations in addition to their studies (Middendorff et al. 2013). These students would not be defined as non-traditional according to the definition previously mentioned, although it is likely that they are particularly challenged by their studies. Finally, psychological higher education research emphasizes that apart from these 'visible' characteristics, there are also 'invisible' individual characteristics to differentiate students, for example, according to their motivations, academic competences and study expectations (Middendorff 2015). It is commonly criticized that the conventional institutional settings of teaching and studying at universities do not sufficiently acknowledge the diversity of students' individual characteristics because universities' (study) structures are still oriented towards stereotypical expectations of how students learn and study (Kreft/Leichsenring 2012).

In other words, the present study argues that an extended definition doing justice to recent trends within German higher education and incorporating actual international and national research findings is needed. Consequently, the present study defines non-traditional students in four different ways, paying attention to students' access routes to higher education, socio-demographic characteristics, living situations and individual competences.

Access routes to higher education are a very important feature of distinction within the German education system as it separates traditional ways of entering higher education from non-traditional ways. Some remarks on the historical roots of this mechanism will clarify what is meant by 'access routes' and explain their importance in the German context. From a sociological point of view, socio-demographic characteristics represent another way of defining non-traditional students by comparing them to the 'ideal' student. Hence my argument continues with a survey of the most important socio-demographic characteristics in the German context. Due to the still strong orientation of German study structures towards students in homogeneous living situations (e.g., financially supported by their parents, no children), the category 'living situations' represents another way of defining non-traditional students. Finally, a point that is often overlooked in discussions about non-traditional students is a more psychologically inclined take on the academic abilities students bring with them upon entering higher education. The category 'individual competences' sheds some light on a paradigmatic shift that has been taking place, which steers away from underlying assumptions about the 'ideal' students' competences and abilities. Such a perspective is often characterized by its focus on students' lack of competences. Against the background of educational initiatives that aim to stimulate a shift from teaching to learning, German universities have begun to diversify individual ways of studying and teaching. This development is accompanied by a more general acceptance of students bringing with them a diverse set of competences, interests and motivations that should be appreciated within the institutional setting of studying and teaching.

The distinction into four categories or ways of defining non-traditional students is only analytical. In practice, they often overlap and research commonly considers them as intertwining. The following sub-chapters try to disentangle the categories used in the context of student diversity, but certain cross-references among those categories will be emphasized. This is to give a better understanding of the complexity of the phenomenon of interest. All these categories are perceived as important because they cover relevant aspects in the general discussion and the political discourse on widening participation and student diversity in the landscape of German higher education.

2.2.1   Access Routes to Higher Education

In Germany, the traditional path to higher education is based on obtaining an academic school-leaving qualification (*Abitur*) from a secondary school

(*Gymnasium*[9]). This is regarded as an indication of the person's possession of the necessary academic competences to successfully complete their studies. The *Gymnasium* still represents the "royal road" (Teichler/Wolter 2004: 66) to achieve the *Abitur*, although access routes have been diversified. While in 2000, 90.5 percent of graduates obtained their *Abitur* at a *Gymnasium*, in 2016 this percentage decreased to 73.5 percent (Autorengruppe Bildungsberichterstattung 2018). The decision to attend a *Gymnasium* is made at the end of primary school on the basis of teacher recommendations. The likelihood to transfer to the *Gymnasium* at a later point in time is still relatively low: Only 10 percent of pupils change to a *Gymnasium* between seventh and ninth grade (ibid.).

The focus on the *Abitur* as the primary access route to higher education can be attributed to the strict institutional segmentation between academic and vocational education, the so-called 'German education schism' (Baethge 2007). This institutional segmentation has been cultivated since the 18th century with the result that the institutional order of 'higher' or 'upper' education became decoupled from practical work. ibid. (2007) distinguishes between central characteristics of institutional orders of higher or upper education and vocational education. Each transport different norms, values and attitudes, which influence the behavior of and interactions between members of organizations belonging to one of the two educational sectors. The institutional order of 'higher' education has been highly influenced by the objective to develop 'educated personalities'. This is commonly associated with the Humboldtian educational ideal of a holistic combination of research and studies to derive more comprehensive levels of general learning and cultural knowledge (Hüther/Krücken 2018). Accordingly, students should not train for a certain vocation but acquire 'education through science'. This perspective was legitimized by the *Gymnasium's* priority to transfer cognitive abilities and theoretical knowledge, while vocational education was not yet established in a consistent way and mostly carried out in accordance with the traditions of the respective craft guilds (Wolter et al. 2014; Baethge 2007). Thus, holders of a university entrance qualification were perceived as having sufficient academic prerequisites for higher education (Wolter 2013a).

Since the 1980s several reforms have been brought underway: on the one hand to professionalize vocational education and intensify abstract knowledge-based qualifications and, on the other hand, to allow persons with vocational

---

[9] In Germany, a *Gymnasium* is an upper secondary school with a strong emphasis on general education in contrast to vocationally-oriented secondary schools. It prepares pupils for higher education. At the end of secondary education, pupils who pass their final exams receive the *Abitur* certificate which entitles the holder to enter any study program at any higher education institution. In this sense, the *Abitur* is not only a school graduation certificate but also a university entrance qualification. In the following, the German terms '*Gymnasium*' and '*Abitur*' will be used throughout this work because of the lack of appropriate translation. For further information on the German education system, see Eurydice (2019).

qualifications without traditional university entrance qualifications to enter higher education. These reforms were the result of several global and national trends, such as the professionalization of the working environment, the comparison to other educational systems in the world, the growing competition of global markets and the need for skilled labor, as well as the Europeanization of educational policy and the growing importance of lifelong learning (Schuetze/Slowey 2002; Teichler/Wolter 2004; Spanke 2017). However, these reforms resulted rather in furthering the differentiation of alternative access routes and educational biographies than in the development of an overall strategy to improve permeability between academic and vocational education (Teichler/Wolter 2004). Nevertheless, the reforms challenged the longstanding legitimation of this institutional segmentation and stimulated discussions among scholars and educational policy actors in Germany.

2.2.2 Socio-Demographic Characteristics

Non-traditional students can also be defined in terms of their social characteristics by comparing them to the social construction of the 'normal' student. This 'normal' student is described in the German context as young, male and coming from a parental home where at least one parent has an academic degree (Mooraj/Wiese 2013; Stöter 2012). Thus, a differentiation is made on the basis of certain social categories that represent the statistically dominant student group within the respective higher education system. In the German context, the most common indicators are gender, socio-economic status, parental educational status, migrant background and international student status (Middendorff et al. 2013; Wild/Esdar 2014). These indicators exemplify to what extent certain student groups are still underrepresented when compared to the 'normal' student.

One of the most common social characteristics referred to in the literature is the educational status of parents. According to international comparisons, Germany belongs to the group of 'exclusive systems' as German university students without an academic family background are underrepresented while students whose parents' education exceeds upper secondary level education are strongly overrepresented (Orr/Gwosc/Netz 2011). Research has shown that pupils with a non-academic family background decide against entering higher education more often than this is the case for pupils coming from an academic family, even if the former has gained outstanding academic achievements. Thus, studies show the significant impact the parents' educational status has on the decision to study (Autorengruppe Bildungsberichterstattung 2018). This is supported by data from the Social Survey, the most comprehensive study about the social and economic conditions of students in Germany

(Middendorff et al. 2013).[10] According to the findings of the Social Survey, an academic family background is the most important distinguishing indicator for the choice of study: 77 out of 100 children with academic parents enter higher education, while only 23 out of 100 children with a non-academic family background enter higher education, resulting in an 'educational funnel' (ibid.). Thus, the educational status of parents determines to a great extent the transition from primary school to a vocational or academic track of education and the ensuing transition into higher education (ibid; Autorengruppe Bildungsberichterstattung 2016; Wilkesmann et al. 2012). This trend is exacerbated by the fact that the probability of a later transition from vocational to academic track of education is rather low in Germany.

Often, socio-demographic characteristics are mutually dependent, resulting in multiple educational disadvantages and the deprivation of certain population groups. The observation of educational inequalities due to several simultaneous repressions found its most prominent expression in Dahrendorf's (1966) notion of 'the catholic working-class daughter from the countryside'. Nowadays, such structurally embedded educational disadvantages have shifted and are represented in the image of 'the migrant boy from the city' (Geißler 2005). Thus, although a society's class structures might have changed, the likelihood to enter higher education is highly dependent on social status and has never lost its currency since the 19th century (Wolter 2011).

One of the most seminal theoretical explanations for the importance of socio-demographic characteristics in educational choices is to be found in Bourdieu's (1992) theory of modern society. For Bourdieu, social capital determines the transitions between different stages within the educational system. To put it differently, social factors such as family background or financial and cultural resources have an impact on the educational paths of individuals (ibid.). Due to an unfamiliar habitus and the culture and practices related to it, social integration within higher education is much more complicated for students with a non-academic family background than for those whose parents have an academic degree (Holmegaard/Madsen/Ulriksen 2017). Further, people from lower social ranks more often chose a vocational educational path because it requires less financial means and has more obvious short-term and mid-term perspectives than the academic educational path (Banscherus/Himpele/Staack 2011). Research indeed indicates that the question of student finance seems to be relevant for decision-making in the German context. Often, children with a non-academic family background wish to be financially independent quickly as they fear the financial burden to them or their parents (Wolter 2011). This is interesting since German (public)

---

[10] The Social Survey, conducted by the German Center for Higher Education Research and Science Studies (*Deutsches Zentrum für Hochschul- und Wissenschaftsforschung*, DZHW), monitors the social and economic situation of students in Germany since 1981. For further information, see Middendorff et al. (2017b).

universities do not charge tuition fees. Thus, free higher education by itself does not sufficiently guarantee equal access to higher education or minimizes the fear of financial strain for students with a particular family background or socio-economic status.

Already in the 1960s and 1970s, the unequal representation of certain demographics was recognized, gaining importance in Germany as well as globally. As mentioned before, the anti-discrimination movement in the United States with their demand for equal rights to participate in society and the fight against discrimination based on race, color, gender and national heritage provided an important starting point for debates about equality in Germany as well (Wielepp 2013). Against the background of the women's movement and the student revolution, Germany focused on the support of persons with supposedly less-educated family backgrounds, gender equality and an assessment of the pro and contra arguments surrounding the inclusion of persons with special needs. However, the effects of these normatively-driven debates in the higher education sector were rather minimal: Apart from isolated measures, like the appointment of women's representatives and representatives for people with disabilities, the topic of socio-demographic diversity played almost no role in strategic considerations (Wild/Esdar 2014). Since the turn of the millennium, the topic of diversity has been gaining importance again in educational policy debates. Among other societal developments, this can also be attributed to the enormous amount of higher education research that continues to emphasize the urgency of social disparity — not only with regard to the question of who enters higher education but also who can successfully complete their studies (Hüther/Krücken 2016).

2.2.3 Living Situations

Non-traditional students can also be defined as students in divergent living situations. This can, for example, relate to people with working experience who want to upgrade their qualifications without discontinuing their profession, students who have to earn a living, students with children or other caregiving tasks, or students with disabilities or chronic diseases (Mooraj/Wiese 2013; Wild/Esdar 2014). Data shows that nowadays an increasing amount of students have other obligations next to their studies due to employment, childcare, but also time-intensive hobbies or competitive sports (Middendorff et al. 2013; Heublein et al. 2017). These students are challenged by their restricted time resources to a high degree and face problems with respect to their academic integration and success (Röwert et al. 2017). At the same time, in Germany, the institutional structures of study programs, service offers and lectures are still oriented towards the image of the 'ideal' student who is unmarried, childless, studies full-time and does not rely on self-financing (Buß 2010; Berthold/Leichsenring 2012; Wielepp 2013; Hanft 2015).

Due to the previously mentioned strict institutional segmentation between academic and vocational education in Germany, there is almost no tradition of introducing flexible study structures in forms of further education (*Weiterbildung*), part-time or distance learning study programs that could acknowledge the heterogeneous living situations of today's students. Thus, the area of postgraduate programs has not been very well developed in comparison to other countries (Teichler/Wolter 2004).

Within German universities, providing more flexible study structures has not been subject to discussions for quite a long time — until the topic of 'lifelong learning' entered the political discourse on the European level (Hanft 2012). In the course of the launch of European initiatives like the Bologna Process and the Lisbon Strategy, higher education systems are requested to transfer universities into 'institutions of lifelong learning' (ibid.). According to the European Commission, structures and offers of universities should be designed to offer possibilities and incentives for continuous learning, while reducing barriers to enable everyone the opportunity to learn. According to Hanft (2015), however, in Germany this demand faces a higher education system that is characterized by its structural homogeneity without any concessions to heterogeneous student groups.

2.2.4 Individual Competences

The previous sections focused on the ways structural barriers in society hamper the participation of those student groups which do not represent the 'traditional' or 'ideal' student with regard to contextual factors (e.g., access route to higher education, educational or socio-economic status of parents, current living situation). In addition to these sociological perspectives on student diversity, there is also a psychological perspective that concentrates on inner-individual differences and their impact on academic performance (Bosse 2015; Richardson/Abraham/Bond 2012). Here, too, the image of a traditional or ideal student is created, only concerning individual competences and academic abilities that predict students' academic success. Following the present study's broad definition of widening participation, the category of 'individual competences' plays an important part as it focuses on the role of individual characteristics for academic success.

This psychological research subsumes studies on the influence of personal traits, motivational factors, self-regulatory learning strategies as well as students' approaches to learning on academic performance (Richardson/Abraham/Bond 2012). Findings indicate that certain features are especially relevant for study success, including cognitive determinants (e.g., intelligence and aptitude, prior discipline-related knowledge), competences and attitudes towards the organization of learning (e.g., management of learning and studying) and motivational determinants (e.g., need for achievement, academic self-concept) (Schulmeister/Metzger/Martens 2012). One of the most important determinants for academic performance is self-efficacy, which refers to an individual's belief in his or her capabilities to succeed in challenging situations or fulfill a task (Bandura 1977).

It should be noted that this perspective is sometimes misunderstood as being deficit-oriented. Deficit orientation emphasizes a lack of certain competences or abilities perceived as necessary for successful participation in higher education. This reaches back to the time of Humboldt: When studying was reserved for a small educated elite, critics took issue with the majority of first-year students supposedly being ill-prepared for academia (Mussmann 1832). This was attributed to their 'bad' attitude towards studying which was thought to be driven by an interest in being trained to earn money rather than being inspired by the idea of academic education. Competences like the ability to adopt new knowledge in a proactive, independent and autonomous way as well as critical reflection skills were emphasized in contrast to the passive reception, repetition or memorization of predetermined knowledge (Hanft 2015). Thus, discussions and complaints about a lack of aptitude for higher education (*Studierfähigkeit*) are as old as the German higher education system itself. Criticism covers all disciplines from mathematics to pedagogy. There are numerous newspaper articles and discussion papers by professors who complain that students are not capable to understand scientific theories, summarize texts in their own words and deal with contradictory statements (Ladenthin 2018).

Driven by recent psychological research about study success, however, a perspectival shift has occurred, which moves away from deficit-oriented views towards an orientation that acknowledges the diverse set of competences, interests and motivations students have (Schulmeister/Metzger/Martens 2012; Arnold/Kolbinger 2012). According to this perspective, a differential approach to studying and teaching is necessary. Such a teaching approach should take the diversity of individual learning personalities into account instead of relying on study structures geared towards one 'ideal' set of competences that students bring with them (Viebahn 2009). This perspective is supported by research in the field of university didactics which advocates for institutional settings of studying and teaching which should acknowledge heterogeneous learning styles and strategies as well as different ways of improving students' motivations (Wildt 1985). Still, it is argued that students' different competences, abilities and motivations are not considered within homogeneous institutional structures of study programs (Bülow-Schramm 2016). As formulated by Döring (2018), the particular nature of university teaching with its common focus on chalk and talk technique

(*Frontalunterricht*) has contributed to the fact that teaching concepts emphasizing individualization have been poorly developed. This criticism can often be found in more general discussions about how the quality of studying and teaching can be improved at German universities.

In summary, student diversity can be conceptualized in terms of access routes, socio-demographic characteristics, students' heterogeneous living situations and individual competences. However, as mentioned before, these distinctions serve only analytical purposes; in reality, those attributions often go hand in hand. For example, persons whose heterogeneous living situations conflict with homogeneous study structures have often entered higher education via alternative routes. Furthermore, educational biographies often correlate with a person's socio-economic status: The probability to go to a *Gymnasium* is 1.8 times higher for children of academics than for children of non-academics (79 percent vs. 43 percent). Therefore, it is more likely for children from a non-academic household to enter higher education via alternative routes with vocational qualifications than via the direct school-based way (Middendorff et al. 2013). Finally, differential categories like access routes or socio-demographic characteristics are often associated with individual competences — e.g., potentially problematic attitudes towards learning and a lack of prior knowledge — although these claims are not supported by research (Hanft 2015).

The literature review undertaken so far should shed some light on the often inconsistent ways terms like 'student diversity' and 'widening participation' are defined in the research landscape of German higher education. There are also no clear and consistent definitions of these terms in the political discourse on widening participation. Rather, the political discourse entails different ideas about equal access and success. Accordingly, the following sub-chapter introduces the necessary background information on the German widening participation agenda. This is particularly relevant for the analysis of the German political discourse on widening participation, which will be presented afterward.

2.3 The German Widening Participation Agenda: Policies to Deal with Student Diversity

Widening participation and student diversity are highly relevant to the German political agenda. In the political discourse, the term 'heterogeneity' is often connected to calls for action on behalf of universities. In other words, there is a strong demand made towards universities to develop appropriate strategies to support heterogeneous student groups according to their individual needs. However, this political demand does not represent a consistent reform agenda.

In order to stimulate organizational change and development, the German government increasingly prefers the use of soft steering instruments like funding programs. Their aim is to support universities financially in their efforts to widen participation (Eurydice 2011; Osborne 2003a). These funding programs differ in their focus on specific target groups and thus with regard to their definition of student diversity. These inconsistencies result in a widening participation agenda with varying emphasis and inconsistent meaning given to the topic of student diversity (Bosse/Mergner 2019). At the same time, the soft steering instruments used by the German government are embedded within a legal framework pushing for widening participation in the German higher education system. This legal framework prioritizes some aspects of student diversity while neglecting others. In order to understand how the topic of student diversity is constructed in the political discourse on widening participation, the following chapter will provide the necessary background information for the German situation. First, the legal framework for widening participation will be introduced as well as central political stakeholders involved in widening participation, followed by a description of the policies and programs for widening participation that were implemented by these central political actors. These policies and programs serve as examples of the numerous soft steering instruments that have been used by the German government over the last years.

2.3.1 Legal Framework for Widening Participation and Central Political Stakeholders

In order to understand how universities deal with student diversity, it is important to understand the legal framework and the governance structures that exist in the German higher education system for widening participation. Most importantly, the German higher education system is a federal system. This means that primarily it is the nation's sixteen federal states (*Bundesländer*) that are responsible for the legislation and administration of education, science and culture in general and for public universities in specific. Thus, the so-called cultural sovereignty (*Kulturhoheit*) lies within the federal states (Hüther/Krücken 2018; Eurydice 2019). This means each state is responsible for its educational and cultural policy. The constitution of each state features detailed regulations, for example with regard to the question who has or is denied access to higher education. The higher education acts of the states describe the general objectives of universities and the general universities (Eurydice 2019). Concerning student diversity, most higher education acts define the contribution to socially support students with specific needs (i.e., those with children or caregivers) to lie within a university's sphere of responsibility (e.g., Lower Saxony Higher Education Act of 2007, §3 Section

1, sentence 7) . Some higher education acts also aim at ensuring that students with disabilities or chronic diseases are not put at a disadvantage (e.g., Bremen Higher Education Act of 2007, §4 Section 6). In addition, most acts point out that universities contribute to achieving gender equality, making sure that the underrepresentation of women in higher job positions and gender-related disadvantages are counteracted (e.g., North Rhine-Westphalia Higher Education Act of 2014, §37a Section 1). Thus, it can be said that the higher education acts of the states define the negotiation of student diversity to be a major task within universities. In this context, student diversity is interpreted in terms of socio-demographic characteristics like parenthood, disabilities/chronic diseases and gender. According to the higher education acts of the states, universities should diminish discrimination and dismantle the structural barriers that might prohibit the participation of these student groups.

To guarantee the coordination and cooperation in areas of (higher) education, research, training and cultural affairs, the federal states established the KMK. The KMK is an assembly of the ministers responsible for education and cultural affairs in the sixteen states. According to its mission statement, the task of the KMK is to address "educational, higher education, research and cultural policy issues of supra-regional significance with the aim of forming a joint view and intention and providing representation for common objectives" (KMK 2019). This joint view is expressed via recommendations and resolutions that are published regularly and discussed intensively. Thus, although decisions or directives formulated by the ministers within the KMK are not legally binding for the states as they need to be transferred into the respective state laws first, the KMK is one of the most crucial bodies for negotiating policy issues in the area of education.

In March of 2009, the KMK set in motion one of the most profound legal changes concerning widening participation: They issued a recommendation allowing access to higher education for vocationally qualified persons without a school-based higher education entrance qualification. According to this KMK resolution (2009), two new access routes for vocationally qualified persons were introduced:

1. persons with vocational advanced training qualifications (e.g., master craftsmen, technicians) have automatically — and without any additional examination — a general higher education entrance qualification (*allgemeine Hochschulreife*). These qualifications are treated as equal to the *Abitur* and allow access to all study programs at universities and universities of applied sciences.
2. persons who completed vocational training and have at least three years of professional experience receive a subject-related higher education entrance qualification (*fachgebundene Hochschulreife)* which allows access to study programs affiliated to the person's

respective professional practice. Additionally, they need to successfully complete a special aptitude test.

The integration of this KMK resolution into federal state law took place at different times, resulting in several amendments with regard to the accreditation of prior vocational training, access to higher education for people without a school-based higher education entrance qualification and the transfer of credits earned by prior experience and professional qualifications (Hanft 2012). This new resolution was not that innovative concerning access options: Some states had quite liberal access regulations for vocationally qualified persons long before. However, the newly introduced agreement was a clear political signal to both sectors (i.e., higher education and vocational sector) to emphasize their equal status and exert pressure on the other states to follow suit (Wolter 2012). There were some differences with regard to the extent of implementation: During the adaptation of the state higher education laws to widen entry options, some states even went beyond the KMK recommendations, while others remained behind (Wolter et al. 2014).

With the KMK resolution's integration into state federal laws, the circle of potential students has broadened substantially. It is predicted that in the future, almost 60 percent of an age cohort will obtain a higher education entrance qualification (Wolter et al. 2014). In 2016, the proportion of persons holding a higher education entrance qualification was already at 52 percent (Autorengruppe Bildungsberichterstattung 2018). However, the number of students entering via these alternative access routes remains to be very low: In 2016, only 3 percent of first-year students entered higher education without a school-based entrance qualification. These students are often enrolled in extra-occupational, part-time study programs, mostly offered by private or distance learning universities. Thus, their proportion among students in full-time study programs at public universities is much lower (ibid.).

Due to states' sovereignty, the Federal Government plays only a minor role in legal educational matters. Here, the BMBF is responsible for general educational policy and the provision of funding for research projects and institutions. The responsibilities of the Federal Government in the field of higher education are defined in the Basic constitution and include general rules of higher education admission, higher education degrees as well as financial assistance for students (Eurydice 2019). Concerning widening participation, one important financial instrument to support educational justice and opportunities is the *Bundesausbildungsförderungsgesetz* (Germany's Federal Training Assistance Act for students, in the following abbreviated as BAföG). This national public student support system was introduced in 1971 and provides students with financial support in the form of loans and grants. In 2016, 18 percent of all students received BAföG (Middendorff et al. 2017a). Whether and to what amount students receive payments depends on the economic performance of their parents. In 2018, the maximum rate was 735 euros per month. Studies show that the recipient status correlates with the educational status of the parents. The greatest proportion of recipients is to be found among students with a low educational background. (ibid.). Thus, BaföG can be seen as one instrument to deal with student diversity, defined in terms of socio-demographic characteristics like educational family background.

Traditionally, the German higher education system is characterized by strong and prescriptive state regulation, e.g., in terms of universities' global budgeting. In response to higher education reforms that have been taking place over the past decades, the states have partly restructured the organization and administration of their universities. The detailed state control traditionally exercised by the states was replaced by strengthening the autonomous actions of universities (Eurydice 2019). By shifting decision-making competences from the state ministries to the governing boards of universities, the main objective of these reforms was to reinforce universities' capacity to act (Schimank 2009). This shift in legal regulations of German universities was influenced by a general new management trend that proved to be consequential for almost all higher education systems worldwide (de Boer/Enders/Schimank 2007; Wilkesmann/Würmseer 2009; Enders/de Boer/Leisyte 2008). This trend is based on the belief that universities should be given more sovereignty and independence in order to fulfill self-interested goals and rational means, whereas the influence of the state should be reduced. Since the mid-1990s, the sixteen federal states in Germany have initiated several reforms to deregulate and give more power to universities concerning financial resources. For example, instead of cameralistic accounting, they introduced lump-sum budgeting (de Boer/Enders/Schimank 2008). Nevertheless, the German higher education system still represents a soft-governmental regime in the sense that the majority of universities' budgets are publicly funded (Wilkesmann 2016b).

The two most important funding models are state baseline funding and third-party funding, while the importance of third-party funding has increased to some extent (Hüther/Krücken 2018; DFG 2020). In 1998, the share of third-party funding at German universities was at 16 percent, whereas in 2012 this value increased to 26 percent. In terms of the funding volume obtained, this represents a doubling of third-party funding revenues over 12 years. Since 2013, however, the share of third-party funding at German universities has stabilized and now makes up between 27 percent and 28 percent of a university's budget (DFG 2020). The majority of these funds stem from competitive initiatives or funding programs using public money. The most important financiers of these competitive initiatives are the *Deutsche Forschungsgemeinschaft* (German Research Foundation, in the following abbreviated as DFG) and joint programs of the BMBF and the states (ibid.). The BMBF has increased its influence on German universities with the help of extensive funding programs. Traditionally, third-party funding has mostly been spent on research issues, but the topic of teaching has become increasingly important for third-party funding as well. The stronger emphasis on funding initiatives for teaching is of special interest for the question how universities respond to widening participation demands as teaching and learning are expected to be more impacted by increased student diversity compared to research. Consequently, it can be observed that a lot of these initiatives incorporate demands for dealing with student diversity, coupling them with more general demands to adapt teaching and studying to the changing needs of today's student population. Some of these policies and initiatives will be introduced in the course of the following chapter.

Other instruments for stimulating organizational change on the part of universities are recommendations by central political stakeholders. One of the most influential political actors in the German higher education landscape is the German Science Council, the most important advisory body for science policy in Germany. It advises the German Federal government and the state governments on key issues concerning higher education and scientific developments (Hüther/Krücken 2018). On that account, it regularly publishes recommendations, positions and statements on the scientific system and related topics, but also on specific scientific institutions.[11] One of these recommendations proclaimed that the German higher education system has to "become accessible for broader sections of the population and to develop strategies to improve the individual study success in the light of a more distinct heterogeneity of its student body" (Wissenschaftsrat 2013). This quote is one of the key examples for the high relevance of widening participation and student diversity on the political agenda in Germany.

2.3.2 Policy Programs and Initiatives Aimed at Student Diversity

As mentioned before, the BMBF has increased its influence on German universities with the help of the funding programs it finances. For example, the BMBF initiated the Higher Education Pact (*Hochschulpakt*) which supports the states financially to help deal with the increase in student numbers. This policy instrument represents an administrative agreement between the federal government and the states to ensure financial support that goes directly either to the universities or the states.

---

[11] The Science Council consists of 24 researchers, who are nominated by the most important German scientific institutions (e.g., German Research Foundation, Leibniz Association) and eight public representatives, who are nominated by the Federal and state governments. Recently, the Council has expanded its original spectrum of tasks. It is now also responsible for to the evaluation of outer-university research institutions, the institutional accreditation of private and ecclesiastical universities, the execution of the Excellence Initiative and the advisory of the Federal Government and the state governments on the structure of research funding. For further information, see Wissenschaftsrat (2021).

Further, there are a number of BMBF funding programs in which student diversity plays a more direct role. One of the most important programs to support widening participation was the funding initiative 'Advancement through Education: Open Universities' (*Aufstieg durch Bildung: Offene Hochschulen*). It focused on the development of flexible study structures and programs, in particular for employed persons or persons with family responsibilities. This funding program sought to contribute to lifelong learning against the background of European initiatives like the Bologna Process and the Lisbon Strategy. According to the European Commission, higher education systems are requested to transform universities into 'institutions of lifelong learning' (Hanft 2012) in which structures and practices are designed in such a way that they offer possibilities and incentives for continuous learning. At the same time, barriers to learning should be removed so that everyone has an opportunity to learn continuously. According to Hanft (2015), however, in the German context, this demand faces a higher education system characterized by its structural homogeneity without accommodating heterogeneous student groups. Consequently, the funding program 'Advancement through Education: Open Universities' aimed at improving the permeability of academic and vocational education and provided universities with financial incentives to introduce more flexible study structures. The BMBF initiated the program in 2010. It completed two contest rounds, one from 2011 to 2017 and one from 2017 to 2020. The first round involved 50 universities and another 46 universities joined the program for the second round. These universities developed concepts for work-compatible study programs, certificate courses, dual courses of study, or study modules with enhanced practical phases.

Besides the development of flexible study programs, the BMBF also introduced the funding program ANKOM. It was designed to support projects at universities that tried to ease the transition from vocational to academic education and allow individuals to successfully complete their studies while working. Especially the recognition and validation of vocational qualifications for study programs became a main point of interest (Wolter 2012; Freitag et al. 2015). The funding program ran from 2006 to 2014. In total, nineteen projects at public and private universities were funded during that time.

These funding programs were accompanied by an Upgrading Scholarship Program (*Aufstiegsstipendium*) for persons with particularly good vocational qualifications which was introduced by the BMBF in 2008. Several state-level initiatives with similar objectives were launched, for example, Lower Saxony's 'Open University' (*Offene Hochschule*) program aimed at supporting universities in Lower Saxony in their efforts to widen participation and open higher education for vocationally qualified persons (Stöter 2012). Another example was the funding program 'Study Models of Individual Speeds' (*Studienmodelle individueller Geschwindigkeit*) in Baden-Württemberg which supported the development of study programs that would shape the first year according to individual needs and aptitudes of diverse students (Mergner/Mishra/Orr 2017).

Despite political efforts, the number of alternative study programs remains relatively low. In 2018, 90 percent of all Bachelor's study programs were designed as full-time study programs (Autorengruppe Bildungsberichterstattung 2018). Only private universities tend to direct their study programs more towards employed persons. Here, one third of all Bachelor's study programs are designed as extra-occupational study programs (ibid.). Nevertheless, the overall number of first-year students enrolled in distance learning study programs has increased from 10.156 first-year students in 2005 to 19.638 first-year students in 2016. The increase of first-year students in dual study programs is even more impressive.[12] In 2005, 2.340 first-year students enrolled in dual study programs, while in 2016, this number increased to 26.089 first-year students. 93 percent of dual study programs are offered by universities of applied sciences (ibid.).

Within the previously mentioned funding programs, student diversity is defined in terms of alternative access routes via which students have entered higher education or the diverse living situations of students that should be acknowledged by the introduction of more flexible study structures. The project initiatives developed at universities in the context of these funding programs mostly entail the development of postgraduate programs and training courses. Postgraduate programs represent an educational sector that is relatively new and unknown territory for German universities (Wolter 2012).

In contrast, the previously mentioned QPL funding program was based on a broader definition of student diversity. It sought to encourage universities to improve the quality of teaching and studying in the face of an increasingly heterogeneous student population. Consequently, this funding program focused on project initiatives by universities within regular Bachelor's and Master's study programs. The QPL Funding Program was financed by the BMBF and represented one of the most extensive funding programs in terms of finances and outreach. It was nation-wide and allocated subsidies to universities with a total funding volume of two billion euros. The program contributed to the general improvement of teaching and study conditions, while it simultaneously emphasized activities supporting the first year of study programs that aim to "acknowledge the heterogeneous student composition" (BMBF 2010: 2). Over the last years, participating universities have developed numerous projects. These projects include the conceptualization of e-learning or blended learning scenarios, the professionalization of lecturers, the improvement of support offers and the introduction of tutoring and mentoring programs as well as introductory weeks and bridging courses. According to

---

[12] Dual study programs combine academic study with vocational training or practical experience in a company. Thereby, students obtain two qualifications, an academic degree and a vocational qualification.

critics, however, universities developed multiple conventional measures without any coherent underlying strategy (Hanft 2015). What is more, the basic conditions in which teaching and studying take place are not affected so that only punctual interventions are possible (Hanft/Zawacki-Richter/Gierke 2015). This is particularly questionable considering the fact that these interventions are only realized based on short-term project financing, although long-term solutions for dealing with student diversity would be necessary.

Still, a closer look at the organizational level reveals that German universities responded to the demand to deal with student diversity very differently in the context of the QPL funding program. The relatively general nature of the QPL funding program provided universities with a high degree of autonomy in choosing to what extent they connect their QPL initiatives with the topic of student diversity. This in particular is part of the reason the present study argues that this Funding Program provides a very interesting example for studying German universities' response to student diversity in the context of the widening participation agenda.

In summary, the political activities in Germany to remove legal barriers to the admission to higher education and improve the credit transfer from previous qualifications are well documented (Freitag et al. 2015; Hanft/Brinkmann 2012). Nonetheless, accounts of their practical implementation and the degree of realization within universities are in most cases absent. This results in an overt discrepancy between the wish to formally open up the higher education system and the restricted permeability between vocational and academic education observed in practice (Wolter et al. 2014). An additional point of critique lies in the observation that widening participation policies focus in particular on the permeability of vocational and academic education. This focus restricts the discussion to access and admission issues on the systemic level. The literature surveyed here suggests that to widen participation with regard to the whole student life cycle, including students' successful participation and completion of higher education, it is necessary to extend the discussion to questions about study organization, study conditions and accompanying support on the organizational level (ibid.). Such an expanded definition of widening participation requires to not only look at how universities respond to widening participation rhetorically (i.e., on the strategy level), but also how widening participation is considered in universities' structures and activities.

2.4 The German Widening Participation Agenda: Discourses on Widening Participation

As it has been reviewed in this chapter, there is no clear and consistent definition of terms like 'diversity', 'heterogeneity' and 'widening participation' in the German political discourse. Rather, it entails different intertwining ideas that transport value-laden expectations about the role of German universities (Mergner/Leisyte/Bosse 2018). Hence, it is necessary to shed some light on the German political discourse on widening participation and disentangle the different underlying meanings and rationales that are connected to student diversity in the widening participation agenda.

To do so and to provide an answer to our first research question (i.e., which perspectives on student diversity can be identified in the political discourse on widening participation), this thesis includes a document analysis of the political discourse on widening participation. This analysis builds on prior research on discourses. According to Boch Waldorff (2013), a discourse is defined as "structured collections of texts, and associated practices of textual production, transmission and consumption, located in a historical and social context". In other words, discourses are established based on texts that are produced by actors that give a certain meaning to certain actions, thereby constituting the social world. This means, in turn, that discourse can be regarded as possessing a form of discursive agency. Here, actors use specific language in order to legitimize new practices or introduce institutionalized rules that provide meaning to society (ibid.). Consequently, research on discourses acknowledges how the macro-level, in the form of the environment or organizational fields in which organizations engage and micro forces, in the form of organizational actors, mutually affect each other (Scott 2010).

Discourses entail patterns of interests, goals and shared assumptions that can be identified via institutional vocabularies. Institutional vocabularies refer to "structures of words, expressions, and meanings used to articulate a particular logic or means of interpreting reality" (Suddaby/Greenwood 2005: 43). In this context, institutional vocabularies are closely related to institutional logics, which are "the socially constructed, historical patterns of material practices, assumptions, values, beliefs, and rules by which individuals produce and reproduce their material subsistence, organize time and space and provide meaning to their social reality" (Thornton/Ocasio 1999: 804). Thus, institutional logic provides a link between individual agency and cognition and socially constructed institutional practices and rule structures (Thornton/Ocasio 2008).

This thesis focuses on political or interest-laden discourses while aiming to identify genres or certain patterns of interest, goals and shared assumptions that are transported utilizing textual material (Suddaby/Greenwood 2005).

Most of the research done in this vein uses a critical discourse perspective, which can be regarded as a very efficient way to identify and display power positions between different actors and show the mechanisms of persuasion and manipulation at work by using language (Boch Waldorff 2013; Vaara/Tienari 2008; van Leeuwen/Wodak 1999). The present study, however, shifts focus by choosing a more content-related than power-related perspective. Thereby, this study wishes to analyze the content of the idea of student diversity within the (political) discourse in order to, firstly, identify the underlying meaning that is given to this topic on the macro-level and to ascertain, secondly, the way universities (re-)interpret these contents and translate them into their local contexts.

The present study focuses on the political discourse because, as mentioned before, the state represents the most important stakeholder within the German higher education system. The state plays such a crucial role because it funds the majority of universities' budgets, and the German higher education system can be described as highly regulated. Although state regulation has decreased in the last years due to the introduction of governance reforms inspired by new public management, institutional pressures from the state are still the most influential for universities (Krücken/Röbken 2009). Here, the study builds on prior research on widening participation discourses in the field of higher education, which will be introduced in the following sub-chapter.

2.4.1 Prior Research on Political Discourses on Widening Participation in Higher Education

Widening participation can be regarded as one institutional concept that is promoted within governmental policies as a means to describe what constitutes a 'good' organization in terms of role identity. In recent years, the topic of widening participation has gained significant interest on the European as well as the national level (Davies 2003). As indicated in several EU documents, there is a political will to increase access to and widen participation in higher education for those groups who have traditionally been excluded (Osborne 2003a), which provided the basis for several countries to start widening participation agendas of their own. Here, the widening participation agenda offers an interesting example for the power of soft steering instruments and for how the framing of the political discourse within the widening participation agenda impacts the choice of measures and instruments on the organizational level of universities.

As international research has shown, within the political discourse terms like 'diversity', 'social inclusion' and 'social equity' are used in an inconsistent way, as they in fact reflect different underlying beliefs and attitudes towards the topic (Archer 2007). By referring to these terms, political accounts to widen participation are legitimized on different grounds, which impacts the enactment of measures to be taken. For example, on the European level, research has demonstrated how different narratives relating to topics of social equality have been activated within the political discourse while the instruments chosen within reform initiatives were rather driven by economic imperatives than social equity rationales (Davies 2003). Research done in an Australian context indicates how political ideologies frame the discussion about social inclusion and the kind of measures which should be used (Gidley et al. 2010). This observation is supported by research dealing with these issues in a British context, where it was shown how the rhetoric of diversity has influenced the framing of the topic of widening participation by giving the discourse symbolic power derived from associations with equity and social inclusion (Archer 2007; Jones/Thomas 2005; McCaig 2015; Lewis 2002; Watson 2006; Davies 2003). Archer (2007) calls this a "moral discourse that silences other competing accounts of widening participation" (p. 635). Here, widening participation is often associated with value-laden expectations that put a lot of moral pressure on universities to respond adequately. According to Watson (2006), this moral finger-pointing leads to the point that he rates widening participation as "the most troublesome item in talk about higher education". However, a systematic understanding of the German political discourse on widening participation is still lacking.

It can be assumed that this moral component is even more apparent in soft steering policy instruments that are more or less open for (local) interpretation. As it has been shown in this chapter, soft regulation instruments are increasingly used by the German government to stimulate organizational responses and support universities financially in their efforts to widen participation (Eurydice 2011; Osborne 2003a). According to Mörth (2005), soft regulations are legally non-binding rules that function nonhierarchically. Additionally, these rules are mostly informal and flexible with regard to their interpretation and adjusted by those who are being regulated (Sahlin/Wedlin 2008). The emergence of soft law comes in a time that is described by Levi-Faur/Jordana (2016) as the "golden era of regulation". Against the background of a shift "from management to regulation, from an intraorganizational to interorganizational focus and from talk of efficiency to talk of transparency" (Sahlin/Wedlin 2008: 231), empirical studies have shown that regulatory and governance activities of all kinds have increased with regard to their scope and breadth (Djelic/Sahlin-Andersson 2006). This trend is usually associated with an increasing societal distrust, which generates a need for activities that improve transparency and set rules with the perspective of building more trust on the part of society. Against the background of the 'audit explosion' (Power 2000), state-centered control might have declined, but it has been offset by the introduction of new regulatory modes, such as standards, rankings and monitoring to "transform the conduct of organizations and individuals in their capacity as self-actualizing agents" (Shore/Wright 2000). Sahlin/Wedlin (2008) speak in this context of a 'responsibility spiral' in which responsibilities become diffused by the multiplication of regulatory and governance activities that have the aim to allocate responsibilities. This is particularly the case with soft regulations that have a tendency to redirect responsibility away from the ones who set rules towards those who follow the rules. However, in the case of soft regulation, there are voluntary rules that are open to translation. Consequently, those who follow the rules are held responsible for the way they interpret the rules to be followed. They are required to explain why they have decided to follow the rules in certain ways. This 'double blurring of responsibilities' (ibid.) can lead to an even greater need for regulation and governance, while at the local level the resistance against soft regulation might increase (Power 2000).

Universities are often criticized for their resistance to change in response to governmental reforms (Kehm 2000). Here most of the research on higher education reform policies refers to the changing governance and steering mechanisms that have been the result of new public management-inspired reforms (Bleiklie/Kogan 2007; Braun/Merrien 1999). However, as Bleiklie/Michelsen (2013) already pointed out, only a few authors have concentrated on alternative policy topics, in particular in the field of soft steering instruments that play such a major role in Germany. On the one hand, soft regulation instruments leave a relatively large scope for action, as universities can choose their own priorities and highlight certain aspects over others. On the other hand, the vague definition of complex concepts like widening participation also produces uncertainty because organizations are required to position themselves and legitimize their actions against the background of this institutional political demand (Boch Waldorff 2013). Therefore, the political call to action within the German widening participation agenda provides an opportunity to gain interesting insights into the ways universities construct their legitimizing accounts for practices to deal with student diversity, while the policy analysis serves as a frame of reference for the analysis of organizational responses. Following an institutional perspective, this study assumes that the political discourse entails references to rules and taken-for-granted assumptions about appropriate behavior on the part of universities. Further, policies are not simply guidelines for action, but they express certain values, beliefs and instruments for (higher education) organizations' role in society (Gornitzka 1999; Bleiklie/Marton/Hanney 1995).

Consequently, the first step in this study is to delineate the background and nature of the identified political discourse and describe its main characteristics. What kind of problems are identified as central? What kind of rationales can be found in the policy debates on widening participation? To provide answers to these questions, the following sub-chapter introduces an analysis of the German political discourse on widening participation.

2.4.2 Analysis of the German Political Discourse on Widening Participation[13]

In order to analyze the underlying perspectives on student diversity in the political discourse of the German widening participation agenda (research question 1), a document analysis of the political discourse on widening participation was executed. Between January and June 2017, text materials were collected. The text materials were policy documents, resolutions and funding program descriptions from central political stakeholders, including the BMBF, the KMK and the Science Council, as they have been identified in this chapter before. The text materials cover the time period between 2006 and 2016. For data collection, the publications on the websites of these central stakeholders were searched for terms like 'diversity', 'heterogeneity' and 'widening participation'. This resulted in a selection of documents that deal with the topics of student diversity and widening participation, for example, BMBF funding programs, KMK resolutions or recommendations by the Science Council. In total 37 documents were collected and analyzed thematically (Schreier 2014), supported by the QDA software MAXQDA. The coding of the data was informed by a literature review on policy implementation and widening participation research in the international and German context (Archer 2007; Jones/Thomas 2005; Kehm 2000; Teichler/Wolter 2004). Since the policy documents were publicly available, the data sources were not anonymized.[14]

The analysis of policy documents revealed that the political discourse on widening participation in Germany is dominated by two different perspectives, the social justice perspective and the economic perspective. Although they are often intertwined, the two perspectives differ in their definition of the main objectives and underlying rationales associated with widening participation.

On the one hand, the policy documents problematize the underrepresentation of certain social groups in German universities. This problem is associated with certain structural and financial barriers that impede the participation of these groups. From this perspective, political actors such as BMBF refer to aims like "increasing the educational opportunities of all citizens" (BMBF 2014) and "improving the educational equality in Germany" (KMK/BMBF 2015: 37). Accordingly, the main institutional vocabularies are 'educational equality', 'equal opportunity' and 'equity of chances'. The underlying rationale of widening participation is defined in terms of social justice, as it is supposed to foster greater social equality through the inclusion of traditionally underrepresented social groups in higher education. These traditionally underrepresented social groups are mostly defined in socio-

---

[13] This sub-chapter has already been published in Mergner, Leisyte, & Bosse (2019).
[14] Since all data material is written in German, the author has translated all following quotations from German into English.

demographic terms with a special emphasis on gender, socioeconomic status and migrant background. For example, policy documents argue, "all people in Germany should have the opportunity to receive good education — regardless of social origin or migration background" (BMBF 2013: 33). Other documents refer to persons in special living situations, like students with care-giving tasks or students with disabilities or health issues.

As this definition of target groups treats financial and structural barriers as the main reason for the underrepresentation of diverse student groups in higher education, the respective policies focus on investment in student scholarships, social higher education infrastructure and student financial assistance, regarding the latter as "the central state instrument to secure equity of chances in education" (KMK/BMBF 2015: 31). For universities, these policies aim to improve study conditions and provide more flexible learning and teaching practices that "acknowledge the increasingly heterogeneous learning needs of different student groups" (ibid.: 35). Accordingly, special support structures are highlighted, like child care services, learning material for students with disabilities, blended-learning concepts, or dual study programs for students who work during the course of their studies. The underlying rationale behind these kinds of actions is that there are structural barriers anchored within society, while universities have the social responsibility to contribute to removing these structural obstacles. Thus, the role of universities is defined as *promoters of educational equality* with the high external expectation that they are able to ensure "equal participation in education with regard to access, progress and successful completion of studies" (ibid.: 30). This assumption is embedded within the wider European reform context of the Social Dimension of the Bologna Process, which is described as "the societal goal that the student body entering, participating in and completing higher education should reflect the diversity of our population" (KMK/BMBF 2010: 1).

On the other hand, the policy documents on the federal level relate widening participation to the central problem of demographic change and a shortage of skilled labor, which threatens the country's economic competitiveness. Therefore, widening participation is associated with the aim of "sustaining the demand for a skilled labor force" (BMBF 2009: 1) to "strengthen the international competitiveness of Germany as a location for science" (BMBF 2014). Regarding institutional vocabularies, the policy documents refer extensively to 'demographic change', the 'need for skilled labor' and the current 'lack of skilled labor'. The rhetoric used in the documents tends to create an atmosphere of pressure and urgency for action.

The solution is seen in increasing the attractiveness of higher education and, consequently, the number of students and (successful) graduates. Thus, by "exploiting the existing pool of talent and knowledge" (KMK/BMBF 2015: 31), widening participation is displayed as a means of raising individual and collective wealth and thereby improving economic performance. Instead of highlighting the impact of structural barriers, this perspective assumes that everyone has the same opportunities if only willing to demonstrate high performance. This economic-oriented rationale sees 'potentials for talents' mostly among one target group, namely, vocationally qualified persons. Consequently, the suggested measures concentrate on improving the permeability between vocational and academic education and the possibilities for lifelong learning. On the part of the policy, the main regulative obstacle for this target group has already been abolished with the political decision of the KMK in 2009 that allows access to higher education for vocationally qualified persons without having school-based university entrance qualifications. To increase the number of students coming from this group, this political decision was complemented by several funding programs to help universities improve the attractiveness of their study programs by developing more flexible study structures and instruments for the recognition of prior vocational learning. In this context, on the part of the universities, the policy documents call for the establishment of "demand-oriented training programs in line with market conditions" (Wissenschaftsrat 2006: 65). According to this perspective, universities are expected to fulfill their role as *providers of professionals* for the economy by operating as drivers of innovation and answering the growing demand for a skilled labor force, both of which are needed to strengthen the national economy. By means of formulations, like "Germany needs professionals and engineers" (BMBF 2015), this ascribed role is legitimized. The future investment in education is supported by statements such as "when we continue to rely on good education, our country is well-equipped for the challenges of the future: digitalization, integration and demographic change" (ibid.). On the European level, such an economic perspective can be rediscovered in the wider context of lifelong learning and the Lisbon Strategy, which aims to make the EU "the most competitive and dynamic knowledge-economy in the world" (Deutscher Bundestag 2006: 4).

Thus, concerning the first research question, it is suggested that the political discourse on widening participation transports two different functional claims regarding the role of universities: on the one hand, by supporting equality in educational opportunities, and, on the other hand, by securing the demand for a skilled labor force. In general, the document analysis indicates that these functional claims are accentuated in the policy documents in different ways, but they are seldom clearly separated. Instead, they are even often intertwined, as illustrated by the following example:

> We can only overcome the challenges of the demographic change and an imminent shortage of skilled labor by relying also in the future on good education for all and supporting all people in our country in the development of their potentials. This is why the improvement of educational equality was and will be a central aim of our work (Wanka 2013: 5).

Both perspectives postulate similar organizational measures to widen participation, but they differ in ascribing meaning to how universities contribute to widening participation due to a different underlying rationale about the key problem and respective solution (see Figure 2.1). According to the social justice rationale, the problem lies within structural barriers that hinder certain social groups from beginning and/or finishing their studies. Inequalities can thus be diminished by removing these barriers. According to the economic rationale, in turn, the not yet fully exhausted potential of talent among vocationally qualified persons is regarded as the key problem. Inequalities can only be reduced by encouraging potential students to participate in higher education. The distinction between these two rationales is often blurred though, as illustrated by the above quote. Further, a lot of policy documents acknowledge both study structures and individual behavior — or, in fact, the relationship between those two parts — as important factors for supporting widening participation. But both perspectives postulate organizational actions regarding widening participation in a rather vague way. As a wide range of possible measures is listed in the policy documents, universities are left without clear guidelines about what actions are required to support widening participation.

In summary, this sub-chapter included an analysis of the political discourse on widening participation. Special focus was put on policy content with regard to identified perspectives on widening participation and student diversity. It should be noted here that the present study focuses on the identification of policy content instead of analyzing the whole policy formation process. Such a focus was perceived as sufficient for the present research objective because the main interest of this study is to examine the level of individual organizations, how they translate policy content concerning widening participation in the local context, and how (different) translations can be explained. Therefore, I decided that an in-depth analysis of the policy processes underlying the widening participation policy agenda, including an identification of key actors and policy arenas, was not necessary. In addition, several studies have already analyzed the (German) policy processes in the field of widening participation and student diversity before, as reviewed earlier in this chapter.[15]

---

[15] For more detailed information about the historical development and policy processes about widening participation, student diversity and lifelong learning, see Wild/Esdar (2014); Hanft (2015); Klein/Daniela (2012); Kreft/Leichsenring (2012).

Figure 2.1   Summarized Findings: Analysis of the German Political Discourse on Widening Participation

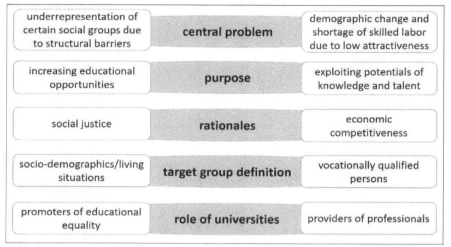

Note. The figure displays two perspectives on student diversity, which were identified in the analysis of the German political discourse on widening participation that differ with regard to the central problem, purpose, underlying rationales, target group definition and the described role of universities. Source: Own illustration.

2.5 Summary

This chapter introduced key concepts and necessary background information on the topic of widening participation in the German higher education context. It started with a definition of key terms like 'diversity', 'heterogeneity' and 'widening participation' (see Chapter 2.1.). A review of the literature on student diversity in the German higher education context revealed that student diversity can be conceptualized in terms of access routes, socio-demographic characteristics, students' heterogeneous living situations and individual competences (see Chapter 2.2.). Chapter 2.3. pointed out that the German widening participation agenda is not so much a uniform reform agenda but rather a conglomeration of policy instruments that differ in their foci and definitions of student diversity. These instruments take the form of either legal regulations, recommendations or funding programs issued by central political actors. All these instruments have the aim to stimulate universities' responses to a predicted increase in student diversity, yet they differ with regard to their underlying perspective on student diversity and appropriate reactions to it. To analyze these differing perspectives on student diversity in more concrete terms, Chapter 2.4. introduced an analysis of the German political discourse on widening participation. The analysis builds on a literature review of prior research on widening participation discourses in the field of higher education. The findings show that the German political discourse is dominated by two perspectives on widening participation. On the one hand, widening participation is perceived as a means to bring about social justice, while perceiving the underrepresentation of student groups according to socio-demographic characteristics as the central problem. According to this perspective, universities as promoters of educational equality should contribute to improving educational opportunities for these groups. On the other hand, widening participation is displayed as a means to secure the pool of skilled labor. Accordingly, the demographic change and the shortage of skilled labor are perceived as the central problem. The focus is particularly on the group of vocationally qualified persons whose potential of knowledge and talent should be exploited by higher education. Hence, universities are seen as providers of professionals.

The findings of the policy analysis align with prior research indicating that the German political discourse on widening participation is dominated by economic as well as social justice imperatives (Archer 2007; Davies 2003). Consequently, universities are confronted with two different perspectives on the central problems, objectives and functions of higher education in the context of widening participation. Accordingly, the question arises how universities respond to these external pressures. This analysis serves as a frame of reference for the analysis of organizational responses, i.e., how the demand to deal with student diversity is translated at German universities. Due to the rather broad and unspecific way these perspectives postulate organizational actions towards widening participation, no specific prototype or model is defined at the macro-level. This also leaves universities without any concrete guidelines on the kind of actions required to support widening participation; rather, a wide range of possible measures are listed in the policy documents.

3 Theoretical Framework and Literature Review

After having made the concept of student diversity in the context of the German widening participation agenda more concrete, this chapter focuses on the theoretical framework needed in order to understand and explain universities' responses to institutional pressures to cope with student diversity and, thus, provide answers to research questions 2-4. After introducing the ontological and epistemological assumptions of the present study, the theoretical chapter reveals why universities can be displayed as a 'special' form of organization (Musselin 2006; Wilkesmann/Schmid 2012), which is important to consider when analyzing organizational responses. This study takes on an institutional perspective (Scott 2013, 2010), which is particularly suitable for this undertaking because the field of higher education can be described as a highly institutionalized environment in which universities face pressures to comply with value-laden expectations such as widening participation (Kehm 2000). More precisely, the study introduces concepts from Scandinavian institutionalism and research on organizational responses to widening participation to explain how German universities respond to student diversity (research question 2). In order to understand local variations in response to this institutional demand, the argument is inspired by research on the role of the local context for explaining organizational heterogeneity in responses to widening participation (research question 3). Finally, to identify organizational practices that deal with student diversity, the study reviews earlier literature on universities' responses to widening participation (research question 4). The chapter ends with a theoretical conceptualization of how the idea of student diversity travels from the political discourse on widening participation to the organizational level of German universities in the context of the QPL initiative.

3.1 Ontological and Epistemological Assumptions

As a first step, it is important to reflect on the presuppositions or world views we bring towards the social world that we wish to examine. How do we position ourselves as researchers and how and with what kind of techniques can we detect and examine the social phenomenon of interest? A discussion of the ontological and epistemological positions of me as a researcher will clarify the subject, theory and methods of this thesis. Therefore, the chapter starts with a short excursion to the epistemological and scientific foundations of this work, embedding it in the field of social science, and, more explicitly, the field of organizational research and higher education research.

The social sciences comprise scientific disciplines concerned with society and the relationships among individuals within a society. In social sciences, the scientific methods used are in part related to the natural sciences as well as to the humanities. All research is guided by certain abstract principles subsuming beliefs about the nature of reality (ontology), how knowledge is created (epistemology) and how we gain knowledge of the world (methodology). According to Denzin/Lincoln (2011) "the net that contains the researcher's epistemological, ontological, and methodological premises" can be called a paradigm, representing "a basic set of beliefs that guides action" (p. 13). These beliefs influence the way the researcher perceives the world and acts in it and reflect the different world views researchers have. They shape their interpretations of the world and guide choices with regard to research topics, theoretical perspectives and methodology (Bess/Dee 2012).

The two most common paradigms in the field of social science are the positivist paradigm and the social constructivist paradigm. According to the philosophic belief of positivism, there is (only) one objective reality that is independent of any observer's perspective. It is assumed that through careful observation, conclusions about reality can be drawn and shared with other observers. As a result, conceptualizations assumed to be generalizable across institutions and societies develop. Common types can then be identified and compared according to a range of performance indicators. Therefore, positivist social scientists often use methods for understanding society that are common in the field of natural sciences. By constructing empirically tested theories, they aim to identify independent variables that explain or predict outcomes for a dependent variable of interest referring to criteria of internal and external validity, reliability and objectivity (Bess/Dee 2012; Denzin/Lincoln 2011).

The social constructivist perspective objects to the positivist view of one objective reality "independent of our volition" (Berger/Luckmann 1966: 13). Alternatively, social constructivism acknowledges the existence of a subjective reality that is constructed by every member of society based on their own experiences and beliefs. Therefore, reality is only accessible through human cognition (Czarniawska 1992). This also means that multiple realities exist which each depend on the respective individual (Lincoln/Lynham/Guba 2011). By depending on such a relativist ontology, this perspective draws attention to the process of 'reality construction' suggesting that people are not passive recipients in organizational settings, but that they can influence and generate the context in which they engage as active agents (Bess/Dee 2012). This construction of reality is created through ongoing communication, interaction and the interpretation of meaning and purpose by the actors (Giddens 1984).

This is the perspective that this research draws on. Social constructivism provides the epistemological background for choosing an interpretative research approach that emphasizes the performance of interpretation of the (inter-)acting human actor (Keller 2009). This so-called interpretivist perspective of social science (Burrell/Morgan 1979; Giddens 1984) is based on the assumption that human action and social interaction require the permanent performance of interpretation. People need to continuously interpret and understand the situations and relationships they are involved in order to be able to act. During interactions, persons are engaged in the permanent efforts of interpreting the signals and messages they send out and receive. The present study follows interpretivist researchers who are interested in the practical-interpretive performances that social actors deliver in their actions, their interactions and the construction of social phenomena and social order (Keller 2009).

Although interpretative approaches can be identified as belonging to a distinct organizational perspective, they also use and integrate concepts from such cognitive psychology, ethnology or ethnomethodology. Still, there are certain characteristics that interpretative approaches share. In the first place, most interpretative researchers agree that what is experienced as reality within organized social systems is constructed by the social (inter-)action of actors. The process of reality construction is only maintained by means of continuous interaction. Secondly, all interpretative approaches emphasize the subjective sense-making efforts of actors while they are engaging and interacting (Wiegand 1996). Wilson (1970) contradicts the interpretative paradigm by arguing that the normative paradigm — in particular the sociological theory of Parsons — explains actions through their orientation along norms and role requirements. According to the normative paradigm, actors must fulfill certain role expectations. Their disregard is sanctioned negatively, while compliance with them is being. The norm here is perceived as "the engine behind what is happening" (Keller 2009: 21). This resembles a rather passive execution of prescribed roles. The interpretative paradigm, in contrast, suggests that actors are actively involved in a permanent process of interpreting their roles and resulting actions and interactions. Thus, it is not the execution of a prescribed role that is emphasized, but rather the way actors plan and design their own actions based on a role that is prescribed by others. Thereby, the acting parties come to a joint perception of the situation (ibid.). It follows that within interpretative approaches, the interpretative power of (inter)acting parties is of central interest.

Further, this research is situated in the field of higher education research, and more precisely takes on an organizational perspective on higher education, since the focus of analysis is on universities as 'organizations' and the organizational actors within those organizations. The interpretative approach is especially suitable in the context of higher education research as both higher education systems and organizations are complex entities (Hüther/Krücken 2016; Teichler 2003). Universities engage in an increasingly complex environment, which makes it virtually impossible to draw on empirically-tested rules concerning their reactions and responses in certain circumstances. In other words, there is no opportunity to create experimental situations in order to test hypotheses by manipulating certain mediating variables. Further, the field of higher education research is interdisciplinary and relatively new. Therefore, there is a lack of basic knowledge and general theory on the organizational processes and responses of universities. This makes a normative methodology of testing hypotheses deriving from certain theoretical assumptions insufficient. In sum, the interpretative paradigm is the most suitable paradigm that can be used in the field of higher education in the current moment in order to analyze such complex entities like universities.

3.2 Universities as a 'Special' Form of Organization

To understand and explain the various ways universities respond to the political demand of widening participation, the present chapter follows the traditions of organizational sociologists who perceive universities as a special form of organization with characteristics that set them apart from 'normal' organizations (Enders/de Boer/Leisyte 2008; Hüther/Krücken 2016; Kehm 2012; Wilkesmann/Schmid 2012). These characteristics have a great impact on the purposes of the organizations, their structure and culture and their internal processes of decision-making (Meier 2010; Musselin 2006).

Universities are complex organizations that represent one of the oldest institutions in the world, predating the challenges of a rapidly changing and diverse environment (Würmseer 2010). They have expanded their mission from serving an elite to the provision of mass education, offering the most important vehicle for the contemporary 'knowledge society' (Wolter 2013b; Trow 2005). Despite the fact that many features of the first universities have survived to the present day, for example, the importance of academic freedom, developments in the modern world and society have changed the role, modes and conditions of universities heavily. This relates to the increasing complexity and differentiation of rapidly emerging disciplines, new challenges deriving from the growing number of students that differ in several characteristics from students before, and the changing role of and the relation to the external environment for the universities (Bess/Dee 2012; Kühl 2010; Pasternack/Kehm 2000). As these examples indicate, universities find themselves in an interdependent relationship with their environment that consists of a wide range of (sometimes conflicting) forces with distinct interests. In this context, universities are neither the powerless victim of environmental determinism nor are they totally unrestricted in their choice of (strategic) actions (Lawrence/Suddaby/Leca 2009). At the same time, from an open system perspective, it can be said that universities do not and cannot exist on their own (Scott 2004; Fumasoli/Stensaker 2013).

The following part introduces the main research findings about the 'special' structure(s) and culture(s) of universities. Although the present study refrains from an in-depth analysis of the structures and cultures of the universities analyzed here, the following part provides the necessary background information for grasping the complexity of universities and their organizational responses to institutional demands.

3.2.1 The 'Special' Structure(s) of Universities

The structural characteristics of universities are marked by their high degree of differentiation and decentralization. This significantly impacts the way universities deal with institutional pressures in general and with the demand of student diversity in particular (Dee 2016). These special structures result from the fact that universities are professional organizations (Mintzberg 1983). In general, this means that professionals (i.e., academics) play a central role for the university and many decisions are made by professional experts. The occupational group of professionals is characterized by the fact that they resolve complex problems and have a high degree of autonomy over their own working processes (Hüther/Krücken 2018). In other words, academics enjoy professional autonomy in their research and teaching (Leisyte 2016). Professional autonomy is particularly high in German higher education due to the Humboldtian tradition that academic freedom represents the strongest asset for being able to fulfill the objectives of universities. The high professional autonomy of academics results in 'bottom-heavy' organizations (Gornitzka 1999: 12) which means that universities' governance structures are characterized by a strong diffusion of power in decision-making processes, low probability of collective action and weak institutional leadership (Cohen/March 1974). Thus, the organizational structures of universities differ from the typical formal-bureaucratic organizational model concerning existing governance and decision-making structures (Hüther/Krücken 2016).

As professional organizations, universities employ professionals that are working in different disciplines. Consequently, the structuring of universities into working units is predominantly characterized by disciplines. A discipline is a specialized form of organization that is clustered around specific subjects or knowledge domains. Hereby, the profession groups specialists of the same knowledge domain (Hüther/Krücken 2018). Unlike being the case with a classic organization, the discipline (and the profession) is not tied to a locality; it rather connects a community that shares the same interests and perspectives involving everyone who 'speaks the language' across different organizations and national systems (Clark 1983). Consequently, interactions within the community, even over long distances (in particular with the help of modern technologies), are more common for academics than interactions with the other distinct groups of experts within their organization.

At this point, it is important to consider that the discipline is the primary source of loyalty for academics because it is costlier for them to leave their field of expertise than to leave their university, especially due to the high level of advanced education they had to complete to be part of this knowledge community (Clark 1983). Consequently, organizational members tend to identify themselves more with the work and the goals of their respective discipline than with the work and the goals of the entire organization (Dee 2016). Due to the relatively high degree of autonomy, the disparate disciplines tend to not only lose contact with the overall organization but also to the other sub-units within the organization, resulting in low degrees of interaction and unit-wide coordination (Clark 1983; Bess/Dee 2012). Consequently, the organizational members of one sub-unit (i.e., discipline), operate rather autonomously and independently from organizational members of other sub-units. This distinguishes universities from other types of organizations.

In his seminal article, Weick (1976) describes educational systems as 'loosely coupled', whereas their sub-units have no direct influence on each other and the opportunities of steering those loosely coupled basic units are enormously constrained. Nevertheless, there are also some advantages associated with this form in contrast to centrally controlled systems as the former can respond more quickly to environmental changes and develop detailed solution strategies. If these solutions turn out to be disadvantageous, the negative effects will be concentrated on the specific basic unit, while the overall organization will be protected by their loose coupling (ibid; Altvater/Bauer/Gilch 2007). What is more, the decentralized and highly differentiated structures of universities promote innovation and experimentation at the level of the respective sub-unit, while the same characteristics can have hindering effects on organization-wide efforts (Dee 2016). The challenge for managers and academics lies in the development of cross-departmental linkages. These linkages are more likely to be established by means of informal networks than formal structures (Kezar 2014).

In the face of external demands, this structural differentiation makes it difficult for universities to coordinate large-scale responses. As mentioned before, studies suggest that in order to support widening participation, whole-institution approaches to studying and teaching are required which acknowledge the diversity of today's student population (Gorard/Smith 2006; Kift/Nelson/Clarke 2010; Kreft/Leichsenring 2012). Since academic departments tend to act independently from each other, it is however unlikely that experiences with successful widening participation practices are exchanged at the departmental or individual level.

Since disciplines are the main differentiating feature of universities, it should also be noted that the kind of widening participation practices deemed appropriate to deal with student diversity might differ according to disciplines. One reason for these differing perspectives might be related to the differentiation between 'hard' and 'soft' sciences that has profound consequences for a wide range of organizational activities (Clark 1983; Bess/Dee 2012). The terms 'hard' and 'soft' sciences refer to a distinction made between disciplines according to the way their knowledge content is structured. Certain disciplines rely on well-developed and relatively clear and universal structures of knowledge, for example, the natural sciences. Within these disciplines, students need to acquire these highly structured contents gradually in a certain pre-defined way. This way of structuring knowledge makes it easier to determine what level of knowledge students should have prior to their studies and at certain points during their studies. Consequently, widening participation practices in these disciplines tend to focus on measuring students' knowledge in terms of pre-defined standard levels and sending them, if needed, to preparatory courses. Other disciplines, in turn, are concerned with ambiguous notions of knowledge, e.g., in the humanities (Clark 1983). On the one hand, disciplines without any agreement on consistent knowledge standards make it easier for students to enter higher education. On the other hand, these disciplines have nevertheless certain expectations towards their students' competences, but these expectations emerge in the form of 'unwritten rules of the game'. This lack of transparency may cause difficulties for students, particularly when they are unfamiliar with the higher education system. Widening participation practices in these disciplines often focus on the social and academic integration of first-year students by matching them with older and more experienced students, for example in mentoring programs.

3.2.2 The 'Special' Culture(s) of Universities

The concept of culture refers to the question of why universities can be so different from each other and how people in those academic organizations think about themselves and their work (Bess/Dee 2012). As mentioned before, institutional culture plays a crucial role in the way universities respond to institutional demands in general and their response to the demand of widening participation in particular (Greenbank 2007).

Academic organizations have strong internal dynamics rooted in the history of the organization. They are expressed by the ways decisions are made, actions are performed and communication takes place, both on an instrumental and a symbolic level (Tierney 1988). The notion of culture includes the common beliefs that help the members of the organization to define who they are, what they are doing and why they are doing it (Clark 1983). These common beliefs have been researched in the context of organizational sagas that refer to "a collective understanding of unique accomplishment in a formally, established group" (Clark 1972: 178). It involves emotionally loaded stories, or even legends "between the coolness of rational purpose and the warmth of sentiment found in religion and magic" that are "intrinsically historical but embellished through retelling and rewriting" (ibid.). Especially normative organizations like universities tend to overstress the importance of symbolic bonding. By this, the organization creates a community that represents an emotionally charged sense of place, thereby generating and supporting loyalty (ibid.). Especially in times of crisis, the depth of belief people have in the values of the institution can decide whether the institution will survive. Stable institutional beliefs are also an important vehicle for securing resources from the external environment by means of institutional reputation and self-image. Here, the strength of the organizational culture is directly connected to the degree of coupling, although there is always a symbolic unity of the whole academic institution (Clark 1983). For outsiders, the symbolic side of organizations is mostly more obvious than their technical structures. These symbols are transported using the official images, logos or public reputation.

Thus, culture in academic organizations includes shared values, beliefs, expectations, attitudes and assumptions that guide the behavior within the social system. Symbols, norms and rituals transport information about appropriate behavior, how this behavior can be rewarded, and how inappropriate behavior can be punished (Bess/Dee 2012). Schein (1990) sums it up as he describes culture as

> the pattern of basic assumptions, invented, discovered or developed by a given group, as it learns to cope with its problems of external adaptation and internal integration, and that has worked well enough to be considered valid and, therefore to be taught to new members as the correct way to perceive, think, and feel in relation to those problems.

However, it is not only the culture of the organization that plays a significant role here in guiding behavior. Rather, academic organizations subsume different "nested groupings that manufacture culture as part of their work and self-interest" (Clark 1983: 73). In universities, several vocational groups manage their everyday working life based on different guiding norms, values and attitudes. At the same time, they rely on each other's cooperation at some moments. The two most dominant groups employed at universities are academics and administrative staff. As mentioned before, professionals have a high degree of autonomy in deciding about their working processes, while solving complex problems (Dee 2016). Dealing with complexity would be hindered by strong external control. Their interactions are characterized by scholarly engagement, common ambitions and shared decision-making that arise primarily from the disciplines of the faculty. Such a culture is described in the literature as collegial (Bergquist 1992). Leaders are selected by their peers for a certain period of time as representatives of their common group interests, being more servants to the group than their masters (Kezar/Eckel 2002). Here, power positions are based on the general agreement about their professionalism rather than on authority based on hierarchy. By demonstrating professional expertise and interpersonal skills, the most influential role of the leader is the definition and exemplification of the common aspirations of the organization (Bensimon/Neumann/Birnbaum 1989).

The work of administrative staff, in turn, is influenced by very different norms and values, like hierarchy and clear and formal structures for decision-making. According to Birnbaum (1988), such a bureaucratic culture emphasizes compliance to formal chains, whereas the behavior of the organizational members relies on a system that is characterized by written rules and reporting relationships. Bergquist (1992) developed a similar archetype, describing the culture as managerial, in which emphasis is put on efficiency and effective governance skills in order to reach the goals and purposes of the institution. The role of leadership within the bureaucratic paradigm is defined as a final authority who is responsible for the well-being of the whole university. His/her task involves synchronization by ensuring that all the separated units work effectively and harmonically together. In this regard, decision-making is described as result-oriented, rational problem solving that follows formal and rational bureaucratic procedures (Bensimon/Neumann/Birnbaum 1989).

Further, universities also consist of several democratic and political elements (e.g., student union, senate) with diverging interests, trying to strengthen their power positions, gain control over institutional processes and pursue their own objectives (Baldridge 1971). Such a political or negotiating culture — as described by Birnbaum (1988) and Bergquist (1992) respectively — is characterized by the establishment of fair and democratic procedures through means of interest group building, confrontation and consensus. Organizational behavior can be described in terms of social exchange where people support certain interest groups, for which, in return, they expect benefits for their own situation (Bensimon/Neumann/Birnbaum 1989). Leaders within these systems have the task to mediate between the shifting power groups. Their power is based on the control of information and the manipulation of expertise, rather than on their hierarchical position (bureaucratic model) or the respect of colleagues due to their professional expertise (collegial model) (Bess/Dee 2012; Kezar/Eckel 2002).

Thus, universities comprise multiple and often conflicting subcultures. Different actor groups, like academics and administrative staff, might differ according to what they perceive as the appropriate way of dealing with external demands in general and widening participation in particular. Even among academics, there is rarely agreement among their beliefs in what constitutes appropriate ways to deal with student diversity (Becher/Trowler 2001; Dee 2016). These different beliefs originate in academics' disciplinary traditions which each constitute a distinct subculture of their own. Further, due to the high degree of structural differentiation previously mentioned, it is likely that the overarching culture of the organization is only weakly developed or not well accepted within the different sub-units (Bess/Dee 2012). This cultural differentiation can be challenging when universities are faced with institutional demands, like widening participation. According to research, organizational members are more likely to select and support widening participation initiatives that are consistent with their own values (Dee 2016; Greenbank 2007). Thus, efforts to enhance widening participation are expected to be more successful if the type of initiative fits in with the cultural values of the educational institution. For example, at a university that has a traditionally high proportion of vocationally qualified students, acceptance for developing study programs and support structures for this non-traditional student group is expected to be higher than at a university where most students enter higher education directly after they have obtained their *Abitur* at a *Gymnasium*.

Further, it should be taken into account that all aspects of an organizational and professional culture are embedded in the culture of the system. The culture of the system relates to the national traditions that guide the status and purpose of (higher) education. For example, one systemic belief over which national traditions can differ significantly lies in the degree of accessibility to higher education (Clark 1983). This belief manifests itself in discussions where some people argue for equitable access, while others fear a loss of prestige. Although nearly all developed countries have experienced an expansion towards mass education, they differ in their opinions about what degree of qualification is necessary to enter the system, which can be related to their traditions and educational history (Clancy/Goastellec 2007).

To put it in a nutshell, literature displays universities as structurally differentiated and loosely coupled, not following strict hierarchies and having rather weak decision-making competences (Weick 1976). Other authors describe them as 'incomplete' organizations because they have unclear hierarchies and their main sources of identity are rooted in the discipline and academic community rather than in the institution with its own set of values and norms (Cohen/March/Olsen 1972; Clark 1983; Brunsson/Sahlin-Andersson 2000).

In light of several university reforms that strengthened institutional autonomy, accountability and competition among institutions (Gornitzka/Maassen 2000; Paradeise/Reale/Goastellec 2009), some scholars argue that universities have become 'complete' organizations with more clearly defined identities (Brunsson/Sahlin-Andersson 2000). However, although current universities can no longer be described as organized anarchies (Cohen/March, 1974), they also do not fulfill the role of a rational actor

(Fumasoli/Stensaker 2013; Krücken/Meier 2006). At the same time, it has to be acknowledged that the environment of academic organizations has also increased in its complexity. Thus, the present study wishes to explore the gaps between contrasting explanations more closely in order to understand how universities deal with institutional pressures while taking into account the complexity of universities as organizations and their environment. Here, the study employs an institutional perspective, which will be further discussed in the following sub-chapter.

3.3 Explaining Universities' Responses: Choosing an Institutional Perspective

Deriving from the ontological and epistemological assumptions and the higher education research context, certain criteria can be deduced that guide the choice of the theoretical framework for the present study. The objectives of the present study require a theory that is suitable for studying both the macro-level of a university's environment and its organizational level because it wishes to examine how the topic of student diversity is constructed in the political discourse, but also how German universities respond to the institutional demand of student diversity. The main research interest consists of the topic of widening participation. As it has been shown in Chapter 2, widening participation represents a value-laden concept that transports inconsistent normative values and expectations that universities face. At the same time, the field of higher education represents a highly institutionalized environment, as has been explained in the previous chapter. Consequently, an institutional theory perspective seems to be a promising way to explain organizational responses of German universities to student diversity.

Institutional theory or, more precisely, organizational neo-institutionalism, can be perceived as one of the most dominant approaches to understand organizations and organizational behavior (Palmer/Biggart/Dick 2008). This is particularly true for the field of higher education (Krücken/Röbken 2009). The field of higher education can be described as a highly institutionalized environment in which universities are pressured to comply with widely endorsed institutional values (Mampaey 2018). One example of such an institutional value is widening participation (Archer 2007; Osborne 2003a). Here, numerous studies have examined how universities respond to the institutional forces they are faced with through a neo-institutional theoretical lens (Krücken/Röbken 2009). Most of these studies use concepts from the classical works of Meyer/Rowan (1977), DiMaggio/Powell (1983), Zucker (1977), Tolbert/Zucker (1983), and Meyer/Scott (1983).

The foundation of neo-institutionalism lies in the critique of the classical rational conceptualization of organizations that portray them as agentic actors capable of responding adequately to situational circumstances (Palmer/Biggart/Dick 2008). At that time in the first half of the last century, prominent technocratic theories focused on the relationship between the organization and their (technical) environment and the ways formal organizational structures were adapted to those technical demands to increase efficiency and ensure an appropriate 'fit'. Even so, Meyer/Rowan (1977) emphasize in their seminal work that organizations are not only influenced by technical expectations (i.e., pressures towards efficiency, accountability), but also by their 'institutional' context which incorporates rationalized myths, i.e., widespread social understandings about what is defined as being rational (Greenwood et al. 2008). These rationalized myths are institutionalized in their environment, emerging as formal and informal rules, social norms and ideologies of society (Meyer/Rowan 1977). While earlier work concentrated mostly on regulative and normative aspects of the institutional context, later neo-institutionalists added the role of symbolic elements, such as behavioral schemata and scripts that shape organizational structures and actions (Scott 2004). Overall, rationalized myths are regarded as a recipe for appropriate behavior. In order to signal their 'social fitness', organizations incorporate practices defined by prevailing rationalized concepts about organizational work, guided by a logic of appropriateness (DiMaggio/Powell 1983; March/Olsen 1984). As Meyer/Rowan (1977) state, "organizations that do so increase their legitimacy and their survival prospects, independent of the immediate efficacy of the acquired practices and procedures". This means organizational action is not solely triggered by the organization's impetus of being rational to increase efficiency, but also by appearing to be rational to secure legitimacy and survival (Meyer/Scott 1983).

Most attention of these early institutional theorists is concentrated on the role of shared meaning, institutional processes and institutional conformity (Lawrence/Suddaby/Leca 2009). Institutional theory builds on observations that organizations often look alike, although their activities might be very different, and that organizational administration tends to take over certain practices that originally stem from disparate sectors (Palmer/Biggart/Dick 2008; Sahlin/Wedlin 2008). In this context, neo-institutionalism is characterized by its two most important contributions to organizational theory, namely the concept of isomorphism and the phenomenon of decoupling.

By conforming to rationalized myths, organizations become isomorphic with their institutional context. DiMaggio/Powell (1983) describe how institutionalization actually takes place through three 'mechanisms of diffusion': coercive isomorphism that results from political influence and the issue of legitimacy, mimetic isomorphism that derives from standard responses to uncertainty, and normative isomorphism that is related to professionalization. Organizations might also enact ceremonial conformity in cases where institutional expectations contradict considerations and requirements of (technical) efficiency (Meyer/Scott 1983). According to Meyer/Rowan (1977), organizations comply with institutional expectations in a symbolic manner by decoupling their formal structures from their technical activities. Thus, in order to secure legitimacy, the expectations and institutional demands are met externally, whereas they have no impact on actual everyday business (Greenwood et al. 2008). Therefore, the main research interest of neo-institutionalist research lies within the similarities between organizations and not their heterogeneity.

The question why organizations or, more precisely, organizational structures, become more alike has also stimulated studies in the field of higher education research. For example, research indicates that an increasing number of universities have begun to implement mission statements (Jungblut/Jungblut 2016; Kosmützky/Krücken 2015; Morphew/Hartley 2006). Mission statements are regarded as legitimate strategic instruments of university leadership. Higher education research has also investigated the three isomorphic mechanisms mentioned above. Schriewer (2007) for example shows that the legal regulations in the context of the Bologna Process (e.g., the introduction of credit points, two-cycle study programs) have resulted in a unique and historically high level of structural harmonization among higher education systems on the European level. This can be described as the result of coercive isomorphism (Krücken/Röbken 2009). Here, the state as the most influential player in public higher education systems has sparked off structural adaptation processes with the help of legal regulations. However, the consistent Bologna framework had to face very diverse European higher education systems, which implemented the Bologna regulations very differently. The consequence is that formally similar models and programs mask considerable variations in concrete activities that might even have counterproductive effects. In the case of the Bologna Process, it seems that the more structured Bachelor's degree programs and the shortened study cycles indeed have hindering effects on the mobility of young students across Europe, which runs counter to the original objective of the Bologna Process (Schriewer 2007). Mimetic isomorphism was identified in the context of universities that adopted academically oriented programs (e.g., Master's and PhD graduate programs) in order to strengthen their reputation and, thus, strengthen their legitimacy (Morphew/Huisman 2002). The underlying mechanism here is imitation. Smaller universities with less academic reputation copy the structures and norms of bigger research-oriented universities which serve as role models within the organizational field. Finally, normative isomorphism results from pressures exerted by the profession. For example, accreditation agencies can exert normative pressures on universities to align curricula and study programs according to specific quality assurance standards (Krücken/Röbken 2009).

The concept of decoupling has been confirmed in numerous higher education studies. For example, Morphew/Hartley (2006) show that the formulation of mission statements is often not followed by any changes in organizational practice. In the context of dealing with student diversity, universities have been criticized to meet this institutional demand on a merely rhetorical basis, while their organizational practices of teaching and learning remain unchanged (Kehm 2000).

However, over the course of time, neo-institutionalism has received extensive critique. In general, institutional theorists fail to provide clear definitions of the concepts of 'institution', 'institutional context' and 'institutionalization' (Czarniawska 2008; Lawrence/Suddaby/Leca 2009). In some cases, these notions are taken for granted and it is left to the reader to make suppositions of what they might entail. In other cases, these concepts are even defined differently within one work, resulting in conceptual ambiguities. According to Greenwood et al. (2008), institutional theorists seem to have different understandings of these terms, but without making their points of view apparent, the authors claim, it is difficult to start a debate about the most important concepts the theory entails (ibid.).

Further, neo-institutionalists' coverage of organizational change has been criticized. This can be traced back to its origin as a counter-movement to traditional organizational theory which — based on the rational choice theory — assumes that change is an organizational norm. Institutionalists object to this assumption by stating that stability, and not change, is the norm (Czarniawska 2008). But according to Czarniawska/Sevón (1996a), reality resembles a rather paradoxical and ambiguous picture, where planned initiatives for change often fail or produce unexpected and unintended results, while simultaneously people convince others — on purpose or by accident — to change their actions and underlying beliefs.

A related critique stems from the assumption of institutional theory that institutional rules are 'out there'. In other words, neo-institutional research assumes that there are certain characteristics of an organization's organizational field that determine whether institutional pressures or expectations are adopted or not. This, in turn, implies the existence of 'one' institutional rule. It is regarded as something definite, invariable and apparent to everyone in the same way. This point of view was challenged by research that acknowledged the complexity of institutional contexts, in which institutional demands are often perceived as conflicting with each other. Therefore, in line with a social constructivist perspective, growing attention was given to the question why and how organizations interpret and respond differently to their contexts. This development questioned previous assumptions of 'objective' and fixed institutional expectations by emphasizing the 'subjective' character of different interpretations and translations organizational actors may depend on (Greenwood et al. 2008).

A similar critique concerns the limited role that agency plays in neo-institutional approaches, as these focus more on processes on the macro-level. This can be explained by the initial concern to explain organizational isomorphism which could not be traced back to competitive pressures or motives of efficiency. Therefore, early institutionalists were mostly interested in the ways institutions affect organizational actions. Accordingly, agency was of secondary interest, mostly ignored or considered as a reaction to institutional pressures by means of adoption, decoupling or ceremonial conformity. Early on, the subordinate role of agency and its over-socialized image was criticized in the literature (Lawrence/Suddaby/Leca 2009). There were several attempts to incorporate concepts of agency into institutional theory, for example by combining approaches from neo-institutionalism and resource-dependency (Oliver 1991). Accordingly, research started to shift its focus from the processes through which institutions affect organizational action towards the processes through which actors affect the institutional practices within which they operate (Palmer/Biggart/Dick 2008). In this context, research on institutional entrepreneurship evolved, referring to "activities of actors who have an interest in particular institutional arrangements and who leverage resources to create new institutions or to transform existing ones" (Maguire/Hardy/Lawrence 2004: 657). Alternatively, studies integrated practice-oriented literature to derive a more balanced understanding of agency and institution (Greenwood et al. 2008). By focusing on the relationship between human action and the cultures and structures the actors are embedded in, these approaches contrast with both, structuralist and voluntaristic views (Krücken/Röbken, 2009).

Krücken/Röbken (2009) argue that current developments in the higher education sector can no longer be grasped by the established concepts of neo-institutionalism. Yet, there are only a few studies to date that argue for an adaptation of neo-institutional theory according to changes in higher education systems worldwide. One example is the study of Kraatz/Zajac (1996) whose findings indicate that the increase of competitive pressures and a tighter coupling of organizational structures due to efficiency resulted in an organizational change of universities which cannot be explained by isomorphic mechanisms or decoupling. Further, Levy's (2006) study on the expansion of the private higher education sector examines the reasons for the increasing heterogeneity of higher education systems, which would counter the neo-institutional assumption of increasing similarities among organizations in the field of higher education. Further, he points out that a stronger actor-oriented perspective is required rather than making the passive changes of universities according to external institutional requirements subject of discussion. He emphasizes the impact of single actors in shaping the way universities deal with challenges they are faced with in a deliberate and intentional way.

The present study follows this criticism and defines two additional criteria for choosing an appropriate theoretical framework for studying the phenomenon of interest. Considering the social constructivist perspective of the present study, the theoretical framework should acknowledge that actors are actively involved in a permanent process of interpretation of the institutional pressures they are faced with. At the same time, the second criterion refers to the observation that actors' actions and interpretations are neither always planned nor always unconscious. In other words, the present study is looking for a theoretical framework that can overcome simple dichotomies that prescribe organizational responses either as a result of strategic actorhood or environmental determinism. Instead, the present study aims to build on a theoretical framework that acknowledges the complexity of higher education systems and institutions.

Here, Scandinavian institutionalism (Czarniawska/Joerges 1996) provides an interesting complementary theoretical lens to understand how external pressures lead to local variations. While institutional theory suffers from the 'either-or'' character of modernist organizational theory which divides the organizational landscape into opposite dichotomies like technical/institutional, change/stability, structuralist/voluntaristic and objective/subjective, Scandinavian institutionalism seeks to overcome those dichotomies, pointing towards a more holistic picture of organizations and their inner processes.

3.4 Scandinavian Institutionalism

Scandinavian institutionalism (Czarniawska/Joerges 1996) is mostly concerned with the question of how organizations respond to institutional pressures. It focuses on understanding how organizations perceive and interpret institutional expectations and how these perceptions and interpretations influence organizational action in their daily lives (Boxenbaum/Strandgaard Pedersen 2009). Thereby, Scandinavian institutionalists acknowledge the heterogeneity of organizational responses, while putting special emphasis on intra-organizational dynamics and processes, which leads to a preference for combining elements of institutional theory with practice-oriented literature (Boxenbaum/Jonsson 2008). Accordingly, they prefer to examine phenomena of interest that are situational, dynamic and emergent, but also ambiguous and fragmented.

This line of theory was first developed in the 1980s and 1990s, based on research on public organizations and public reforms in Norway and Sweden (Brunsson/Olsen 1993; March/Olsen 1989). Scandinavian institutionalism was built around the phenomenon of organizational change by taking up the ambiguity often witnessed concerning change (Boxenbaum/Strandgaard Pedersen 2009). This theory is based on observations within organizational life that show both intentional and contingent factors shaping the process of change. Therefore, Scandinavian institutionalists regard organizations as a combination of change and stability that together represent an organizational norm (Czarniawska/Sevón 1996b).

This strand of theory builds on concepts from neo-institutional, cultural and cognitive approaches, and is influenced by the work of James G. March, Karl E. Weick, Bruno Latour, and Michel Callon (Boxenbaum/Strandgaard Pedersen 2009). Due to their interest in the dynamic elements of circulating ideas this tradition is primarily based on extensive qualitative studies, like case studies and micro-studies of individual decision-making and change processes (Sahlin/Wedlin 2008: 219). Certain concepts, such as translation, sense-making and loose coupling, have shaped the development of Scandinavian institutionalism in a profound way and will be presented in more detail in the following part (Boxenbaum/Strandgaard Pedersen 2009).

3.4.1 Translation and the Travel of Ideas

The most prominent concept within Scandinavian institutionalism is 'translation' (Czarniawska/Joerges 1996). It assumes that institutional demands transport certain underlying ideas which are translated as they travel from one local context to another (Wæraas/Sataøen 2014). During this travel, the idea underlies certain modifications that result in increasingly heterogeneous organizational fields.

The translation perspective of Scandinavian institutionalists was developed as an alternative to the diffusion models of American institutionalists. According to the concept of diffusion, certain elements determine whether the diffusion of an innovation or an idea will take place (Rogers 2002). Here, studies try to identify the 'original' idea and the criteria that determine whether ideas become successful. This perspective, however, appears to be too mechanical and static when applied to the observations made by research. The diffusion process was displayed as a physical process in which a physical unit from one source diffuses to other contexts due to certain powerful properties they entail. But research suggests that "it appears to be not so much a case of ideas flowing widely because they are powerful, but rather of ideas becoming powerful as they circulate" (Sahlin/Wedlin 2008). Ideas become legitimate and popular due to the way they have been displayed, formulated and fitted into their respective contexts by certain actors in the field (Tolbert/Zucker 1983; Røvik 2011). This means that what is diffused from one context to another is not a consistent and premade entity, but rather ideas or practices that are subject to constant translation (Czarniawska/Sevón 1996a). This explains the emergence of management fads and fashions where attention is brought to an idea whose time and space has come (Abrahamson 1996). In other words, ideas do not come out of the blue, but rather circulate all the time. Nevertheless, at a specific local time/space, certain ideas enter the field of attention of organizational actors. Then, ideas and practices are first dis-embedded and then re-embedded in the context they have traveled to (Czarniawska/Joerges 1996). Czarniawska (2008) describes this process with a gardening metaphor, when she emphasizes

> that plants that are to be moved to another place are taken from the bed where they were growing, and then, cleaned of most of the soil in which they sat, are put into a new bed. [...] The plant growing at a new place is never identical to the one that started traveling.

This means that an idea is subject to change every time it is applied in another context because meaning is created by connecting the idea to other elements in the organizational context (Boxenbaum/Strandgaard Pedersen 2009). This puts emphasis on the social aspects of diffusion processes rather than understanding the spreading of ideas in physical terms (Sahlin/Wedlin 2008).

Consequently, this line of institutional research builds on literature about sense-making, which refers to the observation that certain ideas or practices that diffuse under the same term are given different meanings when they are implemented in different organizational contexts (Weick 1979). By trying to make sense of the situation, actors interpret events and actions differently due to their different understandings and interests, which is, in turn, based on their (prior) knowledge, experiences and expectations. Sense-making, in this context, builds on the basic idea that reality is an ongoing act that results from efforts to establish order and make (retrospective) sense of occurrences (Weick 1993). Accordingly, people try to make these occurrences rationally comprehensible by means of sense-making, which "involves the ongoing retrospective development of plausible images that rationalize what people are doing" (Weick/Sutcliffe/Obstfeld 2005: 409). Thus, the literature on sense-making emphasizes the position of actors as "interpreters of institutional pressure and hence as mediators of the institutional pressures on organizations" (Boxenbaum/Strandgaard Pedersen 2009: 190). During the process of trying to comprehend institutional processes, they automatically shape the effects of institutional pressure on the organization.

The literature on translation opposes the traditional institutional assumption that organizations are passive recipients which adopt "the same thing for the same reason" (Abrahamson 2006: 513). Instead, the translation perspective acknowledges the "richness of interpretations that the idea triggers in each actor within a network" (Røvik 2016: 291). Consequently, the travel of ideas is a process of translation and "not one of reception, rejection, resistance or acceptance" (Latour, 1992, p. 116 as cited by (Czarniawska/Joerges 1996).

Actors modify ideas through a process of transformation in order to fit them to the unique needs of the organizational context. By emphasizing the social constructionist principle of institutional thought, the process of translation "implies deliberate and accidental or unintended transformations of ideas as they transfer from one setting to another, and the potential for continuous adjustment and change" (Lawrence/Suddaby/Leca 2009: 17). Thereby, this line of literature allows taking a closer look at local organizational variations in contrast to the conventional notion of organizational homogeneity (DiMaggio/Powell 1983; Meyer/Rowan 1977), while asking "how and why ideas become widespread, how they are translated as they flow and with what organizational consequences" (Sahlin/Wedlin 2008: 219).

3.4.2 Editing Rules and the Role of Agency

Organizational researchers are keen to understand the mechanisms behind organizational heterogeneity and translation as the "key heterogeneity-producing social mechanism" (Røvik 2016: 293). However, there is some disagreement concerning the degree of agency in this process. It is possible to differentiate between agentic approaches that assume actors can manipulate institutional pressures according to their own interests, and the embeddedness approach that assumes, in contrast, that an actor's translations are implicit and unconscious efforts to make sense of certain ideas while making them fit into their local context (Kirkpatrick et al. 2013).

According to Sahlin-Andersson (1996), the perspective of these local actors suggests that change processes are triggered by the construction of local problems. In other words, actors perceive a certain problem by comparing their local situation with that of similar organizations. The respective prototype, idea, or model represents a 'successful' solution to solve this problem so that they imitate these successes. This can be described as an editing process, in which ideas and practices are formulated and reformulated as they circulate. Thus, in each new situation, "a history of earlier experiences is reformulated in the light of present circumstances and visions of the future" (ibid.: 82), while meanings given to the idea or prototype are continuously edited. This process is based on changing situational and institutional circumstances. Here, similarities between the idea and the local setting are emphasized, while differences are downplayed.

Although this process of translation appears at first to be open-ended, Sahlin-Andersson (1996) identifies certain editing rules that guide translations. These editing rules arise from the local context, enable and restrict the modification of circulating ideas by actors, and influence how they translate and fit them to the local context (Sahlin/Wedlin 2008). These editing rules are not explicit or strict rules, but rather implicit "rules which have been followed"

(Sahlin-Andersson 1996: 85) in the process of telling and retelling the stories of editing. Sahlin-Andersson (1996) distinguishes between three kinds of rules, framing ideas according to context, logic or formulation. Firstly, when ideas enter a new local setting, they are decontextualized or disembedded as abstract models or prototypes that enable actors to 'edit' or re-embed social meaning so that the ideas fit into the local context (Sahlin/Wedlin 2008; Czarniawska/Joerges 1996). The respective translation of ideas is, thereby, brought into direct relation to certain aspects of the context. Secondly, elements of logic are added to the story of initiatives and the effects of certain activities. This set of rules includes a certain rationalistic logic that is presented in order to legitimize developments and actions, referring to data, evaluations, statistics or observations (Kirkpatrick et al. 2013). The third set of rules concerns the formulation: while presenting circulating ideas and their effects, these stories might include elements of dramatization, moralization or other attention-tracking justifications in order to make sense of ideas and the way they are translated (ibid; Sahlin/Wedlin 2008).

The concept of editing underlines that organizations are "no passive adopter[s] of trends" (Sahlin-Andersson 1996: 92). At the same time, actors seem to have some interpretative and creative capacities while being confronted with new ideas and practices, although translations follow certain implicit editing rules to make them fit to the local context according to context, logic or formulation. The question remains how much control local actors have over the translation process. Here, an interesting third alternative perspective is suggested by Battilana/D'Aunno (2009) who propose the concept of embedded agency. This concept calls for perceiving agency as a multidimensional concept consisting of elements oriented towards the past, future and present. Agency is conceptualized as a

> temporally embedded process of social engagement, informed by the past (in its habitual aspect), but also oriented toward the future (as a capacity to imagine alternative possibilities) and toward the present (as a capacity to contextualize past habits and future projects within the contingencies of the moment) (Battilana/D'Aunno 2009: 47).

The authors follow the approach of Emirbayer/Mische (1998) who argue that agency consists of three elements, iteration, projectivity and practical evaluation. The first element refers to past patterns of thought and action that actors selectively recognize and apply when interpreting current situations. The second element involves the imaginative conceptualization of future courses of action that emerge from a constellation of habits assumed self-evident which then are reconfigured according to the actor's hopes and desires for the future. The third aspect is oriented towards the present and describes the capacity of actors to make practical and normative judgments about courses of actions as a response to present situations and demands. Consequently, they argue that institutions influence actors, but that the latter can also develop a 'practical consciousness'. In other words, actors might follow habitualized routines and practices, but "they often do so with awareness and purpose, rather than simply acting as institutional automatons" (Battilana/D'Aunno 2009: 47). To find out whether actors behave purposively or not would go beyond the scope of this study. Nevertheless, although the role of agency will not be an explicit focus of the present study, its findings might provide useful insights that future research can build on.

3.4.3 Loose Coupling and Decoupling

The idea of organizations as loosely coupled systems stems from a group of organizational sociologists and social psychologists and was established in the mid-1970s. It was developed by Glassman (1973) and applied to the context of specific types of organizations by Weick (1976) and March/Olsen (1984) in order to challenge the prevalent position of system theory which regarded organizations as coherent units consisting of densely linked and interdependent elements. They stated instead that organizational elements are loosely coupled to one another, either unintentionally or because it was seen as appropriate in a particular situation (Boxenbaum/Jonsson 2008). Decoupling, as previously mentioned, resembles one form of loose coupling. It refers to the disconnection of organizational structure and organizational practice, which is oriented towards the perceived demands of (technical) efficiency as the result of external pressure to conform. The principle of decoupling was later taken up by Scandinavian researchers who demonstrate that organizations also use this technique in situations where they are confronted with multiple and contradictory institutional pressures and expectations (Greenwood et al. 2008). The most famous illustration of this phenomenon is provided by Brunsson (1986) and his distinction between how organizations talk on the one hand, and how they act on the other hand. More precisely, he distinguishes between three organizational outputs: organizational talk, decision and action (ibid.). In general, it can be assumed that talk — the spoken word — and decisions serve the aim to initiate and coordinate internal actions. However, Brunsson (1986: 170) claims that the instruments of talk and decision might also be used to reflect the institutional norms of the environment, serving as "ideological outputs of the organization, beside its output of products". Accordingly, by talking, i.e., rhetorically acknowledging, and by making (ceremonial) decisions, organizations adopt the institutional expectations on the level of externally visible formal structures. These demonstrate their adaptability, while simultaneously leaving the internal structure of activities unaffected (Brunsson 1989). One example stems from a study on a radical reform at Swedish Rail which showed how this reform was formally implemented on the structure level while having had no impact on daily procedures. Management feared that the reform would cause chaos, but instead, they realized that the work of rail traffic and operational supervisors were unaffected by the reform (Brunsson/Olsen 1993; Boxenbaum/Jonsson 2017).

An important additional notion of new Scandinavian institutionalist research is that ideas are not perceived 'just' as containing symbolic value. Rather, it is assumed that transformation takes place in both verbal accounts and actual practices (Kirkpatrick et al. 2013). Scandinavian institutionalist research has shown how over time ideas indeed have long-lasting effects by being adopted into organizational practice, for example by means of newly introduced terminology and models. This perspective suggests that symbolic considerations of legitimacy might trigger the translation process of certain ideas first, while, its subsequent adoption is nevertheless based on sense-making processes about how this idea fits the local context (Wæraas/Sataøen 2014).

3.4.4 Scandinavian Institutionalism in Higher Education Research

Scandinavian institutionalism was driven by research in public organizations and on public reforms (Boxenbaum/Strandgaard Pedersen 2009). More precisely, its research interest was driven by new public management-inspired reforms that resulted in the adoption of management ideas and concepts by public organizations (Waeraas/Nielsen 2016). For example, several studies investigated how management ideas were translated in health care organizations (Boxenbaum 2006; Boch Waldorff 2013; Kirkpatrick et al. 2013). Although Scandinavian institutionalism and the translation perspective can be perceived as particularly useful for analyzing organizational responses of complex entities like universities, it is remarkable that so far this theory has not been used extensively in the field of higher education research.

Studies in higher education research about governance reforms that aim at strengthening autonomy, accountability and competition of universities (Paradeise/Reale/Goastellec 2009) might count as exceptions. For example, Stensaker (2007) examines how the concept of quality can be described as a management idea that has been introduced to higher education. In addition, Mazza/Sahlin-Andersson/Pedersen (2016) analyze how the US academic degree of Master of Business Administration (in the following abbreviated as MBA) diffuses in Europe, resulting in local translations of MBA programs at four European universities. Similarly, Lamb/Currie (2011) explore how business schools in China have copied the US MBA model, yet did not find any evidence for practice variation. For this undertaking, a translation perspective was particularly useful in analyzing the travel of ideas that have the form of concrete models or practices (Sahlin/Wedlin 2017).

As mentioned before, the concept of 'student diversity' is ambiguous, incorporating different value-laden meanings. Consequently, only a few studies have investigated diversity-related concepts from a translation perspective so far. One exception stems from the field of gender studies: Offenberger/Nentwich (2017) analyze traveling ideas of equal opportunities in the context of gender equality reforms at a Swiss University. They emphasize the benefits of a process-oriented theory like Scandinavian institutionalism that understands organizational change as a continuous translation process in which ideas are translated into organizational realities by active interpretative work. Such an understanding is particularly useful for a practical application in gender equality work. The authors suggest that gender equality work requires an ongoing active interpretation of gender equality reforms within the organization in order to move this organization towards a changed understanding of equal opportunities.

Another interesting exception is the study of Mampaey (2018) who examines how the idea of socio-demographic diversity was translated in Flemish universities. He identifies translation rules that shape how heterogeneous definitions of this institutionalized value evolved. However, his research focuses on symbolic or strategic responses of universities in their external communication rather than investigating how they respond to diversity on the level of their actual organizational practices. In contrast to the present study, his research is based on a rather narrow definition of diversity, as it concentrates on the socio-demographic characteristics that approve to be important determinants of diversity in the Flemish higher education context. As mentioned before, the concept of diversity is highly context-sensitive. Consequently, the term 'diversity' has very different connotations and associations in the German higher education context, as the review undertaken in Chapter 2 has shown in more detail. The present study explicitly wishes to keep the definition of 'student diversity' as broad as possible in order to analyze what German universities understand under this term. Narrowing it down to socio-demographic characteristics would be counterproductive for this research objective.

The present study considers the implications of the Scandinavian institutionalist assumption that ideas are not only translated in verbal accounts, but also have an impact on organizational practices. Consequently, the present study wishes to examine organizational responses to student diversity not only on the strategy level but also on the level of structures and action. Here, the study builds on research on organizational responses to widening participation on these three levels. This research will be introduced in the following chapter.

3.5 Research on Organizational Responses of Universities to Widening Participation

Accompanied by several widening participation policy initiatives, universities have begun to open themselves up to non-traditional students and inform, consult and support underrepresented student groups (Banscherus/Pickert 2013). This is not only a worldwide trend but also true for German universities (Watson 2006; Osborne 2003b; Buß/Erbsland/Rahn 2018). Accordingly, the number of studies examining these organizational responses to deal with student diversity has increased substantially.

The German research landscape is characterized by inconsistent statements about how universities interpret and translate the demand to deal with student diversity in their local contexts. Literature suggests, on the one hand, that the demand is only met in terms of rhetoric, while organizational practice remains unaffected (Hanft 2015; Kehm 2000). On the other hand, researchers criticize that universities develop a conglomeration of measures that lack a coherent underlying strategy of how to bring a new consciousness for student diversity into the university (Leicht-Scholten 2011). These inconsistent findings suggest that there are different levels of organizational responses. The strategy level includes universities' statements on definitions of student diversity and their plans to widen participation for certain underrepresented student groups. On a structure level, universities establish formal structures in different areas to support widening participation, for example in the area of information structures, access structures, study program structures and support structures during studies. The structure level can be distinguished from the action level which includes the concrete activities for widening participation in teaching and studying. This third level comprises, for example, activities that aim at improving student performance (e.g., bridging courses), the institution (e.g., practice-oriented teaching) and the fit between the student and the institution (e.g., mentoring programs).

Inconsistent research findings suggest that by investigating organizational responses on all three levels, one gains a more in-depth understanding of the ways universities translate the demand to deal with student diversity. This is of special importance when considering the underlying theoretical background of the present study. According to institutional theory, organizational responses on these levels can differ within one organization, when it is confronted with conflicting or complex demands (Meyer/Rowan 1977). The result is an inconsistency between the way the university presents itself to the outside world (i.e., the strategy level) or establishes formal structures to widen participation (i.e., the structure level) on the one hand, and the way they actually act in the context of studying and teaching (i.e., the action level) on the other hand. Organizations overcome this inconsistency by decoupling these three levels from each other so that they are still able to meet the demand on a rhetorical basis to secure their legitimacy, while their activities remain unchanged to secure their efficiency (Brunsson 1989). Thus, to detect inconsistencies between the different levels of organizational responses and signs of decoupling, the present study builds on recent research on organizational responses on the levels of strategy, structure and action which will be introduced in the next subsections. Since the national (education) context is of crucial importance, the main focus lies on research in the context of German universities. Nevertheless, international research, in particular international comparative studies, will be reviewed as well.

3.5.1 Organizational Responses to Widening Participation: The Strategy Level

Organizational strategies indicate what organizations perceive as important, while they provide a plan how to achieve its desired objectives (Dee 2016). Although strategies can also contribute to the development of an innovative vision for the future, they are mostly reactive to external pressures or they imitate what other organizations are doing (O'Meara 2007).

Universities worldwide have begun to acknowledge widening participation as an important strategic topic. For example, there is numerous research on how British universities have integrated widening participation as a part of their mission statements. This integration was seen as a response to the Labour government's widening participation policy agenda, which aimed to increase the number of 18 to 30-year-olds who participate in higher education to 50 percent (McCaig 2018). Consequently, British universities positioned themselves in prospectus documents and on websites in the discourse on widening participation by stating their institutional commitment to welcome certain non-traditional student groups. Interestingly, depending on their age and profile, differences among universities became apparent. While pre-1992 institutions highlight their elite status and the desire to select the brightest and best students, post-1992 institutions market themselves as welcoming, open and accessible to all students (Graham 2010, 2013). Similar research points to the importance of the institutional culture for the introduction of widening participation strategies, making it easier or harder to pursue strategies of widening participation (Greenbank 2006, 2007). This is in line with the institutional perspective that claims that widening participation requires an institutional change in that sense that universities need to "change fundamentally their modus operandi, their view of the world and their values" (Foskett 2002: 79). However, evidence for institutional change is limited. Rather, researchers like Foskett (2002) suggest that although British universities have indeed discovered widening participation as an important strategic topic, it is mostly understood as a marketing challenge in order to win over new target groups. Consequently, the institutional culture and practices remain unresponsive to the needs of non-traditional student groups (Bowl 2001). Other research from a British context argues that explanations that interpret universities' responses as primarily economically motivated are too short-sighted. Instead, Greenbank's (2006, 2007) analysis of factors influencing the development of widening participation strategies at British universities suggests that a more in-depth analysis of institutional responses to widening participation is required. His research findings show how widening participation strategies emerge out of a complex interplay between economic forces and political factors, mediated by the organizational culture of universities.

Overall, international research points to the importance of including widening participation as a strategic area of activity to get involved in the discussion on student diversity (Gorard/Smith 2006). A strategic approach to widening participation implies the formulation of an institutional commitment that considers the whole student life cycle and takes all of the universities' activities into account. This makes student diversity a cross-sectional task. Such an approach formulates a coherent and sustainable way of dealing with student diversity instead of developing multiple activities on a project basis without any underlying links (ibid.).

In the German context, universities are often criticized for their lack of an overall strategy for widening participation (Hanft 2015). This can be related to the general problem universities have when it comes to building a profile, something which is relatively new and unknown terrain for German universities (Kosmützky 2012). However, as a new trend, some universities have begun to develop diversity concepts comprising the institution as a whole which seek to deal with student diversity in a strategic way (Mooraj/Zervakis 2014). Here, dealing with student diversity is integrated as a cross-sectional task in organizational development and influences the governance of universities' core tasks. These concepts often integrate a more general strategic commitment to connecting student retention and support throughout the student lifecycle with widening participation efforts. Depending on the respective profile of the institution, the definition of widening participation varies within these concepts and what dealing with student diversity means in their local context for teaching, learning and assessment (Mooraj/Wiese 2013). For example, the student profile of the University of Duisburg-Essen is very special since most of the students are regionally recruited. More than half of the students come from a non-academic family, one quarter of the student body has a migration background and two thirds of the students work alongside their studies (Mooraj/Zervakis 2014). Consequently, the university presents itself as having "the chance and responsibility to create framework conditions for study success, regardless of the individual predispositions and students' origin" (ibid.: 4). The university became famous in Germany for its consistent integration of diversity management into strategic areas for action, led by a prorectorate for diversity management. In the area of studying and teaching, different activities which consider the whole student life cycle were developed and coordinated by this prorectorate, accompanied by initiatives that support the development of the staff's diversity competences. This example shows how a strategic approach to widening participation can fit the local context of an institution, comprised of student population, regional factors and historical background.

A strategic approach to widen participation requires the formulation of objectives that are measurable so that universities can examine whether these objectives have been achieved. Hence, monitoring procedures and tracking data are needed to evaluate on a regular basis whether progress has been made towards the fulfillment of widening participation strategic objectives. Research criticizes that universities mostly have poor tracking data about their students and that they are not able to assess the impact of their interventions (Holland et al. 2017). Institutional research might help to inform the organization about the current status of their students and identify areas in need of improvement. On such a basis, targets and interventions can be defined and regular surveys can help to assess the purposed progress (Watson 2006). International experience shows that the way the topic of diversity is communicated on the part of university leadership impacts its adaptation within the organization. In order to increase the internal acceptance of these initiatives, it makes a decisive difference how such a concept is developed: by involving all actors, providing room for skepticism as well as enriching experiences, or by prescribing the development of diversity management in a more top-down-oriented way (Kreft/Leichsenring 2012).

3.5.2 *Organizational Responses to Widening Participation: The Structure Level*

Universities have highly differentiated and decentralized structures. Typically, their structures are characterized by a large number of academic departments that are autonomously responsible for their teaching curriculum and research agendas, depending on their respective disciplines (Dee 2016). Concerning the demand to deal with student diversity, universities have expanded and adapted their institutional structures concerning their information structures, access structures, study programs, study and teacher support structures as well as their coordination structures. The following sub-chapters will introduce the main research findings for these thematic areas and their role in widening participation.

Information structures

Information structures play a crucial role in widening participation because these are the first structures potential students are confronted with. Accordingly, studies show how important the presentation of relevant information on studying and teaching is (Scheller et al. 2013). This does not only relate to the content of the information (e.g., whether information about access and participation opportunities can be found), but also the way this information is presented with regard to language, transparency and consistency. These factors play an even more important role for website information, which presents the main source for potential students to inform themselves about access and study opportunities at German universities (ibid.). However, it can be a special challenge to produce online texts and present relevant information in an appropriate way, which requires special knowledge and expertise in the area of web marketing. Often, German universities do not have personnel resources with the necessary competences to professionalize their web presence. Professional marketing structures are in general a relatively underdeveloped area at German universities, although institutional differences can be detected here. For example, in the face of increasing competitiveness for students, particularly smaller universities of applied sciences have begun to professionalize their marketing and information structures to attract more and new student groups. In the light of widening participation, literature from the German context shows how important it is to integrate information about different entry routes to higher education into institutional marketing and information structures (Kerres/Hanft/Wilkesmann 2012). This is particularly true in the face of research which indicates that non-traditional first-year students make use of this kind of information more often than other student groups (Banscherus/Kamm/Otto 2015). Non-traditional students are characterized by their specific needs for information on admission procedures, the balance between studies and other obligations and so forth (Brunner et al. 2015). Here, some universities have established special advisory services for students without school-based university entrance qualifications to inform prospective students about study opportunities and help them with administrative procedures. Other universities organize information campaigns, like Open Houses, establish contacts with vocational schools or send study ambassadors to inform pupils about study opportunities (Mooraj/Wiese 2013).

Apart from information distributed via websites, other online tools became more and more important in the field of information structures. This is particularly true for the area of widening participation because online tools allow students to inform themselves regardless of time and place (Brunner et al. 2015). The flexibility in time and place is especially interesting for non-traditional student groups who do not have the possibility to visit the universities themselves. Here, German universities have begun to develop online information portals, for example for vocationally qualified persons or online courses for study orientation (Bellen/Tiesler 2015; Heide-von-Scheven/Brauns/Beuter 2015).

Access structures

Access structures represent one of the main obstacles for potential non-traditional students. Although in Germany access to higher education is predominantly determined by federal law, universities have gained autonomy in developing their own admission procedures. A percentage of applicants is chosen according to universities' criteria in order to "ensure a better fit between the expectations of first-year students and study opportunities" (Wissenschaftsrat 2013: 41). Therefore, institutional access structures which are mostly organized at the level of study programs are an important area for widening participation. The most important distinction in Germany lies between study programs with admission and those with restricted admission due to a limited number of places. Admission to restricted study programs is most commonly determined by the grade point average of the higher education entrance qualification and semesters to be waited.[16] The better the grade of the higher education entrance qualification and the more semesters a potential student has waited, the higher the chances of getting a place. Further, some study programs have special selection procedures or performance tests. This is mostly common in the fields of fine arts or sports. Other study programs demand additional criteria, like proof of language competences, letters of motivation or vocational experiences in a relevant professional field. The recognition of vocational expertise is of special interest in the face of widening participation because traditionally the two educational sectors of vocational and higher education have been strictly separated in Germany. However, some study programs are designed to increase permeability between these two educational sectors, while at the same time valuing prior vocational knowledge as an appropriate qualifying criterion.

A related question is whether non-traditional qualifications are accepted by universities or whether they have certain quotas for applicants with a non-school-based university entrance qualification. In British higher education, Watson (2006) reports a wide variation in the acceptance of non-traditional qualifications between universities. Some educational institutions accept less than 1 percent of applicants with these qualifications, other institutions accept up to 70 percent. Such extreme differences are not expected in the German context, but it is anticipated that there are certain differences among organizations due to their different profiles and history regarding widening participation. These differences are not only expected among organizations but

---

[16] 'Semester to be waited' describes the time between receiving a university entrance qualification and the start of studies. One semester is six months.

also within organizations, depending on the respective disciplines and study programs.

Further, for some study programs, in particular at universities of applied sciences, a test assessing the interests and predispositions of prospective students is obligatory. These tests aim to identify at an early stage the best fitting candidates along certain criteria perceived as important for the discipline. This is the case, for example, among medical study programs where selection procedures not only test prior knowledge in physics or biology but also include an examination of individual competences or skills needed for future careers, such as decision-making under pressure or communication with patients. Yet, according to Hanft (2015), only a few universities use these opportunities due to a lack of adequate resources and appropriate diagnostic tools.

Structures of study programs

Study programs represent one of the most important institutional structures that can contribute to or hinder widening participation. One crucial factor here is the flexibility of study structures. As mentioned before, Hanft (2015) emphasizes that more flexible study structures are required in order to meet the demands of current and potential students that have — next to their studies — other obligations to fulfill. Such flexible structures include options for part-time study or accompanying study programs for employed persons. In the context of several funding initiatives, German universities have begun to expand their traditional repertoire of study programs to also offer continuing education programs (Hanft 2012). More innovative forms of flexibility are provided by module or certificate programs that allow students to complete certain parts of their study program in independent time intervals that accumulate over time to complete a recognized study degree (Wolter et al. 2014). However, as mentioned before, the numbers of these study programs and enrolled students are still rather low (Autorengruppe Bildungsberichterstattung 2018).

Another area of widening participation refers to the recognition and accreditation of previous (work-related) experiences and competences in the context of study programs. As mentioned before, in the context of funding programs universities have begun to develop accreditation procedures for certain study programs. With the help of these accreditation procedures, students can shorten their studies by receiving credits for previous vocational qualifications (general accreditation) or individual competences and experiences gained before in different ways (individual accreditation). Research on the topic of accreditation of prior experiences in study programs in Germany indicates that substantial differences in structures, degree of sophistication and experiences with these accreditation procedures exist (Freitag 2012).

Student support structures

Student support structures are essential to support non-traditional students during their course of studies. As studies have indicated, not only access to higher education but also participation and the successful completion of studies are related to social inequalities (Gorard/Smith 2006). One of the most important obstacles that students face here are the costs (McCowan 2016; Gorard/Smith 2006). While tuition fees resemble one of the primary mechanisms for regulating entry to universities, students are also confronted with high living costs and a loss of income resulting from not working (McCowan 2016). Here, special attention should be paid to financial advisory services or financial support programs, like vouchers or grants for certain student groups and to making information on these financial benefits transparent. Further, many universities offer child caregiving services and advising for students with children.

In this context, it should be differentiated between the kinds of support programs that are exclusively directed towards specific (non-traditional) student groups. There is indeed a need for special information and advisory services that address more directly the demands of, for example, potential students with vocational qualifications because they may have very specific questions with regard to admission procedures. However, there are other topics, like student finances or the compatibility between study and family, or study and career, which are not only relevant to the group of students with vocational qualifications. It should be noted that research suggests that non-traditional students felt more comfortable at universities with specific informational and advisory services for them. Based on a qualitative interview study, non-traditional students reported that according to their perception, their questions were answered in a more competent and satisfying way by university support staff who are familiar with the special demands and needs of non-traditional students (Banscherus/Kamm/Otto 2015).

Teaching support structures

Finally, research shows the importance of additional teaching support structures that prepare lecturers for dealing with student diversity (Gorard/Smith 2006). According to university didactics literature, the increase in student diversity also requires a more diverse set of teaching and learning practices to meet the needs of individuals' learning strategies and motivations (Wild/Esdar 2014). What is more, the flexibility of study structures and the development of learning environments that are not bound to specific times and locations demand certain competences from lecturers that had not been required before. Mooraj/Zervakis (2014) point out that current lecturers tend to replicate a more teacher-oriented teaching approach because they were socialized in such an approach as students. Here, authors recommend the shift from teaching to learning that requires a different attitude of lecturers and the use of a broader repertoire of didactic methods. In the context of widening participation, the literature argues that diversity-sensitive teaching in which lecturers critically reflect on their own prejudices and their image of a 'normal student' is of crucial importance (Gorard/Smith 2006). Therefore, universities have begun to develop qualification programs for lecturers in order to support their methodological and didactical repertoire and to improve their teaching settings (Mooraj/Zervakis 2014). More specifically, some universities offer special trainings or coaching courses for diversity-oriented teaching.

One challenge lies in the fact that the shift from teaching to learning demands much more engagement and resources from lecturers than before. However, often such efforts are not sufficiently appreciated. For example, teaching plays almost no role in professors' reputations. Lecturers are not motivated to engage in activities related to widening participation because they are at the same confronted with challenges deriving from increasing student numbers, overburdened study courses, a lack of time for research (which is generally rewarded much more) and administrative burdens (Kehm 2000). Here, universities have begun to use incentives like the provision of financial support, temporal space or teaching awards for lecturers to develop innovative competence-oriented teaching and learning approaches. Thus, in order to stimulate the development of alternative learning and teaching approaches that are suited to meet the needs of a diverse student body, reward structures and supporting qualification measures seem to play an important role to promote a more competence-oriented teaching and learning experience (Mooraj/Wiese 2013).

Coordination and communication structures

In order to pursue a whole-institution approach to widening participation, communication and coordination structures are an essential structural element to incorporate dealing with student diversity into the main educational tasks of teaching and learning consistently and sustainably. Here, the involvement and participation of different universities' actor groups have been proven as crucial. For example, research indicates that widening participation policy developed in a top-down manner often gets lost when "it migrates down the organizational hierarchy" (Greenbank 2007: 209). Alternatively, bottom-up actions that include representatives from all stakeholder groups are more sensible to the institutional culture.

Further, such an approach to widening participation, which considers the whole institution, needs to be communicated to inform the diverse activities of the organization. This requires the establishment of communication channels and networks throughout the whole institution which are utilized on a regular basis. Finally, the diverse activities need to be coordinated in order to ensure that they all fit in with the overall diversity strategy and, thereby, identify possible areas that need to be improved (Mooraj/Zervakis 2014). This requires a coordinating unit responsible for the communication, initiation, coordination and implementation of diversity-related activities. Such a unit can also contribute to an improved exchange about experiences and best-practice examples, facilitating institution-wide communication and engagement, which may, preferably, result in a more diversity-sensitive culture.

3.5.3 *Organizational Responses to Widening Participation: The Action Level*

International and German research indicates that universities have made some progress concerning widening participation strategies, structural aspects like admissions, curriculum and student support. The area of teaching and studying, though, still needs significant change to meet the needs of non-traditional students (Gorard/Smith 2006; Hanft/Brinkmann 2012). As mentioned before, although universities have established several organizational practices on the level of teaching and learning to deal with student diversity, these activities are seldom explicitly linked to widening participation strategies.

The action level of teaching and studying is of particular importance because it is the area that is most affected by a changed student composition since it is characterized by a strong interaction between students and the institution. Research indicates that non-traditional students experience several barriers within the context of teaching and studying. For example, the participation of students in lectures might be prohibited concerning language, physical access, or time resources (Knauf 2016). Further, McCowan (2016) emphasizes that curricula and institutional cultures are more likely to favor dominant social groups, while they contribute to marginalizing disadvantaged groups. Here, Bernstein (1977) distinguishes between two pedagogical codes according to which institutional learning processes are organized. In institutions or study programs that are organized according to the 'collection code', the student needs to accumulate in a pre-defined way knowledge that is separated from each other. In other words, knowledge is provided only in portions without any direct links between the received content. Students are required to make these links on their own without having any influence on the pace, temporal sequence or the way knowledge is transferred. In institutions or study programs that function according to the 'integration code', the borders between knowledge elements are less strict. Lecturers and students both have a share in decisions about the knowledge to be conveyed, and therefore have higher chances to bring their subjective perceptions, prior knowledge, and experiences into the institutionalized learning process. Such a mutual knowledge transfer enables students to connect their individual experiences with curricular academic knowledge. Concerning dealing with student diversity, students gain more opportunities to find their own way through the curriculum here and adapt the processes of knowledge acquisition according to their own needs (Wildt 1985).

Likewise, the learning environment itself is affected because student diversity has an impact on the requirements, strategies, resources, interests, and goals of learning. According to Kreft/Leichsenring (2012), students use different learning methods and strategies due to their different competences and interests, resulting in different learning outcomes. For lecturers, the requirement lies in the creation of appropriate conditions so that the learners are able to learn in their diverse and individual ways. This is not possible when lecturers adduce the concept of 'the average student' to their teaching approach. In that case, some students will feel unchallenged because they already know the subject matter or because they can work fast and are highly motivated. Others will feel overburdened because the topic is new to them or they have difficulties in becoming acquainted with the topic (Knauf 2016). In this context, it is criticized that didactic challenges resulting from students' heterogeneous competences cannot be solved by artificially trying to unify students' divergent performances in order to build homogeneous learning groups (Hanft 2015). As an answer to deal with student diversity, university didactic research distinguishes between different teaching approaches to acknowledge individual differences. For example, Wildt (1985) introduces the approach of external differentiation and the approach of internal differentiation. Within the first teaching approach, additional learning contexts are created for specific subgroups of students. Examples are bridging courses that aim to compensate knowledge deficits of students who have been out of school for several years. However, he also noticed that these extra-curricular courses put an additional burden on the students with regard to what they have to accomplish. It is furthermore highly doubtful that specific bridging courses or introductory courses solely directed at non-traditional students would benefit their social and academic integration into the university. On the contrary, several authors argue that this would separate this group from early on and strengthen their feeling of being 'different'. Besides, Mooraj/Zervakis (2014) show that everyone benefits from such courses, although in different ways and to different degrees.

Activities modeled after the approach of internal differentiation, in turn, try to take differences among students within one learning context into consideration. Their purpose is to acknowledge student diversity by establishing productive ways of dealing with different competences, motivations, ways of learning and preconditions within the regular teaching and studying setting. Within the approach of internal differentiation, the focus is placed on the individual competences which students bring to the university. These are acknowledged instead of emphasizing the lack of competences that needs to be compensated by additional activities (Wildt 1985). Such a competence-oriented teaching approach also allows the competences and knowledge of students to be integrated into teaching. For example, students with vocational qualifications can contribute to teaching by adding their practical knowledge and experience. Such a teaching approach perceives the different entry qualifications of students as a resource. It emphasizes how students' individual competences, diverse backgrounds and experiences can contribute to the learning situation. Some didactic formats seem to be particularly suitable for practical realization, like project-based learning, problem-based learning and research-oriented learning (Seidel 2015). Research also indicates that team-based work has several advantages for the development of competences in students. It does not only contribute to the development of teamwork competences, which are considered to be some of the most favorable skills for graduates entering the labor market. Team-based work also facilitates social integration and strengthens social cohesion. Further, in mixed teams (that is, teams bringing together students with different competences and experiences) students get into contact with persons they may not have interacted with before and can learn from each other's experiences, thereby improving their subject-related, personal and social competences (Viebahn 2009).

Overall, the two teaching approaches of external and internal differentiation refer to the question whether additional measures are necessary to deal with student diversity or whether this should be integrated within regular teaching and learning contexts (Wildt 1985; Bosse 2018). Indeed, opinions among researchers are divided. On the one hand, studies indicate that introductory-level courses can be beneficial for non-traditional students in order to learn the unwritten 'rules of the game' of university life (Read/Archer/Leathwood 2003). Further, induction programs seem to be effective to familiarize students with institutional practices and prepare them for their studies (Gorard/Smith 2006). On the other hand, some authors criticize that many universities concentrate solely on providing additional learning support in the form of tutorials and extra-curricular preparatory courses which aim at closing subject-related knowledge gaps and improving academic writing methods (Hanft 2015; Banscherus/Kamm/Otto 2015). As mentioned before, in most cases those individual activities are developed without any comprehensive strategy and explicit linkages between them (Kehm 2000). It is also questionable whether such activities need to be target-group-specific or could just as well be open to all. Preparatory courses that explicitly address certain non-traditional student groups might be conceived as discriminating if based on the assumption that these student groups lack certain capabilities which they need to acquire to 'fit' into the organization. In this context, students with vocational qualifications complain about their treatment at some universities, where they are obligated to participate in certain advisory services before being able to apply to the university in question (Wolter/Banscherus/Kamm 2016). This indicates how sensitive these topics can be and that careful consideration is needed on the part of the universities with respect to the underlying message that is sent by decisions for certain formats.

In addition to activities of internal or external differentiation, some activities focus on differentiation within study structures. Examples are the temporal extension of the first year of studies or the adaption of structural framework conditions according to the different living situations of students (Hanft/Kretschmer 2014). Structural differentiation might also include individual learning agreements that do justice to the different study objectives students pursue and the various living situations they are in. These learning agreements resemble a contract between lecturer and learner which incorporates the individual resources and interests. These agreements facilitate individual ways of learning and objectives while establishing a high degree of commitment (Gorard/Smith 2006). With the help of new technologies, other forms of structural differentiation to increase the flexibility of the curricular design of learning and teaching settings have been developed. These new technologies take various forms: for example digital scripts, lecture videos, virtual conferences or courses that are offered on electronic learning platforms (Wolter et al. 2014). Much attention has been paid to the development of blended-learning approaches, in which e-learning elements are entwined with regular face-to-face lectures (Euler/Seufert 2005). A central element of these activities is flexibility. This also means that studying increasingly consists of self-learning phases in order to acknowledge the diverse living situations and preconditions of students. Further, teaching in blocks (in units of 3-4 weeks) instead of weekly lectures can facilitate the participation of students who have other obligations apart from their studies (Kerres/Hanft/Wilkesmann 2012).

As has already been indicated, activities can have different underlying assumptions about what the concrete 'problem' concerning student diversity is and what kind of 'solution' is perceived to be most appropriate to deal with student diversity. Based on the preceding literature review, the present study uses a three-fold differentiation of activities that can be distinguished in terms of their perspectives on the central problem and solution. First, some activities define the student as the central problem in widening participation. These activities aim at *improving the student*, for example in the case of bridging courses or subject-related tutorials designed to fill in gaps in knowledge. Second, other activities see the main problem within the institution and its structures that prohibit the participation of non-traditional students. Consequently, these activities aim at *improving the institution*, for example with the help of new technologies to provide more innovative forms of teaching. Third, some activities perceive the lack of fit between the individual student and the respective institution as the main issue at hand. These activities aim at *improving the fit between the student and the institution*, for example in the context of mentoring programs that accompany students in their first year of studies.

3.6 Explaining Local Variations in Organizational Responses to Student Diversity

A closer look at the organizational level reveals that universities differ considerably in the way they approach the topic of student diversity and the extent to which they turn it into a relevant issue for their own agendas. This might be related to institutional differentiations by a number of structural as well as cultural characteristics which result in differences in the composition of the student body and in their experience with widening participation (Banscherus/Pickert 2013; Wild/Esdar 2014). Additionally, literature has identified certain underlying perspectives universities have on student diversity. These perspectives differ with regard to the definition of student diversity, how it is valued (e.g., diversity as a chance or challenge), and how responses should look on the strategic, structural, and practical level. These perspectives, described in the literature as diversity paradigms, will be introduced shortly in the following section.

3.6.1 Institutional Characteristics of (German) Universities

The structural and cultural differences of universities result in variances concerning the composition of the student body and in their experience with widening participation. Some of the most significant structural differentiations in the German higher education landscape are its institutional types of higher education. There are two dominant types of institution: 'university' and 'university of applied sciences'. The purpose of German 'universities' is traditionally defined by the Humboldtian ideal of promoting both research and teaching (Meier/Schimank 2009; Würmseer 2010). In this tradition, universities should convey a form of general and broad education that focuses on furthering human development. In contrast to universities, the educational mandate of universities of applied sciences differs in its core objective. Its core objective is the mediation of competences and skills relevant for specific occupations, thus education is relatively closely related to professional practice (Würmseer 2010).

These institutionalized ideas about the task and function of the two institutional types of higher education result in a need to address different student groups. According to the results of the Social Survey[17], more than 60 percent of the students at universities of applied sciences have a non-academic family background, whereas more than 50 percent of the students at universities have parents where at least one of them has an academic degree (Middendorff et al. 2017a).

Regional boundary conditions are another important dimension of differentiation. Recently, opportunities for action and development of universities have varied distinctly in reference to their location. Demographic and economic dynamics in the different regions of Germany as well as the financial scope of the respective federal state to support their universities are responsible for these differences (Wissenschaftsrat 2010). For example, statistics show that the social composition of the student body in a more urban area such as Hamburg differs from those in other federal states. This manifests in the fact that the amount of students from an academic parental home is disproportionately higher in urban regions (Middendorff et al. 2013). Further, due to their history, areas such as the Ruhr area have a much higher proportion of students with a migrant background than other areas, for example in the federal states that formerly belonged to the GDR (Mooraj/Zervakis 2014). Most importantly, however, regional differences can be attributed to the different federal state laws. Due to the fact that the legal responsibility for higher education lies with the respective federal states, differences can be identified: for example with regard to the rules and regulations concerning access to higher education and the accreditation of prior work experience and qualifications (Duong/Püttmann 2014). Statistics indicate that this results in varying numbers of students entering higher education via alternative access routes (Stöter 2012).

Finally, the profiles of universities can differ substantially. Overall, the main purposes of universities are often described as the trinity of teaching, research and service. With the global trend of diversification and stimulated by a number of reforms, universities have begun to specialize in certain areas and build specific profiles (Bülow-Schramm 2016; Kosmützky/Krücken 2015). In the German context, a distinction is possible between universities with a stronger research focus and universities with a stronger teaching profile. Typically, research-oriented universities are big universities that cover a broad spectrum of disciplines, usually including at least a fundamental spectrum of disciplines within the humanities, mathematics, law and medicine. Professors

---

[17] The data for the 21st Social Survey was gathered from April to September 2016 with the help of a standardised questionnaire distributed among a representative cross-section of students enrolled at public and state-recognized universities.

at research-oriented universities are officially involved in both research and teaching due to the traditionally high relevance given to that combination. Research indicates, however, that the research performance of candidates plays a much more important role for being appointed than their teaching performance (Kleimann/Hückstädt 2018). Teaching-oriented universities are predominantly to be found among universities of applied sciences, as the professors there have a higher number of semester hours to teach than their colleagues at universities (Wilkesmann 2016b). Research, in turn, does not belong to their primary area of responsibility. Also, teaching-oriented universities have a more pronounced tradition of higher education didactics training for teachers. Apart from the differentiation between research- and teaching-oriented universities, there is a third category detectable that refers to the purpose of 'service' in the sense that universities serve the needs of the respective region. They understand their main task in contributing to regional economic development by fulfilling local demands for skilled labor. This requires well-established networks and contacts with the local industry and labor market. These regional-oriented universities can be both, universities or universities of applied sciences. They are mostly characterized by their location and are situated in the periphery of metropolitan areas, in regions with relatively low economic performances (Pasternack 2013).

Thus, due to certain structural factors, universities are assumed to have varying degrees of experience with certain heterogeneous student groups while supporting them. This results in different starting points for the implementation of widening participation initiatives.

Certain intra-organizational characteristics also impact the way universities deal with the topic of widening participation. This involves the vision or mission of universities, their structures and cultures as well as their leadership and/or management styles. As it has been reviewed in this chapter before, universities differ in a number of characteristics that should be taken into account when analyzing organizational change processes on the organizational level. Amongst other things, these characteristics include the multiplicity of purposes, reputation, size, age, the degree of structural differentiation, governance structure and the distribution of authority (Clark 1983; Gornitzka 1999; Hall/Tolbert 2005). Several studies have indicated that cultural features are important factors in the context of organizational change. Universities with very similar missions and structures can perform quite differently due to their different styles of communication with internal and external stakeholders and the varying perceptions these stakeholder groups have about themselves (Clark 1983). As mentioned before, institutional theorists emphasize the importance of a normative match between the identity and traditions of the university and the underlying values and beliefs of a certain policy (Gornitzka 1999). Therefore, it is more likely for ideas to be implemented as they are deemed to fit into the dominant institutional order, which is embedded in the history and culture of the organization (Czarniawska 2009). However, academic organizations also subsume different "nested groupings that manufacture culture as part of their work and self-interest" (Clark 1983: 75). This includes, for example, the culture of the discipline. Research has shown that it is important for change agents to consider the different underlying academic viewpoints and values within the disciplines. In other words, the response to a change initiative might vary even within the organization in accordance with the respective fit of the underlying values of a discipline and the underlying values of a change initiative (Becher/Trowler 2001).

3.6.2 Diversity Paradigms and Ways of Dealing with Student Diversity

Depending on the previously mentioned structural and cultural characteristics, universities differ according to the dominant image or idea they have about their students. In the German higher education context, literature has identified two main ideas of students that affect universities' responses to student diversity enormously. These two ideas are called the homogenization and the heterogenization idea.

The homogenization idea favors the image of the 'traditional' student population in which students with similar needs and requirements enter universities. Such a student is male, white, under 25, unmarried, childless, has no low social origin, is a citizen without migrant background, has gained his higher education entrance qualification via the first educational pathway (*Abitur*), studies full-time, does not work to support himself and has no physical or mental disabilities (Buß 2010; Middendorff 2015; Wielepp 2013). These students share a similar socio-cultural background with their professors due to their academic family background, hence they already incorporate the appropriate cultural codes and social ways of behaving. Thus, it is assumed that students are already equipped with necessary behaviors, prior knowledge and attitudes since they adapted them from their parents and during their school career (Wildt 1985). As mentioned before, in Germany, studying at universities is often still oriented towards the 'ideal' student. According to this perspective, students that do not conform to the 'homogeneous ideal' (Viebahn 2009) should preferably adjust and be unified by means of specific measures. This is related to the assumption that heterogeneous students lack the necessary abilities to study (Wielepp 2013). In other words, this perspective prefers to use the concept of non-traditional students by differentiating them from 'traditional students' in terms of their social characteristics or their educational biography/route. These external characteristics are used as indicators for culturally and socially induced disadvantages, which, in turn, are associated with problematic learning attitudes and competences (Wolter 2013b). Thereby, non-traditional students are equated to students with insufficient academic competences that do not fit as well into higher education as traditional students (Spiegler/Bednarek 2013).

This paradigm is also described by Dass/Parker (1999) as *resistance perspective* that perceives diversity as a threat and has the aim to preserve the exclusive status quo of the dominant, homogeneous majority. Here, universities encounter widening participation with skepticism because student diversity is perceived as oppositional to 'elite education'. In this context, diversity is associated with students whose ability to study is questioned. Such focus on a suspected lack of academic abilities is often associated with a deficit-oriented perspective on students (Seidel 2014). According to this perspective heterogeneous student groups pose several challenges to the organization, a claim which culminates in questions asking "how much heterogeneity is bearable in teaching" (Wild/Esdar 2014: 17). This perspective perceives the individual student as 'the problem', as someone who needs to be adjusted to study requirements, without the institution realizing the necessity, to change the framework or study conditions themselves. Consequently, universities following this perspective often lack an overall strategy how to deal with student diversity. In this context, universities as professional organizations are criticized for being resistant to change (Kezar 2014; Manning 2013; Pasternack/Kehm 2000). According to Kehm (2000), they deal with this complex problem in two different, but generally inappropriate ways. On the one hand, organizations meet these demands on a plainly rhetorical basis in order to fulfill the normatively appropriate behavior, for example by re-defining reform approaches. On the other hand, the problem is answered by developing multiple measures without a coherent underlying strategy. These measures are often criticized for constituting a conglomeration instead of using a more holistic approach that brings a new consciousness on student diversity into the higher education organization (Leicht-Scholten 2011).

Thus, on the strategy level, there is either a lack of overall strategy or the strategy is characterized by referring to political rhetoric and repeating political demands without being very concrete. On the structure level, a cooperating unit for unifying and coordinating activities is missing and communication or an exchange of experiences dealing with student diversity among organizational members is rather low. On the action level, the appropriate way of dealing with student diversity seems to be found in unifying the heterogeneous student body through homogenizing activities to adapt them to the normative expectation of the 'traditional' student (Seidel 2014). According to Hanft (2015), universities that follow the resistance perspective have developed a range of measures that mostly concentrate on the transition phase of the first-year, like consultation services, tutorials and supplementary courses. She questions whether a homogeneity-oriented approach that is still preferred by most universities meets the requirements of an increasingly heterogeneous student body. According to critiques, this deficit-based orientation has the consequence that universities not only deny themselves a productive way of dealing with different starting conditions and diversity characteristics, but they also force students to a one-sided adaptation to the institution and its prevalent cultural norms and attitudes (Seidel 2014).

This is contrasted by the alternative perspective commonly referred to as the heterogenization idea (Buß/Erbsland/Rahn 2018) or the diversity approach (Seidel 2014). This perspective accepts the diverse living situations, requirements and needs of students with which they enter higher education and encourages universities to appreciate these differences, since the diversity of life experiences is perceived as beneficial for academic learning processes. Facilitating wider access to education for different social groups is consistent with the educational mission of universities (Buß/Erbsland/Rahn 2018). Consequently, universities are pressured to improve their own capabilities to adapt and increase their activities to support heterogeneous student groups. This requires to reflect on and transform their normative expectations and the resulting perspective on diversity (Seidel 2014). This perspective is to be found among approaches from diversity management. Diversity management[18] stems from organizational development theory and can be understood as strategies that aim at steering organizational change to support productive diversity, reduce unequal treatment and discrimination and contribute to an improvement of corporate success and efficiency (ibid.). Here, the diversity approach subsumes different underlying logics and argumentations, referring to societal as well as economic reasons. Accordingly, the heterogenization idea can be broken down further.

Thomas/Ely (1996) identify three different paradigms that all share a heterogeneous perspective on diversity: the fairness and anti-discrimination approach, the market approach and the learning and efficacy approach. The *fairness and anti-discrimination perspective* is based on a socio-ethical understanding of diversity while focusing on disadvantaged minorities in the organization. Accordingly, the overall aim is the fair and equal treatment of persons, regardless of individual differences, by reducing prejudices and stereotypes and by improving the demographic representativeness of different groups. In the context of higher education, this perspective focuses on socio-demographic characteristics, like gender or a student's disability status. On the strategy level, a clear commitment to dismiss discrimination and support equality is often formulated. According to this logic, it is the responsibility of universities to ensure formal equality of treatment and diminish structural barriers for disadvantaged groups. On the structure and action levels, concrete activities involve the establishment of equal opportunities offices or special support programs like, for example, mentoring programs for women in the

---

[18] For a more extensive discussion about diversity management in general, see Schulz (2009) and about diversity management in the context of German higher education, see Buß (2010).

natural sciences or the development of alternative learning materials for disabled students.

The *market approach* perceives diversity as a useful resource in the competition for highly skilled labor. This perspective is economic- and results-oriented while focusing on specific demographical characteristics. The aim is to have a competitive advantage by means of smoother access to new markets and customers (Thomas/Ely 1996; Gaisch/Aichinger/Preymann 2017). In the context of higher education, this perspective often focuses on students with vocational qualifications, who are perceived to represent a new customer group for higher education. On the strategy level, widening participation is described as a tool for attracting the brightest and fighting the shortage of skilled labor. According to this logic, the role of universities should be geared towards national and local economic growth by satisfying the increasing demand for professionals. On the structure level and action level, this includes, for example, the introduction of more flexible study structures, the accreditation of prior learning, the development of blended-learning scenarios or the establishment of cooperation with local industry to develop study programs that fit with their needs and interests.

The *learning and efficacy approach*, in turn, is characterized by a more comprehensive perspective that incorporates the moral-ethical argumentation of the fairness and anti-discrimination approach and the economic argumentation of the market approach. As such, this perspective acknowledges diversity as a resource that is worthwhile to be protected and supported. This approach has the aim to share organizational knowledge, promote resource-oriented learning, and, thereby, achieve an open organizational culture. Thus, this approach interprets dealing with diversity as an overall organizational learning process that constantly aspires to find a balance between difference and integration, while adapting dynamically to the diverse ideals, norms and attitudes of the persons involved (Gaisch/Aichinger/Preymann 2017; Thomas/Ely 1996). In the context of higher education, this approach often defines diversity in terms of individual learning personalities that should be acknowledged by different styles of teaching and studying. This competence-oriented and student-centered perspective focuses on the individual competencies the students bring along and their individual study goals, motivations, interests and learning strategies. This is in line with the more general discussion in university didactics about the shift from teaching to learning that emphasizes more competence-oriented and student-centered teaching approaches (Wild/Esdar 2014). According to this perspective, universities and their study programs should focus more attention on the competence profiles of their students and how these competences can be assessed and considered in study structures and individual curricula (Kerres/Hanft/Wilkesmann 2012). This approach calls for a more positive connotation of student diversity by focusing on possible benefits and gains for the whole organization. Such an attitude cannot be evoked by homogenizing efforts. Consequently, on the strategy level, there is a clear commitment to support students in their individual ways of learning. On the structure level, responsibility for multiple activities and actions is often in the hands of a higher education didactic unit which is very much involved in supporting more competence-oriented ways of teaching and learning. On the action level, there is a certain emphasis on developing innovative learning contexts with the help of new technology or more practice-oriented approaches.

Finally, Schulz (2009) adds a fourth approach that he calls *responsibility and sensibility approach*. According to this perspective, diversity is perceived as a social and societal responsibility. Thereby, this approach refers to the humanistic function of organizations in global times and highlights how dealing with diversity should be considered an important contribution to society. Further, it does not only consider single measures, like the approaches before, but focuses on how these measures are connected to the overall organizations' strategies and aims. Thereby, this approach perceives dealing with diversity as a strategic action that addresses internal but also external challenges. It incorporates a humanistic societal orientation, while at the same time pursuing an economic-oriented strategic link (ibid.). In the context of higher education, diversity is understood as an important educational mission, together with research and teaching. It also does not focus on single aspects of diversity but includes measures to deal with diversity with the organization's profile. This results in a university-wide strategy for dealing with student diversity that incorporates several concrete activities to stimulate an overall cultural change of perspectives on diversity (ibid.). In the German context, this perspective is particularly common among universities that participate in diversity audits which have been conducted in the last couple of years. These audits seek to support universities in their efforts to attain a holistic approach to student diversity (Krell 2008). Consequently, on the structure level, a cooperation unit is responsible for coordinating single activities and establishing networks for communicating constantly about efforts and experiences in dealing with student diversity. On the action level, there is a broad spectrum of activities to be identified that fit within the overall strategy (Mooraj/Zervakis 2014).

This latter diversity approach is in line with several other international studies that stress the importance of more comprehensive institution-wide approaches and enhancements (Kift/Nelson/Clarke 2010). Here, similarities to Australian literature and research in the field of first-year experience (in the following abbreviated as FYE) of students can be identified. In Australia, numerous initiatives have been developed with the ambition to improve the FYE of students since this transition period has proven to be of particular importance for later academic success (Tinto 2009). Research shows how the integration, coordination, coherence and bringing academic, administrative and support programs together can be a challenge for Australian universities (McInnis 2003). Kift/Nelson/Clarke (2010) identify three types of FYE approaches: *First-generation approaches* relate to co-curricular initiatives, such as learning support, orientation and peer programs. *Second-generation approaches* are defined as integrated curricular and co-curricular activities, and strategies with a focus on improving the learning experience of students by means of pedagogy, curriculum design and learning and teaching practice. The *third-generation approach* results in a transformation of a whole institution by bringing first and second-generation approaches together to integrate them in a comprehensive and coordinated strategy for all its disciplines, programs and services. As Kift (2009) emphasizes, "third-generation strategies will require an institutional vision for the FYE that is shared by academic and professional staff who form sustainable partnerships across institutional boundaries to ensure its enactment" (p.1). Applied to the context of the FYE of heterogeneous student groups, such an approach assumes an institutional change in a wider sense, where most importantly strategies and programs developed to widen participation first have to be integrated into an overall concept (Bosse/Mergner 2019).

Such a diversity approach acknowledges the importance that student diversity has to become a part of the overall organizational culture (Leicht-Scholten 2011). Research from a German higher education context supports the hypothesis that a cultural change is a basic prerequisite for achieving a way of dealing with diversity in studying and teaching that is well-accepted by the majority of organizational actors (Mooraj/Wiese 2013). According to Foskett (2002: 79), "it is inherently a challenge to internal institutional culture that requires colleges to change fundamentally their modus operandi, their view of the world and their values". One point of critique is the current institutional culture at German universities is unresponsive to the needs of non-traditional students, which influences the experiences of certain minority students in a negative way (Wolter et al. 2014). In the British context, Read/Archer/Leathwood (2003: 263) suggest that students from non-traditional backgrounds are "disadvantaged by an institutional culture that puts them as 'other'". That might even prevent these students to apply to certain institutions. Here, research from the United Kingdom indicates that minority students do not want to go to an institution where they feel like an isolated minority and working-class students do not apply for institutions that they regard as snobbish (Gorard/Smith 2006).

The first application of these paradigms to the context of higher education was undertaken by Gaisch/Aichinger/Preymann (2017). The Table 3.1 is based on their findings, but adapted to include statements about universities' ways of dealing with student diversity on the strategy, structure and action level.

Table 3.1   Diversity Paradigms in the Context of Higher Education

Diversity paradigms	Diversity definition	Validation	Logic of response	Strategy level	Structure level	Action level	Common factor
Resistance (Dass & Parker, 1999)	none	Diversity as a threat	Rejection: striving for excellence	No reference made or vague statement	Lack of coordinating unit	Bridging courses, subject-related tutoring	Preservation of a status quo
Fairness + anti-discrimination (Thomas & Ely, 1996)	Socio-demographic	Diversity as a problem	Political correctness: social permeability	Commitment to dismiss discrimination	Equal Opportunities Officer	Mentoring programs, materials for special needs	Equal opportunities
Market access (Thomas & Ely, 1996)	Educational biography	Diversity as a competitive advantage	New public management, entrepreneurial university	Contribution to economic growth and the supply/demand for skilled labor	Accreditation of prior learning, cooperation with industry	Flexible study structures, blended-learning concepts	Key performance indicators, winning new customers
Learning and efficacy (Thomas & Ely, 1996)	Individual	Diversity as a resource	Organizational learning, competence orientation	Emphasis on individual competences and resources	Higher education didactics unit	Emphasis on measures for internal differentiation	Openness for continuous advancement and transformation
Responsibility and sensibility (Schulz, 2009)	All aspects	Diversity as a social/societal responsibility	Social responsibility in addition to research and teaching	Commitment to student diversity as a central task of universities	Coordinating unit, well-established networks for communication	Broad spectrum of extra- and intra-curricular activities	Building and securing resources in a sustainable way

Note. Adapted and translated by the author from „*Diversitätsparadigmen neu gedacht: Schnittmengen zwischen hochschulischer Vielfalt und unternehmerischer Sinnwelten*", by M. Gaisch, R. Aichinger, & S. Preymann, 2017, presentation at the Research Colloquium of Austrian Universities of Applied Sciences at the IMC FH Krems (Austria), p.5.

This table serves as an indicator for the identification of different understandings of student diversity and relates how these interpretations are materialized on the three levels of interest.

However, it should be noted that the distinctions between the paradigms and the corresponding ways of dealing with student diversity on the levels of strategy, structure and action are only made for analytical purposes. When looking at the organizational level, mixtures of different underlying perspectives and logics are expected. Thus, the present study assumes that the picture of diversity paradigms and ways of dealing with student diversity is much more complex and intertwined. Nevertheless, this table serves as a guideline for providing an answer to the question how organizational responses to student diversity can be explained theoretically and, more precisely, to what kinds of general trends these responses can be related.

To put it in a nutshell, organizational responses of German universities differ according to their local contexts. It is not only institutional characteristics that impact the way student diversity is interpreted or which approaches are perceived as appropriately dealing with it, but also underlying diversity paradigms apparent at German universities.

The following sub-chapter brings the previous findings of this theoretical survey chapter together and assembles them conceptually into the idea of student diversity and how this idea travels from the macro-level of the political discourse on widening participation to the organizational level of German universities.

3.7 Conceptualization of the Idea of Student Diversity

Overall, this study contributes to the increased research interest in how higher-level systems both affect and are influenced by meso and micro forces (Scott 2010). Choosing a translation perspective, it conceptualizes student diversity "as a story of ideas turning into actions in ever new localities" (Czarniawska/Joerges 1996: 13). This idea travels around in the field of (academic) organizations and is materialized within the political discourse that underlies the widening participation policy agenda (Archer 2007; Boch Waldorff 2013) as it transports certain beliefs about what constitutes the role of universities with regard to student diversity (see Figure 3.1). Thereby, we concentrate on the construction of the political discourse on the part of the most important and influential stakeholders in the organizational field. Such a policy analysis serves as a frame of reference for the analysis of the organizational responses, i.e., how the idea of student diversity is translated within the organizational context.

As described in Chapter 2 in more detail, the policy analysis reveals that universities are confronted with two different perspectives on student diversity. According to the social justice perspective, the main problem within the widening participation agenda is the underrepresentation of student groups according to socio-demographic characteristics and living situations. To increase educational opportunities, universities should be promoters of educational equality and diminish financial and structural barriers that these student groups are faced with. According to the economic competitiveness perspective, in turn, the main problem is the demographic change and the lack of skilled labor because higher education has not fully exploited the existing pool of talent and knowledge. The potentials for talents are particularly seen within the group of vocationally qualified persons. Therefore, universities should fulfill their role as providers of professionals by improving their attractiveness for this target group.

After identifying the different perspectives on student diversity within the German widening participation agenda, the question is how the idea of student diversity is interpreted at the local level of German universities. Student diversity can be described as one of several circulating ideas that are translated as they travel from one local context to another. Here, universities seek to create localized meanings of the concept of student diversity through the process of translation (Boch Waldorff 2013). This study aims to retell the narrative behind translating the idea of student diversity in the context of three German universities which each are confronted with the institutional demand to widen participation.

Figure 3.1   Theoretical Framework for Analyzing the Travel of the Idea of Student Diversity

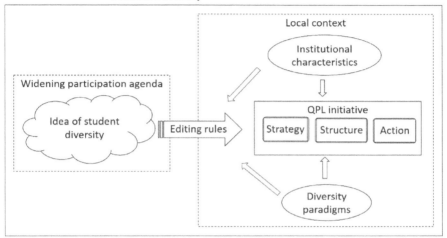

Note. The figure illustrates the travel of the idea of student diversity from the macro-level of the widening participation agenda to the organizational level of German universities in the context of the QPL initiative. Source: Own illustration.

Choosing a concrete example for this institutional demand, the present study focuses on organizational responses of German universities in the context of the QPL funding program. Here, the study examines how universities respond to student diversity not only on a rhetorical basis, i.e., the way verbal accounts are constructed but also by considering how the idea is translated into/onto action on the structural and practical level (Brunsson 1989). In accordance with Brunsson's (1989) distinction between talk, decision and action, the study assumes that the translation of the idea of student diversity takes place on the three levels of strategy, structures and action. More precisely, this study builds on previous research on organizational responses to student diversity by investigating the QPL initiative's strategy (i.e., how student diversity is defined in the QPL initiative's strategy), the QPL-related structures (i.e., what structures to deal with student diversity were created in the context of the QPL initiative) and activities within the QPL initiative (i.e., single QPL projects for dealing with student diversity in teaching and studying).

The translation of the idea of student diversity follows certain 'editing rules' that arise from this context and direct how actors modify and translate circulating ideas and make them fit through context, logic and formulation (Sahlin-Andersson 1996). Based on previous research on the role of the local context, the study wishes to explain local variations of organizational responses. More precisely, the study assumes that the translation process relates to institutional characteristics deriving from the context as well as to some more general trends concerning diversity paradigms that are apparent in the context of higher education (Gaisch/Aichinger/Preymann 2017). These aspects of the local context do not only impact the way editing takes place, but also how universities translate the idea of student diversity within the QPL initiative's strategy, structure and practices.

In line with Scandinavian institutionalism (Czarniawska/Joerges 1996), this study argues that in the long run — despite some sort of decoupling — the diffused idea indeed triggers institutional change in organizational performance. This, it is assumed, is due to the observation that over time ideas turn into organizational practice while retaining their symbolic value (Kirkpatrick et al. 2013).

3.8 Summary

In summary, this chapter introduces the theoretical background perceived to be particularly suitable for answering the research questions of the present study. The chapter begins with a short excursion to the epistemological and scientific foundations of this work, embedding it in the field of social science, and, more explicitly, the field of organizational research and higher education research. Here, the study follows organizational sociologists who perceive universities as a 'special' form of organization (Musselin 2006; Wilkesmann/Schmid 2012). A review of these special characteristics is of relevance for the present study because they influence the way universities deal with institutional demands (Kehm 2012). In order to understand and explain how universities respond to the institutional pressure of student diversity, the course of this study takes on an institutional perspective (Scott 2013, 2010). This perspective is perceived as particularly suitable for this undertaking because the field of higher education can be described as a highly institutionalized environment in which universities face pressures to comply with value-laden expectations such as widening participation (Kehm 2000). In contrast to classic neo-institutional assumptions that are involved in explaining universities' resistance to change or the rhetorical compliance to institutional pressures (Meyer/Rowan 1977), the present study builds on the observation that universities interpret the demand of student diversity very differently. Consequently, it chooses Scandinavian institutionalism (Czarniawska/Joerges 1996) as its theoretical lens to answer how organizations perceive and interpret institutional demands and how these interpretations, in turn, influence organizational action in their daily lives (Boxenbaum/Strandgaard Pedersen

2009). At the same time, this theoretical lens is particularly suitable for studying both the macro-level of political discourse and the organizational level of universities' responses. This chapter introduces the theoretical concepts of 'translation', 'editing rules' and 'decoupling' in order to explain how the idea of student diversity is travelling from the macro-level of the political discourse on widening participation to the organizational level of universities. Since the present study is interested in explaining local variations of organizational responses, a literature survey introduces 1) prior research on organizational responses of universities to widening participation and 2) research on the role of the local context for explaining variations in the organizational responses of universities. The chapter concludes with a final conceptualization of the idea of student diversity and how this idea travels from the political discourse on widening participation to the organizational level of German universities in the context of the QPL initiative.

4 Research Design and Methodology

As mentioned before, the present study takes on a constructivist-interpretive perspective.[19] This perspective draws attention to the process of reality construction by means of ongoing communication, interaction and interpretation of meaning and purpose by the actors involved (Bess/Dee 2012; Giddens 1984). This results in a subjectivist epistemology that assumes that knowledge and understanding are co-created in interactions (Lincoln/Lynham/Guba 2011). Knowledge is thus constructed through our lived experiences and interactions with other members of society. In terms of methodology, this means that as researchers we have to participate in the research process with the subjects studied to make sure that the produced knowledge reflects the study subjects' realities. Such a methodology focuses on processes of reality construction that provide the basis for collective forms of action (Berger/Luckmann 1966). Consequently, social constructivists use qualitative inquiry in order to study each system as a unique entity, gaining 'thick' descriptions of organizational reality. Thereby, they aim for contextual knowledge that might not be generalizable to other social entities.

The constructivist paradigm relies on a naturalistic set of methodical procedures, which means that the inquiry takes place in the natural world — instead of e.g., an experimental setting. Instead of relying on positivist criteria like internal and external validity, reliability and objectivity, the methodology refers to inter-subjective comprehensibility and triangulation which will be explained later in more detail (Steinke 2004; Denzin 1970; Flick 2014). This is regarded as an appropriate way to answer the overall research question of how the idea of widening participation is translated in the organizational context and how variations in organizational responses can be explained.

After clarifying the prevailing paradigm of this research, this chapter introduces the chosen research design and methodology. After explaining the reasons for choosing a multiple case study design, the selection of cases is presented. This is followed by the operationalization in which the research questions are linked to research methods, embedded within the chosen theoretical framework from which indicators are derived to investigate organizational responses to student diversity. The chapter continues with a description of methods of data collection and analysis and ends with a reflection on how this qualitative empirical research meets appropriate quality criteria.

---

[19] According to Denzin/Lincoln (2011), there are four major paradigms within qualitative research, namely the positivist, constructivist-interpretive, critical and feminist-poststructural paradigm. For a more detailed overview, see Denzin/Lincoln (2011).

4.1 Research Design

The research design introduces the purpose of this study by determining the kind of information that is regarded as most appropriate to answer the present research questions and the kind of strategies that are most effective for gaining the information (Denzin/Lincoln 2011). Thereby, the research design describes a more or less flexible set of guidelines that connect the theoretical paradigms firstly, to strategies of inquiry and, secondly, to methods for collecting empirical material.

Following the Scandinavian tradition, this research design is highly influenced by a narrative approach. Organizational narratives as the main mode of communication and knowledge transfer have become a central topic in organizational studies (Czarniawska 2010, 1998). This is also true for the field of higher education research, starting with the work of Clark (1972) on organizational sagas. Clark collected circulating ideas or 'tales of the field' of three US colleges. These narratives were deeply rooted in the colleges' histories, paradoxically each emphasizing their uniqueness, while at the same time following similar narrative patterns.

Narrative knowledge is "the main bearer of knowledge in contemporary societies" (Czarniawska 2010: 59). Narratives resemble a common form of communication to entertain, learn, teach or interpret. At the same time, narrative reports complement, illustrate and question logical-scientific forms of presentation. As Czarniawska (1998) points out, it has been shown that these narratives can teach students the practices of the field in a much more efficient way than scientifically written texts.

Narrative approaches are common among researchers in the tradition of Scandinavian institutionalism, which is primarily due to the similarity of story-telling to sense-making, as it is described by Weick (1995: 60f.) in the following way:

> If accuracy is nice but not necessary in sense-making, then what is necessary? The answer is, something that preserves plausibility and coherence, something that is reasonable and memorable, something that embodies past experience and expectations, something which resonates with other people, something that can be constructed respectively but also can be used prospectively, something that captures both feeling and thought, something that allows for embellishment to fit current oddities, something that is fun to contrast. In short, what is necessary in sense-making is a good story.

In other words, the process of story-telling can be regarded as "the never-ending construction of meaning in organizations" (Czarniawska 1998: 15). From a constructivist perspective, stories mediate reality. Stories are a basic instrument used by people to communicate, create and exchange understanding with other people and for themselves (Feldman et al. 2004). A story[20] serves as a frame of reference that is developed, adapted and refined in a way that new events can be more easily absorbed (Czarniawska 2010). In this context, stories are used to make sense of organizational life and communicate the created sense retrospectively (Weick 1995).

Choosing a narrative approach guides the choice of the appropriate research design. One common research design for narrative approaches is a case study design (Czarniawska 1998) which has the aim to collect organizational stories. Collecting stories can be useful to understand how actors make sense of the demand of student diversity, how it is translated into the local context and transferred into concrete strategies, structures and practices. These stories contain actors' understanding of specific 'recipes' for dealing with change (Feldman et al. 2004).

4.2 Case Study Design

Following the Scandinavian tradition, this study uses a process-oriented and qualitative methodological approach that focuses on the organizational level by employing a case study design (Boxenbaum/Strandgaard Pedersen 2009; Sahlin/Wedlin 2008). A case study design is particularly useful as it foregrounds the 'what' and 'how' questions central to our study since we examine how universities perceive and respond to the institutional demand of widening participation and how they translate the idea of student diversity into the local context. Here, the contextual conditions are highly relevant to gain an in-depth understanding of the phenomenon of interest (Yin 2003). Further, case studies are thorough in that they comprise in-depth and qualitatively rich descriptions of the units under study (Flyvbjerg 2011). Therefore, it is common to gather multiple data materials, while reconstructing the collective understandings and beliefs within the individual unit (Yin 2003). Since the research takes place within a natural setting and the research interest focuses on the processes and actions underlying the organizational responses to student diversity, it is important to take into consideration that the case evolves over time so that data materials should be gathered from different points in time.

As mentioned before, the widening participation agenda is particularly appropriate for studying translation as it does not represent a consistent

---

[20] Often, the terms narrative and story are used in an intertwined way. However, I argue for the distinction based on Feldman et al. (2004) who emphasize that a story is a subset of narrative. Thus, a narrative provides the grand conception that encompass several stories illustrating the overall narrative. Stories resemble interpretations of actions in a chronological order, while describing "from the storyteller's perspective how things used to be and how they are, as well as how they should be" (Feldman et al. 2004: 150).

legislative reform but is rather embedded within a broad range of different political initiatives that call for various ways of responding to this demand. In this context, the German government makes increasing use of soft steering instruments like funding programs that aim at supporting universities financially in their efforts to widen participation (Eurydice 2011; Osborne 2003b). However, due to the high complexity of universities as professional organizations (Mintzberg 1983), it remains unclear what kind of impact these political impetuses really have. In more concrete terms, the widening participation agenda represents a policy that a) has a high political and societal relevance, b) universities have varying experience with (overall it is regarded as relatively new to universities), c) requires some changes in the formal and informal procedures of the organization and d) a changed understanding of their core functions for society and their educational mission (Kehm 2000). In this context, research on the role of educational policy instruments is important. This is not merely due to their widespread application in the field of higher education and the increasing financial resources they entail. Rather, it is due to their voluntary character, which leaves universities with a larger scope of action for how to deal with the political demand of widening participation and, more precisely, the (re-)interpretation for and translation into their own respective local contexts.

Germany provides an example for introducing political reforms to promote wider participation in a higher education system characterized by a traditionally high level of social exclusion (Mergner/Mishra/Orr 2017). As mentioned before, Germany belongs to the countries with the lowest degree of permeability between different levels of education (Orr/Hovdhaugen 2014). This can be traced back to the institutional separation between academic and vocational education in Germany, the so-called "German education schism" (Wolter et al. 2014: 12). Concerning the social composition of the student body, studies suggest that despite the substantial increase in student, this expansion has not automatically resulted in fewer inequalities in higher education access and participation (Middendorff 2015; Wolter 2011).

As a concrete analytical example for German policy initiatives that promote widening participation, the QPL funding program was chosen for to three reasons. First, this program represents one of the most extensive programs in Germany in terms of finances and outreach. It was a nation-wide funding program that allocated subsidies to universities with a total funding volume of two billion euros. During their first funding period (2011-2016), 253 projects at 186 universities were subsidized, and for the second funding period (2016-2020) the follow-up applications of 156 universities were accepted (BMBF 2017). Second, the QPL funding program sought to contribute to a more general improvement of the quality of teaching and study conditions, while simultaneously emphasizing measures focusing on the design of first-year study programs that aim to "acknowledge the heterogeneous student composition" (BMBF 2010: 2). This very general nature of the QPL funding program provided universities with a high degree of autonomy in choosing to what extent they connect their projects with the topic of widening participation. Due to this autonomy, this program provides a very interesting example of how universities translate the topic and relate it to their own strategies, structures and activities. Third, due to this focus, the QPL funding program allows to study project initiatives of universities within the wide range of regular Bachelor's and Master's study programs since the research interest of the present study lies in how the traditional activities of teaching and learning are affected by widening participation. Other project initiatives with a more explicit focus on widening participation mostly encourage the development of postgraduate programs and training courses. Postgraduate programs represent an educational sector that is relatively new and unknown at German universities and clearly provides an interesting alternative research area for further studies.

4.3 Selection of Cases

Since the study examines variations in organizational responses of universities to the institutional demand of student diversity, a multiple case study design with universities as the unit of analysis is chosen. The first criterion for case selection is the participation of the university in the QPL funding program. In order to account for institutional differentiation that maps out different levels of experience and attitudes towards student diversity, three additional selection criteria are selected: they include the type of higher education institution (university or university of applied sciences), the location (metropolitan/periphery) and the institutional profile (research-oriented, teaching-oriented and regional-oriented).

As mentioned before in Chapter 3, universities differ fundamentally in a number of structural and cultural characteristics. This results in differences concerning the composition of their student bodies and their experience with widening participation. One of the most significant structural differentiations in the German higher education landscape is the type of higher education institution. Here a distinction is possible between universities that focus on the provision of general and broad education from a scientific perspective and universities of applied sciences that aim at a more specialized, practice-oriented education (Würmseer 2010). Regional boundary conditions are another important dimension of differentiation, while metropolitan universities show a different social composition of their student body compared to universities in rural areas. Finally, it is possible to differentiate between the profile of higher education institutions, having either a stronger orientation towards research, teaching or regional needs (Kleimann/Hückstädt 2018; Pasternack 2013). Consequently, three universities were selected as case studies. The first university is the University of Hamburg. It is located in a metropolitan region and is characterized by a strong research orientation. The second university, the University of Kassel, is located in a more peripheral region with a stronger regional orientation. Finally, the third university, the HAW Hamburg, is located in a metropolitan region with a stronger teaching orientation since this is a university of applied sciences.

4.4 Operationalization

This operationalization serves the purpose of deriving indicators, which result from the theoretical framework (see Chapter 3), for answering the research questions of the thesis. At the same time, the operationalization indicates the research methods and data sources the empirical research is based on. [21]

Organizational responses of German universities to student diversity in the context of the QPL initiative (research question 2-4) are analyzed within a qualitative multiple case study design. Multiple data materials were collected at the three analyzed universities, including text materials (websites, mission statements, project descriptions, reports, n=129), protocols from participatory observations (n=11), expert interviews with organizational actors involved in QPL management and/or single QPL projects (n=6), group discussions with persons working in single QPL projects (n=3 á 5-8 participants) and interviews with lecturers involved in single QPL projects (n=7). To analyze organizational responses to student diversity, sociological constructed coding is informed by literature on Scandinavian institutionalism and its related concepts of translation, editing rules and decoupling (Czarniawska/Joerges 1996; Sahlin-Andersson 1996; Sahlin/Wedlin 2008; Brunsson 1989). Further, previous studies about responses of universities to demands of widening participation and student diversity inspire the coding process (Buß/Erbsland/Rahn 2018; Hanft 2015; Harris-Hümmert/Mitterauer/Pohlenz 2015; Knauf 2016; Mooraj/Zervakis 2014; Wild/Esdar 2014; Wildt 1985).

In order to answer the second research question, a case-specific analysis examines how the institutional demand to deal with student diversity is translated at the three case study universities in the context of the QPL initiative's strategy, its structures and activities. A summary of the main findings of the case-specific analyses of the three universities can be found in

---

[21] For a detailed overview of the operationalization of research questions, see Table 4.A in the online appendix.

Chapter 5.[22] In order to explain local variations of organizational responses (research question 3), a cross-case analysis aims to identify editing rules that are used in the context of the QPL initiative at the three universities (see Chapter 6.1). Further, by retelling the narrative of how the three universities deal with student diversity in the context of their QPL initiatives, the analysis aims to identify aspects of the local context (i.e., institutional characteristics and diversity paradigms) that impact the way the idea of student diversity is translated in the local context (see Chapter 6.2.). Finally, to answer the fourth research question, a cross-case analysis is executed to identify organizational practices to deal with student diversity in the context of the QPL initiative (see Chapter 6.3.).

4.5 Methods of Data Collection

The process of data collection in the present study for analyzing organizational responses (research question 2-4) was inspired by principles of grounded theory (in the following abbreviated as GT), which represents "a method of inquiry in which data collection and analysis reciprocally inform and shape each other through an emergent iterative process" (Charmaz 2011: 360). In other words, the researcher goes back and forth between the process of collecting and analyzing data. This process involves analyzing fragmentations of the present data using comparative methods, working with interim codes and asking analytical questions that, in turn, guide the further process of data collection, a strategy called theoretical sampling (Glaser/Strauss 1967). Theoretical sampling does not restrict the process of data collection to certain types of data materials, although the main focus lies on manifest artifacts (recordings, interviews, text materials). The main characteristic of theoretical sampling lies in the circular nature of the inquiry: the criteria for data collection are developed on the basis of the data material that has already been analyzed (Meier/Pentzold 2010). Therefore, the processes of data collection and analysis go hand in hand, informing each other continuously.

The use of GT strategies is especially useful when the aim of the research is to study actions and processes instead of themes and structures (Charmaz 2011). Further, deriving from a constructivist GT perspective it is acknowledged that knowledge is always located in a certain time, space and situation and is co-created in the interactions between participants and researcher. Accordingly, GT requires researchers to interact constantly with participants, data, codes and interim categories that have been developed. Such

---

[22] For a more detailed insight into the case-specific analyses, see Case Studies I-III in the online appendix.

an interactive approach is especially suited for the specific research context in which this study took place. In particular, data collection was partly executed in the context of the accompanying research project, StuFHe whose aim was to evaluate project initiatives at four partner universities in the context of the QPL funding program. However, from early on I did not regard myself as an external evaluator from a distance, but rather as a close partner who is interested in the practical relevance of the findings. Further, since data materials are highly context-specific, it was acknowledged from the beginning that the interpretation of data is only possible in close cooperation and interaction with the partner universities from which the data was gathered. These joint interpretations took place regularly via workshops, presentations and co-organized conferences. These events, in turn, provided the basis for additional data materials in form of observatory protocols. Further, I visited the partner universities periodically to present tentative results and discuss with the local partners how these results could be interpreted and how the results could be used to change organizational practices. During this fieldwork, organizational stories were collected that helped to improve understanding the contextual conditions, as it is described by Czarniawska (1998: 4) in the following words:

> It is impossible to understand human conduct by ignoring its intentions, and it is impossible to understand human intentions by ignoring the settings in which they make sense. Such settings may be institutions, sets of practices or some other contexts created by humans and non-humans – contexts that have a history, that have been organized as narratives themselves.

Thus, in order to understand the underlying intentions and settings in which organizational action took place, the discussions with actors of the universities were essential. Consequently, I was part of the organizational change processes and actions in the context of the QPL initiatives at the three partner universities because I contributed by presenting tentative research findings to internal discussions about how the universities deal with student diversity. On the one hand, this involvement represents a necessary condition for conducting constructive-interpretive research to gain insight into the collective understandings of the case at hand. On the other hand, this also requires a more profound critical reflection on the role of the researcher, which will be discussed in this chapter.

Thus, the process of data collection was inspired by GT guidelines in order to sample, select and structure the data material for this study. First, a first round of document collection was carried out between January and April 2015.[23] Since the study is interested in the way the institutional demand of student diversity is interpreted in the context of the QPL initiatives of German

---

[23] For a detailed overview of the data collection process concerning organizational responses to student diversity, see Table 4.B in the online appendix.

universities, the project descriptions of the three universities' QPL initiatives were collected from the QPL project database, the universities' websites of the QPL initiatives and press releases. Over the course of time and on the basis of interim codes, further text materials from the three universities were collected, including descriptions of the institutional profile on the website, mission statements, annual reports and other communication materials having either a reference to the QPL initiatives, the topic of dealing with student diversity or relate to general characteristics of the universities. In total, document collection ran from January 2015 to June 2018.

Since all these documents are also accessible to non-members of the organization, these documents can be understood as means for (self-)representation to the outside world. Such a public image has the original task to legitimate the organization by being a center of reflection that displays how the environment is scanned by organizational actors, and external expectations are connected to organizational processes (Sandhu 2014). Consequently, it was decided to not anonymize these documents, since they were publicly available.

Second, a first round of expert interviews was carried out between June and August 2015 with persons involved in the QPL initiative at the three case study universities. These semi-structured interviews had the aim to complement the previous document analysis in that they should add an inside perspective to the outside representation. In line with Meuser/Nagel (2009), we define an expert as a person with institutionalized authority to construct reality in that they set the conditions for actions for other organizational members. First, persons involved in the management of the whole QPL initiative were selected according to their expertise about the overall QPL approach, the motives for application, and how the QPL initiative was implemented. Second, persons working in single QPL projects on the operational level were selected according to their expertise about specific QPL projects that focus on student diversity. These persons with the status of spokesmen can be regarded as experts in that they provide "crystallization points" (Bogner/Littig/Menz 2009: 2) for practical insider knowledge about the organization. Thus, the interviewee is of interest as a functionary and not as a private person. The subject matter of the interview is the special knowledge the person acquired during carrying out these functions. The expert represents a perspective that is typical for the organizational context in which this person has acquired their knowledge and acts accordingly, typically including a theory about the problem, a solution and decision-making structures (Meuser/Nagel 2009). The interviews took between 49 minutes and 131 minutes. During the semi-structured interviews, the persons were asked about the institutional profile, the motives behind the application and focus of the QPL initiative and specific projects respectively, and their experiences during the process of project implementation and coordination. For analytical purposes, the interviews were audio-taped and transcribed verbatim.

To analyze organizational responses of the three case study universities, the expert interviews were useful in that they provided first insights into the different interpretations of the topic of student diversity, which in turn result in various organizational practices. However, the present study aims to gain a more complementary picture of organizational understandings and underlying beliefs about student diversity. More concretely, based on the assumption that these understandings and beliefs are embedded within collective interactions, the main research interest in the following research period followed an identification of 'group opinions' (Mangold 1960) at the three universities.

Therefore, between July and November 2017 three group discussions were carried out at the three universities respectively. Group discussions provide the opportunity to rather focus the analysis on interactions within their social context than looking at individual actions (Bohnsack 2004). Thus, other than individual interviews, group discussions are less concerned with the individual construction of meaning, but more with collective attitudes and orientations towards a specific topic of interest and rooted within a common environment of experiences (Przyborski/Riegler 2010). Thereby, group discussions provide an empirically-based access to the collective body, which entails collectively anchored orientation patterns that are the product of shared experiences and prior collective interactions which are updated during the discussion (Bohnsack 2013). This is relevant because the present study aims to identify these collective attitudes and orientations with regard to the topic of widening participation and student diversity at the case study universities.

Participants for the group discussions were selected based on their responsibilities for single QPL projects within the university's QPL initiative. They, therefore, share a similar background experience. Thus, group formation was oriented towards homogeneity, while reflecting a 'real' group composition in the sense that although members of the group came from different departments and disciplines, they knew each other from the context of the QPL initiative and had interacted before on a regular basis. The three-hour group discussions consisted of five to eight participants. They were moderated by the senior researcher of the junior research group and me by giving selected stimulus materials (Barbour 2014). Stimulus materials were tentative research findings, for example, quotations from the expert interviews about student diversity. For purposes of data analysis, the group discussions were minuted, but also audio-taped and transcribed verbatim.

During the process of data analysis, the findings indicated the important role of lecturers, who are actively engaged in the course of the QPL projects. Following GT guidelines (Glaser/Strauss 1967), it was decided to conduct a second round of expert interviews with committed lecturers involved in QPL projects. The goal here was to detect common understandings and beliefs about student diversity and the ways these understandings and beliefs provide the basis for the daily actions of teaching and learning. Between March and July

2018, seven expert interviews were conducted at the three partner universities. Since knowledge about the organizations varied, it was decided to have a variable number of interviews. This can be traced back to different reasons. First, due to fact that I was situated at one of the university's studied, most knowledge and data materials were already available in the case of the University of Hamburg. Consequently, in comparison to the other two universities, I already had established a good rapport with academic staff and QPL employees. Further, I was regularly asked to present findings in the context of informal and formal events at this university (e.g., teaching events). These events were protocolled in order to use the protocols as data material for interpretation. According to the principle of theoretical saturation (ibid.), data material about this university was already comprehensive so that I decided to execute only one interview. This interview supported the assumption that theoretical saturation had been accomplished so that it was decided to stop data collection. At the University of Kassel, in contrast, the contact with the institution was sparse due to distance, although regular meetings and events were held at least twice a year. Therefore, it was decided to conduct the highest number of interviews featuring four experts at this university. As the third case study, the HAW Hamburg is located in the same city as the University of Hamburg, so a lot of events and interactions with this university took place during which I also got into contact with lecturers. Therefore, I decided that the data material was already sufficiently comprehensive, so that only two additional interviews with academic staff were to be conducted. The interviews took between 45 and 72 minutes. They were audio-taped and selectively transcribed verbatim for purposes of data analysis.

Finally, as mentioned before, I presented and discussed research findings with the case study universities in QPL related workshops, meetings and events. Most importantly, yearly joint workshops with the case study universities[24] were organized. They served as updates on the latest developments at the case study universities and their QPL initiatives. These workshops also enabled the participants of the case study universities to exchange experiences and information about their approaches to deal with student diversity across their institutions. Participants of these workshops were representatives for the QPL initiatives at their respective universities, including administrators on the management level and persons working in single QPL projects on the operational level. In total, five protocols of joint workshops between December 2014 and May 2018 were collected.

---

[24] In addition to the three universities examined in the present study, there was a fourth university under investigation in the context of StuFHe, namely the *Technische Hochschule Mittelhessen* (THM). It was decided to exclude the THM for practical reasons. For example, data materials were quite extensive at the three chosen universities. Gathering additional data materials from the THM would have been too costly due to the distance and the lowest degree of contact. Finally, the three universities provided a consistent sample of universities concerning a) type of institution, b) profile and c) location.

Further, one protocol from a QPL workshop at the University of Hamburg, one protocol from a QPL-related teaching event at the University of Kassel and four protocols from QPL-related events at the HAW Hamburg (1 teaching event, 2 workshops, 1 presentation) were gathered between 2015 and 2018. These protocols were part of the second round of collecting documents. In addition, in June 2018, information from the universities' websites was collected in a more systematic way, including universities' websites of the QPL initiative and single projects, QPL-related documents (e.g., project proposal, press releases) and other university documents (e.g., mission statements, annual reports). A special focus was put on information that documented changes between the first funding period (2012-2016) and the second funding period (2016-2020).

For the purpose of anonymization and transparency, it was decided to choose acronyms indicating the type of data material and data source. Document data are abbreviated by 'doc', interview data are abbreviated by 'int' and group discussion data are abbreviated by 'gb'. Documents are numbered consecutively; interviews with higher education administrators are abbreviated as 'intA', interviews with project assistants are abbreviated as 'intB'. Data materials from the three universities are abbreviated by referring to the University of Hamburg by 'UHH', the University of Kassel by 'UK' and the HAW Hamburg by 'HAW'. Following this coding logic, data sources from the three universities can be distinguished (e. g., UHH_doc_4/2). To indicate in the findings chapters of this study which empirical evidence the findings are based on, however, it was decided to refer to the names of document data sources, when these document data sources are publicly accessible (e.g., QPL final report).

Most of the data material was only available in German, including documents, interviews and protocols, but also the names of the universities' QPL initiatives, their single QPL projects and the names of university units. I decided to translate data material from German into English in the findings chapters of this thesis to improve readability and traceability. Where an official translation by the university was available, I used this official translation and indicated the source in a footnote.

4.6 Data Analysis

All data materials were analyzed according to GT principles (Glaser/Strauss 1967) with the help of MAXQDA. The GT method was perceived as the most appropriate method for data analysis due to three reasons. First, the main research interest was in the definition of student diversity and its relation to certain ways of dealing with this topic as well as in an analysis how this is, in turn, connected to characteristics of the university at hand. This requires an in-depth analysis that identifies underlying relationships among these categories for which the GT method is especially suitable (Cho/Lee 2014). Further, the present study wishes to examine the underlying understandings and beliefs that guide the translation of the idea of student diversity within the organizational context. Thus, research was interested in identifying the underlying structures of meaning, i.e., the collective orientations that guide organizational members' actions. Methods of abduction (Charmaz 2011) can be useful here since knowledge about the phenomenon of interest is fragmented and previous research findings have raised questions about the reasons for the different translations of the topic of student diversity in the local context. Abduction then provides the opportunity for the researcher to formulate hypotheses including possible ways of interpretations for these findings, which are then subsequently tested based on new data (ibid; Cho/Lee 2014).

The whole process of data analysis was computer-assisted with the help of MAXQDA. After the first phase of data collection, the data materials from the document analysis and the expert interviews were triangulated and integrated into one MAXQDA dataset. All data materials were read intensively and repeatedly (Schmidt 2004). In accordance with GT principles, the first step during the reading process was to ask questions about the data materials by using open coding (Corbin/Strauss 1990). Here, data is divided into units of meaning that are interpreted. The process of interpretation is guided by asking questions about the phenomenon of interest (e.g., what is the phenomenon of interest, what is identified as the cause, what kind of rationales are given, what kind of strategies are used and what kind of consequences are anticipated?) (Wendt 2009; Böhm 1994). Here, memos and a log book were used to record the researcher's interpretations and thoughts about preliminary codes, theoretical questions and hypotheses (Strauss 1998). It is important to reflect that open coding is strongly influenced by the researcher's own prior theoretical knowledge and the research questions that guide attention to specific topics of interest (Schmidt 2004). There are two sorts of codes that can be assigned: natural codes (in-vivo codes) and sociological constructed codes. In-vivo codes are concise terms that stem directly from the data material. Sociological constructed codes are theoretical general terms that the researcher chooses on the basis of theoretical knowledge (Wendt 2009).

Open coding was particularly helpful to retell how the idea of student diversity was translated at the three German universities in the context of the QPL initiative and how these translations materialized on the levels of strategy, structure and action. In this context, it was helpful to identify and collect text passages that are relevant for the topic of student diversity. As a first step, draft analytical categories were determined during the intensive and repeated reading of the material. Relevant passages in the text were coded according to the analytical categories. Second, while processing more and more material, these categories were assembled into a guide of analysis and coding, including detailed descriptions of the individual categories (Schmidt 2004). The main categories that were identified were 'student diversity', 'characteristics of the university' and 'QPL initiative'. Third, after coding the whole material according to the coding guide, these main categories were further differentiated in an inductive-deductive way. This means some categories originated out of the data material, while other categories were built inspired by the previously mentioned literature. During the whole process of data collection and analysis, the categorical system was continuously adapted, while new data sources were triangulated with previous data sources.

Since the main interest was directed at the translation of dealing with student diversity, the first main category 'student diversity' was divided into sub-categories that specify the contained information in the material with respect to this main category, namely 'definition of student diversity', 'attitudes towards student diversity' and 'dealing with student diversity'. The first sub-category refers to text passages in which diversity is defined by referring to certain student characteristics (e. g. students from a migrant background, international students). The second sub-category includes text passages in which judgments towards diversity are articulated, while giving the topic a specific meaning (e. g. diversity as a challenge, diversity as a chance). The third sub-category refers to text passages that involve descriptions of how the interpretation of diversity is converted into concrete activities.

Further, the second main category 'characteristics of the university' involves text passages in which statements about the university were made. This includes cultural characteristics, like their profile, history, tradition and educational mission, but also structural characteristics, like the size, number of faculties and departments, number of students and statistics about their student population and financing.

The third main category 'QPL initiative' involves text passages in which information about the aims, structures, measures and developments of the project was provided. In order to develop an answer to the research question how the demand of student diversity was translated in terms of strategy, structure and action within the QPL initiative, the category subsumes the respective sub-categories 'strategy', 'structure' and 'action. The sub-category 'strategy' includes data materials in which information about the QPL initiative's strategy, motives, aims and purposes is provided. The sub-category 'structure' includes information about the structure of the QPL initiative, for example, the institutional anchoring of the overall initiative and its components and the faculties and departments involved. The sub-category 'action' refers to information about the single projects that are part of the overall QPL initiative. A first helpful distinction was the differentiation of activities that aim either at improving the student, improving the institution, or improving the fit between student and institution. Activities that aim at improving the student include, for example, bridging courses that perceive the student as lacking certain competences necessary for a successful completion of studies. Therefore, these kinds of actions see the student as the main 'problem' that needs to be adapted according to the expectations embedded within the institutional system. Activities that aim at improving the institution, in turn, perceive insufficient or inflexible institutional structures or realities as the main problem. Therefore, these activities, for example teacher trainings, have the purpose to improve the quality of teaching or the conditions in which teaching and studying take place and adapt them more to the needs of the current student population. Finally, activities that aim at improving the fit between the student and institution perceive the interplay of both factors as important for a successful study. These activities, for example online-self-assessments, provide support for the students to reflect about their own interests, abilities and aims, while they also encourage the institution to make their expectations concerning students' interests, abilities and aims more transparent (see Figure 4.1).

Based on the coding, the final step of data analysis included the production of detailed case interpretations (Schmidt 2004).[25] Next to these single-case interpretations, the present study also seeks to examine between-case differences. Here, the research design follows a narrative and process-oriented approach in order to provide an answer to the research question of how variations in organizational responses to student diversity can be explained. First, text passages with a high interactive and metaphorical density were identified in which certain incidents, processes, changes or particularities were described. These incidents are regarded as potential indicators of the phenomenon under study and are labelled conceptually according to editing rules of context, formulation and logic (Corbin/Strauss 1990). Editing rules concerning context include text passages in which the respective interpretations of student diversity are connected to contextual factors like the university's educational mission, profile, experiences and prior projects, other funding programs, financial situation and current developments. Editing rules concerning formulation embed the translation of student diversity into a wider storyline, using dramatic linguistic turns and give ideas special labels. Finally, editing rules concerning logic include arguments for certain perspectives and activities that are reformulated in rationalistic terms, referring to evaluations, statistics, but also means-and-ends based on personal experience and observations. The findings for editing rules are presented in Chapter 6.1.

---

[25] The single-case analyses for the three universities concerning their responses on the strategy, structure and action level can be found in the Case Studies I-III in the online appendix.

Figure 4.1 Categorical System for the Analysis of Organizational Responses to Student Diversity

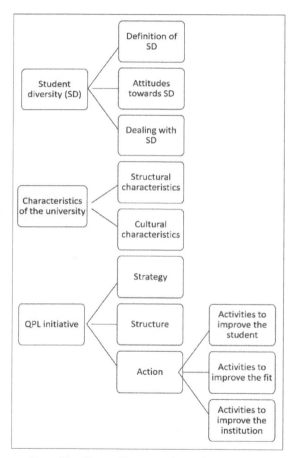

Note. The Figure illustrates the main categories and their corresponding subcategories that were used in the coding process of qualitative data analysis. Source: Own illustration.

As a next step, the aim was to identify the 'overarching narratives' at the three universities in order to provide an answer to the question of how variations of organizational responses to student diversity can be explained. This step is a common technique described in the GT literature as selective or theoretical coding (Corbin/Strauss 1990). Here, the researcher examines and sorts all code lists and reads the memos and the logbook intensively again. Further, literature on diversity paradigms was consulted to inspire thought processes about how organizational responses on the strategic, structural and practical levels are connected to each other. Here, summaries and tables helped to conceive of a story-telling in more abstract terms, attempting to conceptualize in a few sentences how the idea of student diversity was translated. This summary helped to reveal the aspects of the local context that guided the translation process substantially and, consequently, resulted in local variations of the idea of student diversity. Such a way of selective coding resulted in the identification of the core category by which all categories are unified (Corbin/Strauss, 1990). This core category is called 'local context'. The findings concerning the 'overarching narratives' of the three German universities are presented in Chapter 6.2.

In addition, axial coding was used to provide an answer to the research question about the kinds of organizational practices dealing with student diversity that could be identified in the data material. This step served the differentiation of previous concepts and categories, while examining their underlying relationships and interconnections. The main data sources for this analytical step were the group discussions, since it was suggested that they provided the best opportunity to identify the common understandings and underlying meaning structures that provide the basis for collective actions (Bohnsack 2003). Here again, text passages with a high interactive and metaphorical density were identified. They were directed at defining student diversity in specific terms and provided certain ways of dealing with this sort of student diversity. In order to examine the underlying interpretative patterns of student diversity, i.e., developing an understanding of the conditions under which these concepts emerge and how these concepts are connected to each other, the coding paradigm (Corbin/Strauss 1990) was applied. The coding paradigm offers a guide for the focused analysis of central phenomena of interest to examine not only the characteristics but also their relation to other concepts based on the data material. Here, the central *phenomenon*, which is in the present case the translation of student diversity ("what do you understand in the context of your QPL project under 'diversity'?"[26]) is brought into relation to the causes, strategies, conditions, consequences and contexts (see Figure 4.2).

---

[26] In German, the term *Heterogenität* was used in order to avoid the often strong normative character of the term *Diversität*, as it is described in more detail in Chapter 2. Therefore, in German, the group discussants were confronted with the question *"Was verstehen Sie im Kontext Ihres QPL-Projekts unter Heterogenität?"*

In more detail, around the main phenomenon of interest, the data material is analyzed according to

- the proclaimed *cause* for the occurrence of the phenomenon,
- the *conditions* or underlying assumptions that are associated with the phenomenon,
- the *context* in which the phenomenon occurs,
- the *strategies* to deal with the phenomenon and
- the *consequences* that result from dealing with the phenomenon.

Through constant comparison, it is suggested that interpretative patterns can be identified that link translations of diversity with concrete approaches for action. These interpretative patterns are expected to be not only found within subjects, but rather represent collective interpretative patterns that organizational members share (see Figure 4.2).

Figure 4.2   The Coding Paradigm According to Corbin/Strauss (1990)

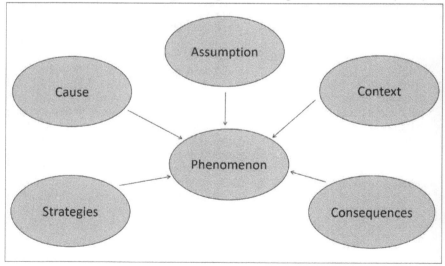

Note. This figure illustrates the coding paradigm according to Corbin/Strauss (1990). Adapted and translated by the author from "Grounded Theory – wie aus Texten Modelle und Theorien gemacht werden" by A. Boehm, 1994, in A. Boehm, A. Mengel, T. Muhr (Eds.), Texte verstehen: Konzepte, Methoden, Werkzeuge (p. 132). Konstanz: UVK Universitätsverlag. Source: Own illustration.

The analytical process can best be described with the help of an example. When asked about how student diversity in the context of their respective project is defined, one participant in a group discussion answered:

> The diversity is very clearly given among first-year students. Especially within mathematics the kinds of prior knowledge they arrive with here differ markedly from each other. By means of this first knowledge test, the individual obviously learns, 'where are my individual weaknesses that I need to compensate for?' And here we give justice to diversity in that the individual recommendations that are made via the system become clearly visible on the personal online desk. The one person with a lot of prior knowledge is required to do less rework. The one who lacks a lot of prior knowledge, of course, has to rework a little bit more. That's the one thing: visibility of the differences in prior knowledge via the test (HAW_gd/306).

Here, the phenomenon "of interest is the definition of diversity that can be labeled 'prior mathematical knowledge'. As a next step, this text passage is compared with other text passages in which similar or different incidents are described. By comparing incidents and giving phenomena of the same kind the same label, concepts for these incidents evolve that become more abstract as the analysis continues (Corbin/Strauss 1990). Applying the coding paradigm, the analysis reveals for this definition of student diversity that the cause for this phenomenon is attributed to divergent educational biographies and different school-leaving certifications of first-year students. Based on the condition that there is a certain performance standard that should be present at the beginning of studies, it is regarded as an appropriate strategy to identify and give the students feedback on their individual weaknesses in comparison to this standard. As a consequence, the deficits on the part of students are expected to be compensated.

These interpretative patterns are constantly compared to derive categories on a more abstract level. These link perspectives on student diversity with specific organizational practices and identify the underlying meaning and understanding that is given to this topic. In total, the present study identifies seven organizational practices to deal with student diversity. The findings are presented in Chapter 6.3.

4.7 Quality Criteria in Interpretive Qualitative Research

Based on the social constructivist perspective, the present study acknowledges that the 'lifeworld' (*Lebenswelt*) is a world interpreted by social actors, established by so-called first-order cognitions and constructs (Altheide/Johnson 2011). The researcher is only able to interpret the meanings of actors and produces second-order constructs that are constructed within a certain social, cultural and historical context and with a focus on a specific audience (ibid.). For the audience to follow these second-order constructs, transparency of the qualitative research process is central. By reconstructing the way in which qualitative research was conducted, the reader should be able to relate to the researcher's interpretations (Wilkesmann 2019). However, it is also true that the reader — due to his or her different experiences, perspectives and knowledge background — might arrive at alternative interpretations that make more sense to them. The traceability of researcher's interpretations is of special importance for qualitative social research because social 'data' are constructed in a special social context. In other words, in qualitative social research, data is not available as an objective value that can be accessed anytime. Rather qualitative data is generated in an interactive process between the researcher and the research object under scrutiny. Consequently, to ensure traceability, qualitative social researchers are called on to emphasize the context of the data collection process (ibid.). In this context, it is of central importance for the quality of qualitative research to ensure that the research meets certain criteria.

This research takes the position that it is not possible to adapt quantitative criteria to qualitative research since both are based on completely different epistemological and ontological assumptions (Flick 2014). Consequently, quantitative criteria have been developed in the context of methods (experiments, tests) that differ substantially from the methodological settings in the context of qualitative research (Steinke 2004).

However, qualitative research should nevertheless be built on evaluation criteria to avoid randomness and arbitrariness and to strengthen the recognition of high-quality qualitative research within the scientific community. Therefore, it is necessary to clarify beforehand which criteria are regarded as appropriate in the context of the present study. We agree with qualitative researchers stating that the formulation of quality criteria should be based on the general theoretical, methodological and procedural character of qualitative research (Steinke 2004; Flick 2014; Przyborski/Wohlrab-Sahr 2013). Subject comprehensibility and triangulation are regarded as appropriate core criteria for ensuring the high quality of the qualitative research process. Finally, in accordance with choosing an interpretivist approach, a reflection on the role of the researcher will be provided.

4.7.1 Inter-Subject Comprehensibility

This quality criterion means that persons other than the researcher performing the work should be able to comprehend the research process so that methodological decisions and procedures made during the research process can be evaluated in as detailed a manner as possible (Steinke 2004). According to

Steinke (2004) there are three ways to fulfill this quality criterion. First, documentation of the research process is the ultimate path. This includes not only the documentation of the researcher's prior understanding and expectations based on previous knowledge, but also documenting the process of data collection including the documentation of context factors that have influenced data collection and the documentation of methods of analysis. Further, decisions and problems that came up during the process of sampling, choice of method of collection and analysis should be documented accurately. Second, interpretations in groups are a good way to verify tentative hypotheses and concepts developed during the process of data analysis. Third, the use of codified procedures ensures a more systematic and rule-based strategy to arrive at the interpretation of data. By developing a coding frame that describes the characteristics of the present codes in more detail, other persons besides the researcher performing the work can comprehend the coding process and replicate the process of interpretation (ibid.).

All these criteria for inter-subject comprehensibility have been met in the context of the present study. First, the research process was documented thoroughly, including the researcher's understanding and expectations through memos, a log book and literature reviews that were written during that time. The process of data collection was documented as well, including ideas and decisions about new additional data material and choices about appropriate methods and tools for data analysis. As mentioned before, the process of data collection and analysis went hand in hand with the principles of theoretical sampling.

Second, the interpretations of data material were discussed in several groups in order to collect alternative interpretations and verify preliminary hypotheses. Interpretations were discussed with the other researchers of the junior research group StuFHe. This had the big advantage that these researchers were highly knowledgeable and sensitive about the local context from which the data materials were collected. Further, these researchers came from different disciplinary backgrounds, including psychology, sociology and linguistics. Their multiple perspectives coming from different academic backgrounds on the phenomenon of interest made an important contribution to the interpretations of data material. In order to check these 'insider' perspectives against perspectives from people who have no direct links to the present study, I exchanged my interpretations with an additional interpretation group consisting of doctoral students involved in interpretative higher education research. These regular exchanges of interpretation results and data material among the two groups contributed to high inter-subject comprehensibility.

Finally, the use of MAXQDA for data analysis with its functions of writing memos, assigning text passages to codes, sorting these codes into concepts and categories and keeping a log book about current thoughts and ideas helped substantially to ensure a systematic and rule-based procedure for data analysis that can be reproduced by other researchers.

4.7.2 Triangulation

Triangulation should be used to avoid one-sided or distorted findings that resulting from using only a single method, theory, or database. There are different ways of using triangulation as a validation strategy with the aim of developing a deeper understanding of the phenomenon under investigation (Flick 2004). According to Denzin (1970), to add depth to the analysis, researchers may use four different forms of triangulation, including methodological triangulation, data triangulation, theory triangulation and investigator triangulation.

First, methodological triangulation can be realized by using different methods (between-method) to ensure different modes of access to the phenomenon of interest (Flick 2004). The present study takes methodological triangulation into consideration. Group discussions were triangulated with document analyses and expert interviews.

Second, data triangulation combines data that has been collected from different points in time, from different sources, at different places or with different persons (Flick 2014). The present study uses data triangulation as well: It combines documents from different points in time and produced by different actors, transcripts from interviews as well as group discussions that were conducted at different points in time with different stakeholders.

Third, theory triangulation describes the analysis of data material by looking through different theoretical lenses (Flick 2004). In the present study, the data analysis not only follows Scandinavian institutionalism and the travel of ideas (Czarniawska/Joerges 1996) but also editing rules (Sahlin-Andersson 1996) and the translation of discourses into practices (Boch Waldorff 2013) to gain a better understanding of the translation processes at the universities in question. Literature on university didactics research complements these theoretical lenses with more practical-oriented research (Wildt 1985; Viebahn 2009; Wild/Esdar 2014). However, here it is important to note that one should only combine those theoretical perspectives that share the same epistemological assumptions about the phenomenon of interest.

Finally, investigator triangulation refers to the quality criterion that suggests interpretations of data should always be carried out by more than one researcher or, at least, the subjective interpretations gained by one researcher should be discussed on the basis of the original data material within groups (Flick 2014). In the present case, most research was carried out in a group of two to three researchers who interpreted the data material together and discussed tentative concepts and categories on a regular basis seeking to ensure high inter-coder reliability (Steinke 2004). However, the final in-depth interpretations, in particular by using analytical tools from grounded theory, were done by myself alone. As mentioned above, to check subjective interpretations, I met with two groups of researchers regularly to discuss those interpretations on the basis of data material.

4.7.3 Reflection on the Role of the Researcher

A reflection on the role of the researcher is of special importance in higher education research because researchers mostly examine their own organization in which they interact every day (Wilkesmann 2016a, 2019). According to Bleiklie/Enders/Lepori (2015), such an approach of self-ethnography (*Eigenethnographie*) can have several advantages. For example, as organizational members, researchers have easier access to information than non-organizational members. This is particularly true for researching organizational behavior in real-life situations. Within their organization, researchers can also easily gather data over a very long period of time and with minimal use of resources. Finally, such an approach is particularly helpful in explorative designs that aim to reveal real-life patterns of organizational behavior. However, self-ethnographical research approaches bear the danger of 'self-objectification' and 'hubris' (Wilkesmann 2019).

Self-objectification means that higher education researchers as organizational members are involved in a conflict of interest that influences their perspectives on the research topic. Higher education researchers, according to Schmid (2016), have a special interest in the field they examine because their research has practical implications for their organization and, thus, their own work environment. Additionally, empirical evidence points to the fact that there is a correlation between the university status and university members' statements in surveys (Enders/Teichler 1995). For example, professors will assess their potential influence on inner-university decision-making processes differently compared to non-professorial academic staff. Accordingly, Wilkesmann (2019) argues that a professor who examines the situation of a professorate can design the research in such a way that it strengthens the professor's own interests. In this case, evidence-based practical guidance might transport hidden interest-driven politics.

Further, the problem of hubris (Wilkesmann 2016a) refers to the fact that organizational members perceive themselves as experts for the field of higher education research because they are themselves researchers. However, these persons tend to generalize their personal experiences or their subjective perspective in an illicit way. What they do not reflect in this context is that their personal experiences stem from a special discipline, a special disciplinary culture, experiences made in their faculty or their university, which might be different in a different setting. Thus, experiences made in a special discipline or type of higher education institution are generalized incorrectly to apply to other disciplines or cultures (Wilkesmann 2019).

To avoid self-objectification and hubris, Bleiklie/Enders/Lepori (2015) suggest that higher education researchers should install mechanisms in the design of the study that create distance and promote reflectivity. For example, the case study reports should be written in constant confrontation with the underlying theoretical assumptions and be repeatedly rewritten to promote reflectivity and distance from personal experience. Further, it can help to define a set of points of observation, establish links between theory and written reports, and focus the reports on certain theoretical dimensions. Finally, it is important to contrast the present cases by systematic confrontation with different perspectives.

The present study represents a self-ethnographic research design only to some extent. I worked in two of the three institutions, but I had also several contacts with the third institution through workshops, seminars and so forth. Further, this research is interested in the way different organizational actors interpret and translate the idea of student diversity in the context of their local context or, more precisely, in the context of the QPL initiative. In this sense, its main interest lies in detecting 'first-order constructs' (Schütz 1971), which describe the subjective theories that actors have about their everyday actions. Here, the study examines not only the perspectives of the actor group which I am part of (i.e., doctorate students or academic staff) but also involves the interpretations of other actor groups, like professors and administrative staff. Consequently, it is suggested that the probability for the problem of hubris to emerge is relatively low.

Following the qualitative explorative research design, the main research interest is not to arrive at research findings that can be generalized to fit other higher education institutions. Rather, choosing a translation perspective, the theoretical assumption is that the specific local context of universities plays a crucial role in the way universities translate the demand of widening participation and derive organizational practices to deal with student diversity. In this sense, this study is also interested in 'second-order constructs' (Schütz 1971), which encompass the theoretical explanations why and how actors attain first-order constructs. In this context, this study aims to sensitize readers to the impact of institutional characteristics on organizational change processes which develop out of the constant confrontations with institutional demands that the organization has to deal with. Whether the results can be explained by this theoretical approach, and do not only reflect the author's subjective experiences (i.e., the problem of self-objectification), it is still important to interact openly with other researchers (Wilkesmann 2019).

Thus, since elements of self-ethnography are detectable in the present research design, the extent to which it was possible "to keep a sufficient distance from the object of study" (Bleiklie/Enders/Lepori 2015: 878) should be discussed. Referring to Bleiklie/Enders/Lepori (2015), the GT methodology (in that data collection and analysis went hand in hand) is perceived as particularly useful for guaranteeing the constant interplay between writing up results and reflecting on theoretical assumptions. Since data had been collected since 2015, I worked throughout the whole period of data collection and analysis simultaneously on literature reviews and theory chapters. Further, research findings were constantly written down and revised. Such a textualization of research findings varied in format and concerned different target groups. For example, in the context of StuFHe, research findings were presented and discussed with persons involved in QPL initiatives at the three case study universities. This sort of communicative validation (Wilkesmann 2019) was perceived as particularly helpful to test whether interpretations of research findings were sensitive to the special features of the local context. Further, research findings were presented and discussed at several scientific conferences. Since the present study is situated in the interdisciplinary field of higher education research, I visited international and national conferences that subsumed a broad spectrum of different disciplines, including sociology, organizational theory, university didactics, pedagogy and psychology. At these conferences, I was able to reflect on the theoretical and methodological approach as well as on the research findings in cooperation with researchers of different disciplinary backgrounds. In addition, some parts of the study were published in peer-reviewed scientific publications. Both sorts of argumentative validation (ibid.) (i.e., at conferences and in publications) were important to make sure that the study follows the rules for ensuring good scientific practice, which lowers the probability of self-objectification.

4.8 Summary

This chapter introduced the research design of the present study, following a narrative-interpretive qualitative research approach. The thesis is based on a multiple case study that examines in depth the organizational responses to student diversity at selected universities in the context of the QPL initiative. Since research is interested in identifying potential local variations of organizational responses, three case study universities were selected. They vary according to type of higher education institution, location and institutional profile. Following GT principles (Glaser/Strauss 1967), methods of data collection and data analysis went hand in hand. Data sources for the multiple case study include text materials from the three case study universities, expert interviews with persons involved in the QPL initiative, group discussions with persons working in single QPL projects and protocols from participatory observations from QPL-related events at the three case study universities. Data was triangulated and analyzed according to GT principles with the help of MAXQDA. First, open coding was helpful to retell how the idea of student diversity was translated in the context of the QPL initiative at the three case study universities on the levels of strategy, structure and action. Second, with the help of selective coding, the 'overarching narratives' at the three case study universities were identified to account for local variations in the translation of the idea of student diversity in the context of the QPL initiative. Finally, axial coding supported the identification of organizational practices dealing with student diversity at the three case study universities. The chapter ends with a discussion on how the present study meets appropriate quality criteria for interpretive qualitative research, like inter-subject comprehensibility, triangulation and a reflection on the role of the researcher.

5 Case studies

The following chapter introduces the three single case universities, including background information, statistics about the universities' student profile in comparison to the national average student population and a short description of their QPL initiatives. Further, a summary of the main findings of the single-case analyses will be presented, providing a short overview about the university's strategy of the QPL initiative, its QPL structure as well as the QPL activities or, in other words, the single projects that are part of the QPL initiative.[27] These findings provide the basis to give an answer to the research question of how the idea of student diversity is translated in the context of the QPL initiatives at German universities.

5.1 Case 1: The University of Hamburg

The University of Hamburg is a large university in a metropolitan region with over 42.000 students in 170 study programs (Jahresbericht 2016). It comprises eight faculties: Law, Business, Economics and Social Sciences, Medicine, Education, Psychology and Human Movement, Humanities, Mathematics, Informatics and Natural Sciences (in the following abbreviated as MIN) and Business Administration. Due to this broad spectrum of disciplines, the University of Hamburg can be defined as a comprehensive university (*Volluniversität*). There are 660 professors and 3,700 academic staff members supported by 6,000 non-academic staff members (Jahresbericht, 2016). In 2016, the proportion of third-party funding among financial resources amounted to 32 percent (Jahresbericht 2016).

The university was founded in 1919 by local citizens as the first democratically founded university in Germany. According to its mission statement, the university understands itself as a "gateway to the world of knowledge" (UHH_doc_40/2) and education should be facilitated through "science and scholarship" (UHH_doc_41/3).

5.1.1 Student profile

The following statistics gathered in Table 5.1 help to gain a better understanding of the student composition and give an impression of the

---

[27] For a more detailed insight into the case-specific analyses, see Case Studies I-III in the online appendix.

diversity of the University of Hamburg's student population compared to the national average. As indicators for student diversity, the present study takes the following into account:

- socio-demographic characteristics like gender, age, migrant background, family educational background;
- living situation, like health, student employment, completed professional qualification, parenthood;
- university entrance qualification.[28]

In comparison to the national average, there is a significantly higher proportion of women enrolled at the University of Hamburg. Only one third of the students at the University of Hamburg are male, while on national average half of the students are male. Concerning the age structure, the student population at the University of Hamburg is in general younger: 65 percent of the students are under 22 years, while the national average of students belonging to this age group amounts to 38 percent. With regard to the factors of 'migrant background' and 'family educational background', there is no significant difference to the national average: 21 percent of the students at the University of Hamburg and 20 percent of students in general have a migrant background. 56 percent of the students come from academic families, while the national average amounts to 52 percent of the students with an academic family background.

Concerning the category of health, students at the University of Hamburg reported health problems impeding their studies more often than their peers: 30 percent of the students at the University of Hamburg say they feel hampered in their studies because of health problems. The national average is 11 percent. However, concerning student employment, completed professional qualification and parenthood, there are some differences between the University of Hamburg and the national average. 38 percent of the students at the University of Hamburg are working beside their studies and 27 percent of students have a completed professional qualification. On national average, 31 percent of the students are employed and 22 percent of them have completed a form of professional qualification before entering university. Concerning parenthood, only 6 percent of the students at the University of Hamburg have children already. The same applies to the national average.

Finally, the amount of students entering university via alternative access routes is higher at the University of Hamburg than on national average: 28 percent of the students have an alternative entrance qualification, whereas only 16 percent of the national student body enter university with an alternative entrance qualification.

---

[28] The choice of indicators was driven by previous research as discussed in Chapter 2.

Table 5.1   Student Profile at the University of Hamburg

Socio-demographic characteristics	University of Hamburg (2016)[a] n	%	Social Survey (2016)[b] n	%
Gender				
Female	405	68	26.325	48
Male	187	32	28.165	51
Age				
Under 22	386	65	20.794	38
Between 23 and 26	100	17	15.680	29
27 and above	110	19	18.359	33
Migrant background				
With migrant background	95	21	11.085	20
One parent from abroad	40			
Both parents from abroad	55			
No migrant background	352	79	43.969	80
Educational family background				
Non-academic family background	188	44		48
Academic family background	137	56		52

Note. [a]Data for the University of Hamburg stem from the research project StuFHe.
[b] Data for the national average student population stem from the 21st Social Survey. Data compiled by the author.

Table 5.1   Student Profile at the University of Hamburg (continued)

Living situation and university entrance qualification	University of Hamburg (2016)[a] n	%	Social Survey (2016)[b] n	%
Health				
No health problems	317	53	40.212	77
Health problems not impeding studies	101	17	6.381	12
Health problems impeding studies	180	30	5.847	11
Student employment				
No	227	38	15.809	31
Yes	374	62	35.760	69
Completed professional qualification				
No	368	73	43.129	78
Yes	82	27	12.045	22
Parenthood				
No	564	93	51.963	94
Yes	37	6	3.047	6
University entrance qualification				
Abitur obtained at a *Gymnasium*	325	72	45.86	84
Alternative entrance qualification	125	28	8.798	16

Note. [a] Data for UHH stem from the research project StuFHe at the University of Hamburg. [b] Data for the national average student population stem from the 21st Social Survey. Data compiled by the author.

5.1.2 QPL Initiative

The university participated in both the first (2012-2016) and second round (2017-2020) of the QPL funding program. For the first round, the title of the QPL initiative was "Bridges to the University – Pathways to Academia" (*Brücken in die Universität – Wege in die Wissenschaft*[29]) and it received over 12.8 million euros of project funding. In this context, the university established the *Universitätskolleg*[30] in 2012, which "provides a conceptual, institutional and administrative framework for a multitude of projects" (UHH_doc_1/2). Overall, 45 projects focusing "on the transition from school or job to university and the cultivation of skills required for academic pursuit" (UHH_doc_1/4) were funded. Conceptually, these projects were united under the umbrella of the *Universitätskolleg* while their practical implementations were realized within the faculties or central service units. Thematically, these projects covered a broad range of topics, e.g., online assessments for student orientation, coaching programs for accompanying first-year students, courses for scientific writing and tutorials compensating deficits in prior knowledge. They were assigned according to their content to seven clusters (see Figure 5.1). The four clusters 'School Projects', 'Assess your own Knowledge', 'Expanding Knowledge' and 'Shaping Transitions' belonged to the category of projects serving to 'Build Bridges' in the transition from school or job to university. The two clusters 'Learning to Study' and 'Accompanying First-Year Students' focused on first-year challenges and prepared students on 'their Pathways to Academia'. The final cluster 'Accompanying Research and Evaluation' evaluated the projects and provided feedback for the further development of teaching and learning.

---

[29] Official translation by the University of Hamburg (2017b).
[30] In the following, the German term '*Universitätskolleg*' will be used throughout this work due to the lack of an appropriate translation.

Figure 5.1 Structure of the QPL Initiative at the University of Hamburg (First Round)

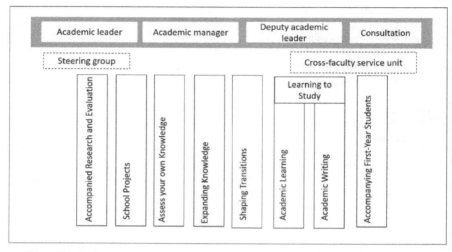

Note. Figure shows the structure of the QPL initiative "Bridges to University – Pathways to Academia" at the University of Hamburg for the first round of the QPL funding program. Adapted and translated by the author from "Jahresbericht Universitätskolleg 2013 — Dokumentation des zweiten Jahres" by the University of Hamburg, 2013, p. 79 (https://www.universitaetskolleg.uni-hamburg.de/publikationen/uk-schriften-004.pdf).[31]

In 2017, the university launched the *Universitätskolleg 2.0*, this time under the title 'Diversity as a Chance' (*Diversität als Chance*). For this second round of the QPL initiative, the university received almost 11 million euros. Compared to the first round, the focus was broadened in that the projects were to serve the "general improvement of studying and teaching" (UHH_doc_2/2) while focusing on different stages of the academic life cycle. Overall, the *Universitätskolleg 2.0* featured six measures grouped into three different clusters (see Figure 5.2). The cluster 'Preparation' comprised activities for prospective students, including online self-assessments and activities within the measure 'Welcome Culture and Chances of Digitalization'. The cluster 'Studying' focused on extra-curricular courses for students for promoting

---

[31] This image was created by the author in MS Powerpoint. The text of the original image in the report is written in German. The graphical representation of the original image was reconstructed to make the QPL initiative's structure more transparent to readers.

subject-specific and general competences and the Writing Center. Finally, the cluster 'Teaching' offered support for lecturers, including the two measures 'Teaching Laboratory' (*Lehrlabor*) and 'Student Participation in Sustainable Teaching'.

Figure 5.2   Structure of the QPL Initiative at the University of Hamburg (Second Round)

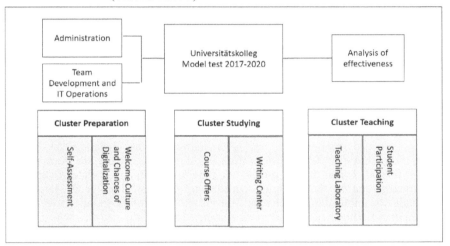

Note. Figures shows the structure of the QPL initiative "Diversity as a chance" at the University of Hamburg for the second round of the QPL funding program. Adapted and translated by the author from "Universitätskolleg QPL" by the University of Hamburg, 2018, retrieved from https://www.universitaetskolleg.uni-hamburg.de/universitaetskolleg-2-0.html.[32]

5.1.3 *Summary*

The single-case analysis of the University of Hamburg revealed some general findings about the university's response to the demand of student diversity in the context of the QPL initiative on the level of strategy, structure and action.

Concerning the strategy level, the shift of strategic focus had implications for the structural and agential levels. In the first round of the QPL initiative, the QPL initiative's strategic focus was on the transition period between school

---

[32] This image was created by the author in MS Powerpoint. The text of the original image in the report is written in German. The graphical representation of the original image was reconstructed to make the QPL initiative's structure more transparent to readers.

and university. The first year of studies had been identified as a 'problem zone'. Judging from reading the strategy papers, this transition period was perceived as problematic because students were not well prepared for academic studies. The *Universitätskolleg,* therefore, was to integrate measures to prepare students for their studies and make the transition to university easier. After the first round, however, the *Universitätskolleg* was evaluated by an external evaluation agency which criticized the QPL initiative's strategy for focusing too much on students' deficits. According to the university's QPL management, such a strategy ran the risk of making the *Universitätskolleg* look like a 'repair shop'. This conflicted with the university's objective to qualify as an elite university in the context of the Excellence Initiative, another funding program that aimed to support top-level research at universities. Consequently, the QPL initiative's strategy was altered substantially for the second round of the QPL initiative. In the second round, the QPL initiative's strategy was not only linked to additional highly value-laden demands, like diversity and sustainability, but its activities were expanded to include the whole student life cycle. Despite this thematic expansion, the number of projects decreased enormously, from 45 projects to only 6 projects remaining.

The structure of the first QPL initiative was characterized by its considerable size: 45 single projects were gathered under the roof of the *Universitätskolleg*. It took quite some time to find an appropriate governance structure and the right people for leadership positions. Further, the huge size made documentation and channels for the exchange of information even more important. There was an enormous amount of publications in the context of the QPL initiative. Persons working in the QPL projects were regularly asked to document their current project status. Nevertheless, the degree of exchange among the single QPL projects was rather low because of the sheer number of projects, the size of the university and the distance between faculties and central service units in which the projects were realized.

In addition, the *Universitätskolleg* was established as the University of Hamburg's first cross-faculty institution. The establishment of such an institution was met with skepticism on the part of the academic staff working in the faculties who traditionally enjoy a considerable degree of autonomy and decision-making power. Consequently, they perceived the *Universitätskolleg* as a competitive threat to their own activities. These structural challenges, in combination with the agency's recommendation to change the *Universitätskolleg*'s strategy, resulted in an overall change of the *Universitätskolleg*'s structures in the second round of the QPL initiative. Not only did the number of projects change, but also the structural anchoring of the projects was altered. During the first round, most of the projects were realized within the faculties and central service units. For the second round, the six remaining projects were directly tied to the *Universitätskolleg*. Consequently, staff working in the QPL projects were employed centrally. This new structure of personnel was accompanied by an extension of administrative support.

In the first round of the QPL initiative, the activities of the *Universitätskolleg* were characterized by their diversity, which can be attributed to the sheer amount of involved projects. The projects were organized by the faculties or central service units and the degree of exchange among the projects was relatively low. All of these projects were driven by different underlying assumptions about student diversity and appropriate ways of dealing with it. Consequently, there is no single or simple answer to the question how the University of Hamburg responded to the demand to deal with student diversity in the context of their QPL activities. In summary, the University of Hamburg seemed to be of the opinion that the academics working in faculties knew best how to deal with student diversity. This can be attributed to the faculty projects' emphasis on the specificity of the challenges for students in the different disciplines, as this was repeatedly pointed out in their project descriptions. The interviews and the group discussion support this assumption. The appropriate way to answer to student diversity, thus, was seen in developing faculty projects that take the specific disciplinary background into account. This disciplinary background could for example consist of special requirements or structures of programs that needed to be made more transparent to the students, or that the students needed to be prepared for with the help of extra-curricular courses. Statements about the benefits of faculty projects were mostly to be found among persons who worked in faculty QPL projects. In QPL projects organized by central service units, in turn, the perspective prevailed that specific student groups experienced similar challenges. A lack of experience with the (German) university system would have been an example for that aspect. This also included international students or working persons without school-based entrance qualifications. The appropriate way of dealing with these kinds of challenges was seen in offering low-threshold opportunities to get into contact with more experienced students with a similar background. These social contacts between new students and experienced students were also established among different faculties. However, the QPL employees in these cross-faculty projects emphasized that their activities were only to be understood as a sort of starting aid. In the long run, the aim was for students to establish social contacts in the study programs so that cross-faculty activities were no longer needed.

5.2 Case 2: The University of Kassel

The University of Kassel is a relatively young, medium-sized university in the city of Kassel in the Northern Hessen region of Germany. In the winter semester 2017/18, the university had 25,538 students in 140 study programs (UK_doc_1/9). Its eleven faculties comprise a relatively broad range of subjects, including Engineering, Agriculture, Natural Sciences, Humanities, Social Sciences, as well as a School of Art and Design. In 2017 it employed 334 professors, 1,602 academic staff members and 1,242 non-academic staff members (UK_doc_33/3). In 2017, the total amount of third-party funding was 60.5 million euros which are 19 percent of the total budget of 315.7 million euros (UK_doc_1/11).

The University was founded in 1971 as a *Gesamthochschule*[33], a type of institution combining characteristics of both universities and universities of applied sciences. It was possible to study there in so-called integrated study programs with entrance qualifications other than the general school-based university entrance qualification. Some of these integrated study programs followed a staged design, which means that it was possible to obtain a so-called 'diploma I', indicating a reduced course of scientific studies, or a 'diploma II', corresponding to a regular university diploma. These staged study programs at a *Gesamthochschule* can be seen as forerunners of the Bachelor's and Master's degree system.[34] With the Bologna Process, this type of higher education institution lost its status. Since 2003, all former *Gesamthochschulen* are now by law universities. With such a history, the university describes itself in its mission statement as a "pioneer" in the development of modularized courses (UK_doc_37/7). The university's profile has a strong regional orientation that emphasizes knowledge transfer and close co-operations with regional and international businesses and companies. The university also displays itself as interdisciplinary due to the "unconventional profile with fields of expertise in nature, technology, culture and society" (UK_doc_35/7).

5.2.1 Student profile

Compared to the national average student population, the proportion of women studying at the University of Kassel is higher (see Table 5.2). 68 percent of the student population in Kassel is female, while on national average only 48 percent of students are. Against the national average, the students are also younger: 60 percent of the students at the University of Kassel are under 22

---

[33] In the following, the German term *'Gesamthochschule'* will be used throughout this work as it lacks appropriate translation.
[34] For further information on the history of the University of Kassel, see Kluge et al. (1981).

years, compared to 38 percent of students on national average. Concerning the migrant background and the educational family background, there are few differences to be found between students in Kassel and the average national student population. At the University of Kassel, 22 percent of the students have a migrant background; on national average, every fifth student has a migrant background. 54 percent of the students at the University of Kassel and 48 percent of the students in Germany come from a non-academic family background. Thus, the proportion of students from a non-academic family background is higher at the University of Kassel.

Concerning health, 29 percent of the students at the University of Kassel report that they experience health problems that impede their studies. On national average, only 11 percent of German students experience health problems impeding their studies. Further, there is a much higher proportion of students working beside their studies in Kassel. Every second student reported that they are employed during studies, while on national average this concerns only 31 percent of the German students. Nevertheless, only 20 percent of the students in Kassel have completed a professional qualification before entering university. This proportion is almost as high as the national average (22 percent). What is interesting is that one out of three students has children already. This is a quite high proportion when compared to the national average, according to which only 6 percent of the German students reported about parenthood.

Finally, more students in Kassel enter university via alternative access routes compared to the national average. 38 percent of the students obtained an alternative entrance qualification. In comparison, of the average national student population, only 16 percent of German students reach university via an alternative entrance qualification.

Table 5.2   Student Profile at the University of Kassel

Socio-demographic characteristics	University of Kassel (2016)[a] n	%	Social Survey (2016)[b] n	%
Gender				
Female	231	68	26.325	48
Male	110	32	28.165	51
Age				
Under 22	206	60	20.794	38
Between 23 and 26	93	27	15.680	29
27 and above	45	13	18.359	33
Migrant background				
With migrant background	53	22	11.085	20
One parent from abroad	17			
Both parents from abroad	36			
No migrant background	193	79	43.969	80
Educational family background				
Non-academic family background	129	54		48
Academic family background	112	47		52

Note. [a]Data for the University of Kassel stem from the research project StuFHe. [b]Data for the national average student population stem from the 21st Social Survey. Data compiled by the author.

Table 5.2   Student Profile at the University of Kassel (continued)

Living situation and university entrance qualification	University of Kassel (2016)[a] n	%	Social Survey (2016)[b] n	%
Health				
No health problems	178	52	40.212	77
Health problems not impeding studies	67	19	6.381	12
Health problems impeding studies	100	29	5.847	11
Student employment				
No	172	50	15.809	31
Yes	175	50	35.760	69
Completed professional qualification				
No	200	80	43.129	78
Yes	49	20	12.045	22
Parenthood				
No	230	67	51.963	94
Yes	114	33	3.047	6
University entrance qualification				
Abitur obtained at a *Gymnasium*	154	62	45.860	84
Alternative entrance qualification	94	38	8.798	16

Note. [a]Data for the University of Kassel stem from the research project StuFHe. [b]Data for the national average student population stem from the 21st Social Survey. Data compiled by the author.

5.2.2 QPL Initiative

The university participated in both the first (2012-2016) and second round (2017-2020) of the German federal QPL funding program. The title of the QPL initiative for both rounds was "Growth and Quality — Professionalization of Studying and Teaching" (*Wachstum und Qualität — Professionalisierung von Studium und Lehre*). It was funded in the first round with 11.3 million euros (2.3 million p.a.) and in the second phase with almost 9 million euros (2.5 million p.a.).

The QPL initiative of this university comprised three clusters: 'Professionalization of Propaedeutics', 'Professionalization of the Didactic Quality of Teaching' and 'Professionalization of Quality Management and Counseling' (see Figure 5.3). Each cluster focused on a different target group, namely students, academic staff involved in processes of teaching and learning and administrative staff working at central service units. Further, each cluster subsumed six single projects that incorporated a broad spectrum of activities. For example, the cluster 'Professionalization of Propaedeutics' involved advisory services, academic competence workshops, mathematical propaedeutics and foreign language courses. The cluster 'Professionalization of the Didactic Quality of Teaching' incorporated activities like higher education didactic training, the integration of practical experience and research-oriented approaches and the use of e-exams. Finally, the cluster 'Professionalization of Quality Management and Counseling' included projects that aimed to improve the quality of service units responsible for study coordination, quality management, examination offices, advisory services for international students and psychosocial counseling. In parallel to activities within the projects, a central project administration team was responsible for process support and evaluation.

Figure 5.3   Structure of the QPL Initiative at the University of Kassel
              (First and Second Round)

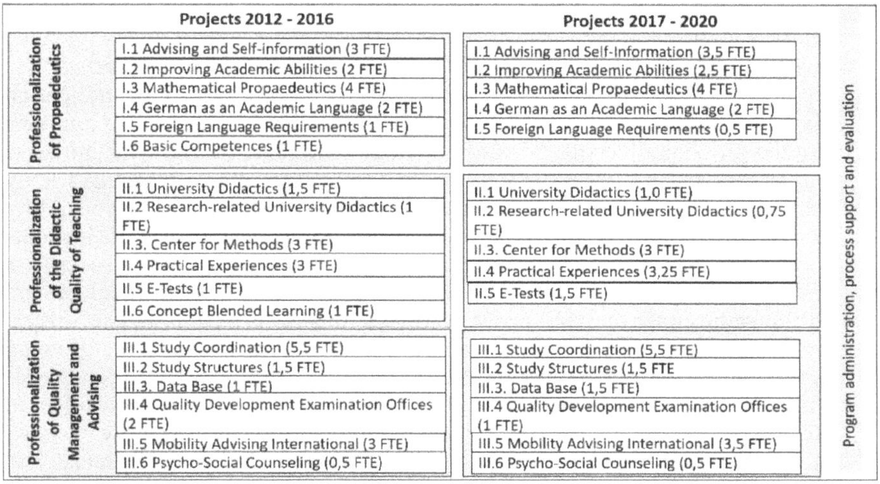

		Projects 2012 - 2016	Projects 2017 - 2020	
Professionalization of Propaedeutics		I.1 Advising and Self-information (3 FTE)	I.1 Advising and Self-Information (3,5 FTE)	Program administration, process support and evaluation
		I.2 Improving Academic Abilities (2 FTE)	I.2 Improving Academic Abilities (2,5 FTE)	
		I.3 Mathematical Propaedeutics (4 FTE)	I.3 Mathematical Propaedeutics (4 FTE)	
		I.4 German as an Academic Language (2 FTE)	I.4 German as an Academic Language (2 FTE)	
		I.5 Foreign Language Requirements (1 FTE)	I.5 Foreign Language Requirements (0,5 FTE)	
		I.6 Basic Competences (1 FTE)		
Professionalization of the Didactic	Quality of Teaching	II.1 University Didactics (1,5 FTE)	II.1 University Didactics (1,0 FTE)	
		II.2 Research-related University Didactics (1 FTE)	II.2 Research-related University Didactics (0,75 FTE)	
		II.3. Center for Methods (3 FTE)	II.3. Center for Methods (3 FTE)	
		II.4 Practical Experiences (3 FTE)	II.4 Practical Experiences (3,25 FTE)	
		II.5 E-Tests (1 FTE)	II.5 E-Tests (1,5 FTE)	
		II.6 Concept Blended Learning (1 FTE)		
Professionalization of Quality	Management and Advising	III.1 Study Coordination (5,5 FTE)	III.1 Study Coordination (5,5 FTE)	
		III.2 Study Structures (1,5 FTE)	III.2 Study Structures (1,5 FTE	
		III.3. Data Base (1 FTE)	III.3. Data Base (1,5 FTE)	
		III.4 Quality Development Examination Offices (2 FTE)	III.4 Quality Development Examination Offices (1 FTE)	
		III.5 Mobility Advising International (3 FTE)	III.5 Mobility Advising International (3,5 FTE)	
		III.6 Psycho-Social Counseling (0,5 FTE)	III.6 Psycho-Social Counseling (0,5 FTE)	

Note. Figures shows the structure of the QPL initiative "Growth and Quality — Professionalization of Studying and Teaching" at the University of Kassel for the first and second round of the QPL funding program. Adapted and translated by the author from "Fortsetzungsantrag im Rahmen des Qualitätspakt Lehre" by the University of Kassel presented at the Conference of Deans of Studies on 20th May 2015, p. 15. FTE = full-time equivalent employment.[35]

As indicated in Figure 5.3, the QPL initiative hardly changed with regard to its overall structure in the second round of the QPL initiative. Only two projects ended with the first round: project 1.6 'Basic Competences' in the cluster 'Professionalization of Propaedeutics', and project 'Concept Blended Learning' in the cluster 'Professionalization of the Didactic Quality of Teaching'. Small additional changes were only to be found in terms of the allocation of personnel resources in the single projects. For example, the personnel resources for project I.1 increased from 3 full-time equivalent employment (abbreviated in the following as FTE) positions to 3.5 FTE positions.

---

[35] This image was created by the author in MS Powerpoint. The text of the original image in the report is written in German. The graphical representation of the original image was reconstructed to make the QPL initiative's structure more transparent to readers.

5.2.3 Summary

The single-case analysis of the University of Kassel revealed some general findings on the university's response to the demand of student diversity on the level of strategy, structure and action in the context of the QPL initiative.

In the QPL strategy for both rounds, widening and increasing participation played a crucial role. Against the background of increasing student numbers and the growing diversity of students' study requirements, the QPL initiative was intended to provide an opportunity to develop activities in the area of study structures and organization. The university emphasized its social responsibility to include persons that enter university via alternative entrance qualifications. This social responsibility was legitimized based on its historical roots as a *Gesamthochschule* and its regional role as a promoter of regional development. At the same time, the University of Kassel was described as facing several challenges, pertaining to increasing student numbers, the growing heterogeneity of the student population, the fear of losing academic standards and the lack of appropriate funding for studying and teaching. This resulted in the perception that dealing with student diversity challenged the daily business of studying and teaching, particularly in the face of scarce (financial and personal) resources. Consequently, the QPL funding was perceived as filling in for missing funding opportunities to improve the quality of studying and teaching without lowering academic standards. In general, a continuous urgency for action became eminent in the data material. This contributed to the construction of a threatening scenario the university perceived itself to be confronted with.

The structure of the QPL initiative was legitimized on the basis of a SWOT analysis that indicated the need to professionalize propaedeutics, the didactic quality of teaching and the quality management and advisory services. This resulted in the establishment of three clusters subsuming eighteen projects. The central management of the QPL initiative was in the hands of the Department for Development Planning, which was mostly responsible for the allocation of personnel resources for the faculties and service units in which the single QPL projects were realized. Further, the QPL management team evaluated the success of the single QPL projects regularly, based on evaluative questionnaires and statistical information. The positive results of these evaluations, displayed prominently on the QPL initiative's website, were used to legitimize the argument for why the overall QPL structure remained almost unchanged in the second round. Nevertheless, the degree of interaction and communication about the experiences made in the projects can be described as relatively low.

The activities in the QPL initiative were oriented towards three target groups, namely students, lecturers and administrative and support staff. Thus it appears that in this case dealing with student diversity was not restricted to the responsibility of students, but also considered the institutional setting in which studying and teaching take place. First, the activities aimed to contribute to a professionalization of propaedeutics. Propaedeutic activities were largely characterized by defining student diversity as a lack of certain academic competences. This lack of academic competences was identified by comparing study performance to a certain academic standard that was more or less opaque to the students. Students who lacked these competences were requested to participate in compensatory extra-curricular activities. Other propaedeutic activities focused on the social integration of first-year students. For example, via tutoring or mentoring programs more experienced students accompanied new students on their way. Other propaedeutic activities aimed to improve self-information and self-reflection on the part of the students. These activities were inspired by student-centered teaching approaches, a principle that had been held high in several strategic papers of the University of Kassel. Other activities focused on the professionalization of the didactic quality of teaching. These activities aimed to improve lecturers' teaching competences and stimulate the development of research-related or practice-oriented teaching approaches by lecturers. Other activities explored the integration of blended learning concepts or e-exams into teaching settings. Finally, activities that focused on the professionalization of quality management and counseling mostly entailed the provision of additional personnel resources. The intention here was to fill positions with experts in these areas. These persons were supposed to relieve lecturers from administrative tasks that are usually not part of their job description.

5.3 Case 3: The HAW Hamburg

The HAW Hamburg is the second-largest university in Hamburg and the third-largest university of applied sciences in Germany. In the winter semester 2018/19, the university had 17,092 students in 41 Bachelor's and 37 Master's degree programs. It employed 401 professors, 492 contract teachers, 399 research assistants and 486 technical and administrative staff (HAW_doc_1/12-16). The university consists of four faculties, the Faculty of Design, Media and Information, the Faculty of Life Sciences, the Faculty of Engineering and Computer Science and the Faculty of Business and Social Sciences. In 2014, the global budget amounted to 76,939 million euros (HAW_doc_36/68).

The university was founded in 1970 as one of the first universities of applied sciences in Germany. According to their website (2018), as a university of applied sciences and with lecturers who had industry jobs before joining the university, teaching focuses on the practical implementation of science. Here, the university formulates the objective to provide their student with "practical insight into their field of study through projects, lab work, internships and theses rooted in industry" (HAW_doc_47/6). Its mission is to develop "sustainable solutions for society's challenges of the present and the future" (HAW_doc_2/1), while "the main focus is on the excellent quality of teaching and studying" (HAW_doc_2/3). Since, as it is argued on their website (2018), the university also hosts students from over 100 nations, it perceives "its diversity as their special strength" (HAW_doc_2/5). Student diversity seems to be at least partially equated with the international character of the student body.

5.3.1 Student profile

Concerning gender, there is a significantly higher proportion of women enrolled at the HAW Hamburg (see Table 5.3). While 59 percent of the students at the HAW Hamburg are women, on average only half of the German student population are female. Also, the student population at the HAW Hamburg is comparably young: 61 percent of HAW students are under 22 years, while on national average 38 percent of the students belong to this age group. Concerning migrant background and educational family background, the numbers of the HAW Hamburg and the national average show some differences. While in Germany one of five students have a migrant background, every fourth student at the HAW Hamburg has a migrant background. Further, at the HAW Hamburg, 57 percent of the students come from a non-academic family background, while on national average only 48 percent have a non-academic family background.

Concerning health, the students at the HAW Hamburg reported more often health problems impeding their studies. Here, 33 percent of the students say that they feel impeded in their studies because of health problems. The national average is 11 percent. Further, there are fewer students at the HAW Hamburg that work next to their studies (52 percent) than there are on national average (69 percent). However, concerning the aspect of a completed professional qualification, there is no significant difference between the HAW Hamburg and the national average. 23 percent of the students at the HAW Hamburg and 22 percent of the general German student body have completed a professional qualification before enrolling at university. Concerning parenthood, 23 percent of the students at the HAW already have children, while on national average this is true for only 6 percent of German students.

Finally, the proportion of students entering university via alternative entrance routes is higher at the HAW Hamburg than there is on national average. Every third student entered the HAW Hamburg with an alternative entrance qualification, whereas on national average only 16 percent of the German students come to university via an alternative route.

Table 5.3   Student Profile of the HAW Hamburg

Socio-demographic characteristics	HAW Hamburg (2016)[a] n	%	Social Survey (2016)[b] n	%
Gender				
Female	52	59	26.325	48
Male	36	41	28.165	51
Age				
Under 22	54	61	20.794	38
Between 23 and 26	23	26	15.680	29
27 and above	11	13	18.359	33
Migrant background				
With migrant background	16	25	11.085	20
One parent from abroad	7			
Both parents from abroad	9			
No migrant background	49	75	43.969	80
Educational family background				
Non-academic family background	35	57		48
Academic family background	27	43		52

Note. [a]Data for the HAW Hamburg stem from the research project StuFHe. [b]Data for the national average student population stem from the 21st Social Survey. Data compiled by the author.

Table 5.3   Student Profile of the HAW Hamburg (continued)

Living situation and university entrance qualification	HAW Hamburg (2016)[a] n	%	Social Survey (2016)[b] n	%
Health				
No health problems	49	56	40.212	77
Health problems not impeding studies	10	11	6.381	12
Health problems impeding studies	29	33	5.847	11
Student employment				
No	43	48	15.809	31
Yes	46	52	35.760	69
Completed professional qualification				
No	50	77	43.129	78
Yes	49	23	12.045	22
Parenthood				
No	68	77	51.963	94
Yes	20	23	3.047	6
University entrance qualification				
Abitur obtained at a *Gymnasium*	43	66	45.860	84
Alternative entrance qualification	22	34	8.798	16

Note. [a]Data for the HAW Hamburg stem from the research project StuFHe. [b]Data for the national average student population stem from the 21st Social Survey. Data compiled by the author.

5.3.2 QPL Initiative

The university participated in both the first (2012-2016) and second round (2017-2020) of the QPL funding program. The title of the QPL initiative for both rounds was "Piloting Teaching. Dialogue-oriented Quality Development in Studies and Teaching" (*Lehre lotsen. Dialogorientierte Qualitätsentwicklung in Studium und Lehre*). It received 6.2 million euros (2011-2016) for the first and 5.4 million euros (2017-2020) for the second phase.

In the first round, the QPL initiative was divided into university-wide projects and faculty projects (see Figure 5.4). The four university-wide projects included the installation of faculty quality managers for implementing dialogue-oriented quality management, a mentoring program for students' transition to the job market, the development of a new method for measuring and monitoring study success and teaching-learning coaches for improving teaching. The faculty projects involved improving the supervision of laboratories (Faculty of Design, Media, and Information and Faculty of Life Sciences), the development of study programs (Faculty of Life Sciences), the development of blended-learning concepts for preparatory courses (Faculty of Engineering and Computer Science), and advising on the use of new media and e-learning-tools (Faculty of Business and Social Sciences).

In the second round, the focus was put on university-wide projects (see Figure 5.5). Projects that had been faculty projects in the first round were extended to all faculties, for example, curricula development and coaching. Thus, according to the project documents, projects that had been developed and proved to be effective were used as best-practice examples and transferred to the whole university. Another emphasis was put on strengthening networking among the projects. Overall, five projects were funded, including dialogue-oriented quality management, study program monitoring, media 4.0 in studying and teaching, curricula development and coaching, and mentoring for students in vocational training.

Figure 5.4   Structure of the QPL Initiative at the HAW Hamburg (First Round)

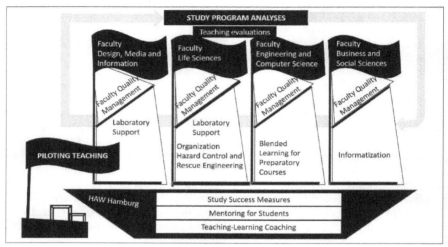

Note. Figure shows the structure of the QPL initiative "Piloting Teaching. Dialogue-oriented Quality Development in Studies and Teaching" at the University of Hamburg for the first round of the QPL funding program. Adapted and translated by the author from "Lehre lotsen 2011-2016 — Erste Förderphase" by the HAW Hamburg, 2016, p. 12.[36]

---

[36] This image was created by the author with MS Powerpoint. The text of the original image in the report is written in German. The graphical representation of the original image was reconstructed to make the QPL initiative's structure more transparent to readers.

Figure 5.5　　Structure of the QPL Initiative at the HAW Hamburg (Second Round)

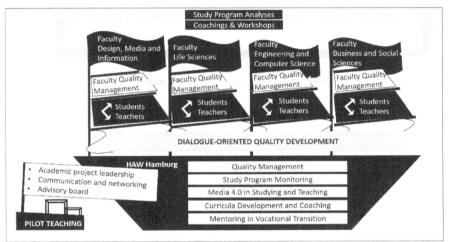

Note. Figure shows the structure of the QPL initiative "Piloting Teaching. Dialogue-oriented Quality Development in Studies and Teaching" at the University of Hamburg for the second round of the QPL funding program. Adapted and translated by the author from "Qualitätspakt Lehre lotsen" by the University of Hamburg, 2018, retrieved from https://www.haw-hamburg.de/lehrelotsen.html.[37]

5.3.3　Summary

The single-case analysis of the HAW Hamburg revealed some general findings on the levels of strategy, structure and action about the university's response to the demand of student diversity in the context of the QPL initiative.

Overall, the aim of the QPL initiative was to develop a dialogue-oriented quality culture and optimize steering processes in the context of quality assurance and development. With such a focus, the QPL initiative concentrated on improving the institutional settings in which studying and teaching take place instead of improving students' competences. The QPL strategy was heavily influenced by the university's teaching profile, which can be attributed to the fact that the HAW Hamburg is a university of applied sciences. This type of higher education institution regards teaching as its main educational task.

---

[37] This image was created by the author with MS Powerpoint. The text of the original image in the report is written in German. The graphical representation of the original image was reconstructed to make the QPL initiative's structure more transparent to readers.

Consequently, questions concerning the provision and conceptualization of high-quality teaching were debated extensively. 'Good' teaching was defined here in terms of competence-oriented teaching, which required a re-thinking of classical teaching-and-learning-formats. Student diversity played a role to some extent and was defined as the varying set of competences with which students enter higher education. The university emphasized its responsibility to establish teaching-and-learning scenarios that acknowledge and make deliberate use of the differences in students' competences, particularly against the background that as a university of applied sciences, the student composition varies in terms of entrance qualifications, socio-demographic characteristics (e.g., age) and living situation (e.g., working next to their studies).

The QPL initiative's structure was displayed as a sailing ship, whose hull comprised university-wide projects and its masts consisted of faculty projects. Overall, prior projects and experiences with improving the quality of teaching and studying laid the basis for the QPL structure. These prior projects were initiated by the same inner circle of committed administrative and academic staff that surrounded the Vice President for Studies and Teaching. The Vice President had a significant influence on the overall QPL initiative because she was not only involved in writing the QPL proposal but also responsible for the QPL initiative in the first and second rounds. The QPL initiative was very dear to the Vice President as it allowed her to pursue her vision of the HAW Hamburg as a learning organization that facilitates continuous, self-reflective and competence-oriented learning on the part of its members. The inner circle of committed staff was highly involved in various activities at the HAW Hamburg and exchanged experiences via formal and informal channels. Often, the exchange of experiences resulted in spill-over effects of single QPL projects, when members realized that a certain activity might also work well for their respective work unit. Thus, the degree of interaction and communication among persons in this inner circle can be described as high. However, the documentation of activities was rather sparse, which particularly became a problem in times of personnel fluctuation. Further, the communication about QPL activities with organizational members who had no links to this inner circle of committed employees was underdeveloped because formal communicative channels or tools were missing.

The activities in the QPL initiative were concerned with questions of improving the quality of studying and teaching. This was accomplished by improving the institution or, more precisely, the institutional setting in which studying and teaching take place. Consequently, the activities were mostly oriented towards academic or administrative staff. Nevertheless, student diversity played an important role for legitimizing the QPL initiative as a whole. The increasing heterogeneous student population was used as a reason why it was so important to improve the quality of studying and teaching in general and support the shift towards competence-oriented teaching in specific.

Within the QPL projects, additional administrative staff supported organizational members to join the dialogue on the quality of studying and teaching. The QPL employees worked closely together with academic staff in the faculties to understand the respective faculty culture and identify their needs. As experts or moderators, they accompanied processes of communication and collaboration, but let faculty members themselves realize their ideas on how to improve studying and teaching. At the same time, the QPL employees identified and supported the spread of 'best-practices' to other study programs, departments, or faculties, particularly when these practices resembled the guiding principle of competence orientation. Competence orientation was relevant for the discussion in that it focuses on the competences with which students enter higher education, their acknowledgment in the context of studying and teaching and the set of competences graduates should leave university with. In some places, this competence orientation led lecturers to re-think their perspectives on students and the desired levels of competences they should enter higher education with.

Even before those implementations, the HAW Hamburg had a relatively broad spectrum of extra-curricular activities that aimed to improve students' competences or the fit between students and the institution. These projects were based on different underlying assumptions about student diversity. For example, the viaMINT preparatory courses were based on the assumption that students enter university with differing levels of prior knowledge. The appropriate way to deal with student diversity was seen in identifying possible knowledge gaps and assigning students to online modules they should take to compensate for those gaps. The first-semester tutorials, in turn, were based on the assumption that first-year students differ with regard to their individual abilities, but also their prior experiences and current living situations. The appropriate way to deal with this student diversity was seen in providing a space in which they can exchange their experiences with other students and develop appropriate strategies that fit their individual situation to overcome the challenges in their first year of studies.

6 Cross-case Findings: Organizational Responses of German Universities to Student Diversity

In line with Scandinavian institutionalism (Czarniawska/Joerges 1996), student diversity can be described as one of several circulating ideas that are translated as they travel from one local context to another. This translation follows certain 'editing rules' that arise from this context and direct how actors modify and translate circulating ideas and make them fit by means of context, logic and formulation (Sahlin-Andersson 1996). Chapter 6.1. introduces the findings concerning editing rules that have been identified at the three German universities under review here. These editing rules guide the translation process of the idea of student diversity on the strategy, structure and action level in the context of the QPL initiative. In other words, these findings show how universities responded to this demand not only on a rhetorical basis, i.e., in the construction of verbal accounts but also how the idea is translated into/onto action on a structural and practical level (Brunsson 1989).

As already indicated, organizational responses to student diversity differ among the three universities. The research question following from that asks how variations in organizational responses to student diversity of German universities can be explained. According to Scandinavian institutionalism, the translation or the editing of the idea of student diversity is determined by the respective local context in which the translation takes place (Sahlin/Wedlin 2008). As mentioned before, what is being transferred from one local context to another is not the idea per se, but rather certain materializations of the idea. These materializations can be identified in the edited narratives that are told in the organizations. In these 'overarching narratives', the idea of student diversity is presented or framed in a widely accepted or familiar way so that it makes sense to the addressees. This act of interpretation or framing is steered by institutional beliefs and norms that derive from the local context and depend on several structural and cultural characteristics of the organization (Czarniawska 2009; Greenbank 2006). Further, organizational actors' interpretations also reflect different underlying diversity paradigms that are apparent within the organization (Gaisch/Aichinger/Preymann 2017). Consequently, differences in the wider institutional and local context of universities might help to explain variations in the translation of the idea of student diversity (Kirkpatrick et al. 2013). Chapter 6.2. introduces the 'overarching narratives' prevalent at the three German universities, emphasizing the role of the local context for explaining variations in organizational responses to student diversity.

Third, the present study argues that particular attention should be paid to identifying how the idea of student diversity is materialized on the level of concrete actions at German universities (Czarniawska/Sevón 1996a). More precisely, the case study analyses of the action level reveal that the QPL projects at the three German universities are based on different understandings of student diversity. Chapter 6.3. introduces seven different organizational practices that directly result from those understandings and which have been identified in the context of the QPL initiative.

6.1 Editing Rules

Editing rules refer to rules deriving from the local context that enable and restrict how organizational actors translate circulating ideas and make them fit to the local context in the process of telling and retelling the stories of editing or translation (Sahlin-Andersson 1996). The present study was able to identify three kinds of editing rules that guided the translation process in the context of the QPL initiatives at the three German universities. Following Sahlin-Andersson (1996), these are called editing rules concerning context, formulation and logic, which will be explained in more detail in the respective sub-chapters. More precisely, these editing rules were not only to be found where actors translated the idea of student diversity on a rhetorical basis, i.e., in the construction of verbal accounts. Rather, editing rules also framed the translation of the idea of student diversity into/onto action on structural and practical levels. These editing rules could be identified in the stories that were told by organizational actors at the universities about the strategy behind the QPL initiative, the structures that have been established and the activities or, more precisely, the single QPL projects that have been developed in the context of the QPL initiative. These edited stories were found in the triangulated data materials by identifying text passages with a high interactive and metaphorical density (see Chapter 4.6). In the following sub-chapters, findings will be presented according to the respective editing rules used in the translation of the idea of student diversity according to 1) context, 3) formulation and 3) logic. The sub-chapter will end with a table that summarizes the most important findings concerning editing rules in the context of the present study.

6.1.1 Editing Rules of Context

The data analysis reveals that organizational actors at all three German universities used editing rules of context to bind the idea of student diversity more concretely to their respective local situation. On the level of the QPL initiatives' strategies, the respective interpretations of student diversity were linked to the profiles, mission statements and traditions of the universities. Concerning the QPL initiatives' structures and QPL related activities, contextual factors like prior experiences, the size of the universities, but also the institutional anchoring of the QPL initiatives provided the background for translating the idea of student diversity. The following sub-chapters will first introduce the editing rules that have been identified on the strategy level, followed by the editing rules that were found in the data materials on the structure and action level.

Editing rules of context: Mission statements and profiles

At the University of Hamburg, the definition of student diversity in the context of the QPL initiative's strategy was heavily influenced by its mission statement 'Education through Science and Scholarship' and its research profile. The aim within the first round of the QPL initiative was to support skills that were regarded as necessary for academic studies, "given the rapidly increasing diversity of the student population" (UHH_doc_34/5). In other words, the increasingly diverse student body was used to legitimize the need to support academic abilities. The QPL proposal was based on the assumption that the transition phase between university and school undergoes new challenges due to the increasing heterogeneity of incoming students. In an interview, this transition phase was displayed as a "problem zone" (UHH_intA/28) that needed adequate measures to prepare students for their way to higher education. Thus, the data suggest that organizational actors at the University of Hamburg perceived students as not well enough equipped for beginning their studies. Such an emphasis is characterized by an understanding of student diversity as a lack of competences necessary for academic studies. Academic organizational actors at the University of Hamburg perceived these abilities as particularly important since, as the mission statement implies, the university saw it as its responsibility to "educate future citizens through science", so that students develop into "strong personalities" who take responsibility in society (UHH_doc_34/3). This emphasis on academia and science is also linked to their profile as a large university that is characterized in project documents as having a "high degree of diversity" in terms of their "attractive richness of subject and research areas with about 70 disciplines" (UHH_doc_34/2). Thus, the term "diversity" is used to highlight their distinguishing feature as "one of the biggest universities in Germany" with a broad spectrum of subject areas and "excellent research opportunities" (UHH_doc_34/2).

The strategy of the QPL initiative of the University of Kassel was strongly influenced by the university's mission to "enable and ensure the full range of access to education without social, gender-related, ethnic or national selection" (UK_doc_42/1). At the same time, the university described in project documents the challenge of "the enormous growth in student numbers and their growing diversity" (UK_doc_46/5), while the support structures in studying and teaching had not been able to keep pace with this growth. In the QPL proposal, the growth in student numbers was directly linked to the guiding principle of „widening educational opportunities" (UK_doc_42/1) to which the university has committed itself. Thus, diversity played a prominent role for the University of Kassel in general and the QPL strategy in particular, while diversity was mostly interpreted in terms of socio-demographic characteristics and educational biography. The university emphasized its tradition of already comparatively broad access for certain non-traditional student groups, like for example people with vocational qualifications instead of school-based university entrance qualifications. The prominent role of student diversity, as argued by organizational actors in interviews and documents, is deeply embedded within its history since it originated from a *Gesamthochschule*, established as the first of its kind in 1971. As such the university perceived itself as a 'pioneer' in developing study programs for students entering higher education via different access routes.

In the case of the HAW Hamburg, the definition of student diversity was connected to its institutional type that has a strong teaching orientation. The status of a university of applied sciences was used to legitimize the traditionally higher proportion of people who enter university via alternative access routes. Further, the number of students who have worked before taking up studies is much higher than at universities. According to the interviews, the broad spectrum of students' competences, including students holding the *Abitur* and students who enter university based on vocational qualifications, should be used in a positive way. In other words, the dominant perspective here was that students enter university with different sets of competences, based on their educational biography. The university should accept and use these differences in its teaching and learning settings, which is in line with the overall emphasis of the HAW Hamburg on a competence-oriented way of teaching. Thus, organizational actors at the HAW Hamburg saw it as the task of the institution to provide a broad spectrum of different subjects — some with a stronger academic orientation, others with a more practical outlook — so that all students can make use of their skills respectively. Next to this external differentiation of teaching and learning scenarios, the university saw it as equally important to contribute to internal differentiation by encouraging "teaching or studying that does justice to the different learning types or the individual personality" (HAW_intA/36). Thus, according to the university's self-understanding, teaching should be developed further to be more adaptable to the diverse ways students are learning and studying. This calls for a definition of student diversity in terms of an individual's learning personality that should be considered in the context of studies and teaching.

Editing rules of context: Traditions, prior experiences and institutional anchoring

At the University of Hamburg, prior experiences and traditions played an important role in the translation process for dealing with student diversity on the structure and action level of the QPL initiative. The QPL initiative involved the establishment of the *Universitätskolleg* that represented the conceptual roof for 42 single QPL projects. These single QPL projects, however, were actually realized within the faculties or central service units during the first round. Here, traditions played a crucial role for the QPL initiative's structures as the university had no prior experience with such a cross-faculty institutionalization of teaching and learning as realized in the *Universitätskolleg*. The *Universitätskolleg* was the first cross-faculty institution and no existing examples of cooperation and collaboration between the faculties existed before. This lack of cooperative experience was related to the specific structural characteristics of the university where "the faculties define the dominant structure of the university" (UHH_IntA/18), as it was described in one interview. Consequently, due to the historically high autonomy and strong power of the faculties, the establishment of a non-faculty institution was met with skepticism on side of the academic staff because the *Universitätskolleg* held decision-making-powers and financial resources that the faculties rather would have liked for themselves. The dominance of the faculties also had consequences for the choice of activities dealing with student diversity. In the institutional documents, a general consent could be observed where the faculties were perceived as very specific and different in their own functional logics and ways of studying and teaching. Here, organizational actors at the University of Hamburg re-embedded the idea of student diversity within the general belief that "academics know best" what kind of activities were needed to deal with student diversity because, allegedly, the needs and requirements were so different between the faculties. Overall, the *Universitätskolleg* subsumed activities that aimed to prepare students for higher education by supporting the development of academic competences. Here, organizational actors in the faculties argued that the kind of academic competences required in the respective disciplines differed from each other. Consequently, no central institution was to decide on the respective set of competences, but the academics within the faculties themselves had to define these competences and prepare their students for the beginning of their studies.

At the University of Kassel, prior existing structures and discussions affected the structure and action level of the QPL initiative. The discussion about how to deal with student diversity had a long history at the university and was institutionalized by a task force called 'Heterogeneity' established in 2008. This task force published its recommendations in a final report in 2009, which influenced the QPL proposal and the choice of appropriate tools to deal with student diversity in a substantial way. The task force's recommendations pointed out that the faculties should define 'performance profiles' to help prospective students understand the kind of competences or study requirements demanded from them. Further, the recommendations suggested that students' lack of competences should be compensated as early as possible. In the end, these recommendations found their way into the QPL proposal where student diversity was defined in terms of certain competences that students lack at the beginning of their studies. The appropriate way of dealing with this aspect of student diversity was seen in making study requirements more transparent to the students. Further, compensating measures were to be developed in order to 'homogenize' students according to the required competences, but also to broaden the spectrum of teaching and learning scenarios. Consequently, the QPL initiative included project activities like bridging courses and introductory lectures, e-learning offers, advising, additional tutoring and mentoring, project-based learning projects and discipline-specific team-teaching with specialists for academic writing.

At the HAW Hamburg, the size of the university and existing networks played an important role for the QPL initiative's structures and activities. The QPL initiative was structurally anchored to the position of the Vice President for Studies and Teaching who was surrounded by an inner circle of highly committed administrative and academic staff. This circle shared the Vice President's vision of the HAW Hamburg as a learning organization that facilitates continuous learning on the part of its members in a self-reflective and competence-oriented way. Accordingly, student diversity was also defined in a competence-oriented way, while emphasizing that students enter higher education with a diverse set of competences that should be acknowledged in the context of studying and teaching. The same group of committed employees was highly involved in developing new project activities to deal with student diversity in a competence-oriented way. This inner circle was very well connected among its members and exchanged their experiences through several formal and informal channels. This exchange of experiences was facilitated by the medium size of the university. Thus, although project activities were realized within different faculties and service units, these units were closely connected to each other through joint projects, committee memberships, participation in round tables, but also through personal contacts that were established.

6.1.2 *Editing Rules of Formulation*

The present study was able to identify editing rules of formulation for all three universities which framed the idea of student diversity within a wider storyline. On the level of the QPL initiative's strategy, editing rules of formulation were activated to interweave the idea of student diversity with current discussions and developments at the university, while other institutional demands were either connected or played off against each other. Concerning the QPL initiative's structure and QPL related activities, editing rules of formulation were used by organizational actors at the three universities to tell stories about best-practice examples for approaches to deal with student diversity. The following sub-chapters will first describe the findings concerning editing rules of formulation that have been identified on the strategy level. Second, the findings concerning editing rules of formulation on the structure and/or action level in the context of the QPL initiatives at the three case study universities will be displayed in more detail.

Editing rules of formulation: Other institutional demands, dramatization and symbolic language

At the University of Hamburg, editing rules of formulation were enacted in the context of a strategic shift that had been taking place within the QPL initiative's strategy. In the first round of the QPL initiative, student diversity was mostly defined in terms of a lack of academic competences with which students enter university. During the preparation of the QPL proposal for the second round, an external agency evaluated the QPL initiative to identify strengths and weaknesses. One of their main findings was that the QPL initiative's strong focus on the elimination of deficits carried an inherent risk of reputational loss in that the *Universitätskolleg* might be regarded as a 'repair shop'. This worry was described by a person from QPL management as conflicting with the university's aim to be regarded as an excellent research university. The emphasis on 'excellence' can be retraced to the Excellence Initiative, a different funding program the university had applied to at the same time. In the application for the Excellence Initiative, the President of the University of Hamburg described his vision for the University of Hamburg to become a 'University for a Sustainable Future'. To avoid a conflict of institutional demands, the strategic perspective of the QPL initiative was changed accordingly. The recommendations of the agency were adopted on a one-to-one basis, while more emphasis was put on the notion of 'Diversity as Chance' to integrate the *Universitätskolleg* into the university-wide sustainability strategy as part of the more general objective to become an 'elite university' in the context of the Excellence Initiative. As a result, the title of the overall QPL initiative was changed from 'Bridges to the University — Pathways to Academia' to 'Diversity as a Chance'.

At the University of Kassel, elements of dramatization could be detected on the strategy level of the QPL initiative. Overall, in the interviews, organizational actors constructed a story about the precarious situation of the University of Kassel and the way the university was confronted with an incredible number of external challenges. It was told in repetitive and dramatic ways how drastic the increase in student numbers was and how challenging it was to deal with the diverse study and learning requirements of students when they began their studies. In these stories, the university was displayed as bravely trying to get a hold of the situation, although it was badly equipped in terms of finances and personnel and received almost no external support, which further aggravated the situation. These stories were dominant for the university's understanding of student diversity as they welded the actors together while providing a common understanding of the central problem and solution. Increasing student numbers and the heterogeneous study and learning requirements of the students were perceived as the main problem, in particular in the face of scarce resources. However, this problem was always described by organizational actors as a problem with a certain currency or topicality that required immediate reaction. The solution to this problem was seen in filling gaps by means of third-party funded projects. In other words, the third-party funding of the QPL initiative was to compensate for the support structures in studying and teaching that had not been able to keep pace with the "enormous growth in student numbers and their growing diversity" (UK_doc_46/5). This approach of 'filling gaps' was criticized by some organizational members because they did not see any long-term plans for dealing with the topic of student diversity as a permanent task that required steady financing and support.

A different form of formulation rule can be found on the strategy and structure level of the QPL initiative at the HAW Hamburg. Here, the university made extensive use of symbols and symbolic language that played an important role in external perception. Some of the QPL funding was used to employ a graphic design agency to develop a branding concept with a maritime theme that fit with 'Piloting Teaching', the title of the QPL initiative. This resulted in the image of a big sailing ship illustrating the project structure, with a hull including the cross-disciplinary projects and four masts representing the faculties and their inner-faculty projects. Further, the language of the project presentation was adapted accordingly, using maritime terms in project descriptions, such as 'piloting teaching', 'the compass of competence orientation' or that 'students should take the steering wheel into their own hands'. This symbolic language was frequently used by the Vice President for Studies and Teaching and her team of committed academic and administrative staff. As mentioned before, this group of employees resembled a closed inner circle who spread their ideas and expectations with the help of continuously new innovative projects in order to achieve their vision of competence-oriented teaching. On the strategy level, they used interpretive patterns of buzz-words, like competence orientation, dialogue orientation and their idea of a 'learning organization' in a very repetitive to support sense-making among other members of the university.

Editing rules of formulation: Best-practice examples and networking

All three universities used editing rules of formulation on the action level of their QPL initiatives in the context of best-practice examples. These best-practice examples were found in stories about single projects that were deemed successful in the eyes of the organizational actors who told these stories. These stories were used to indicate a changed perspective on student diversity and how to deal with this topic.

At the University of Hamburg, one best-practice example was told in the context of the 'Teaching Laboratory' project. This project was successful in that its concept was first tried in one faculty and then expanded to include other faculties as well. In the context of this project, lecturers were invited to apply for financial resources with new innovative teaching concepts. Here, QPL employees working in this project reported a changed mindset in participating lecturers when it came to the question of dealing with student diversity. One of these stories of a changed mindset was told by a person working in this QPL project about a teaching project in physics. According to the interview, the project started with the lecturer's impression that students did not read the study materials and were badly prepared for the lectures. Such an implication can be associated with a deficit-oriented view on students and student diversity as the main focus is put on the lack of preparation. In the context of the project, the lecturer started to develop small tests and then added additional learning tools like videos and interactive scripts. After a while, he realized that students selectively chose these learning tools, according to their personal preferences ("some of them preferred to read. Others liked to watch a video, and others used scripts", UHH_gd/209). Irrespective of the learning tool used, the lecturer observed that the students' level of expertise increased. Thus, over time, the lecturer became aware that students learn differently and that teaching should take these different learning types into account. The underlying logic changed from assuming the appropriate way of dealing with student diversity was to confront students with one traditional way of mediating content that they then needed to adapt to, towards a broadened perspective in which institutional practices are adapted to allow different learning routes. However, structural barriers at the University of Hamburg limited the spread of this perspective change to other units and faculties. Due to the huge size of the university in general and the QPL initiative with its 45 projects in particular, the exchange of experiences about perspectives on student diversity was relatively low. Nevertheless, as the project was refunded in the second round of the QPL initiative and even expanded to include two faculties, some lecturers indeed reported how the exploration of new and innovative forms of teaching and learning led to a changed understanding about student diversity on their part.

At the University of Kassel, rules of formulation were used to legitimize changes in the QPL project's focus on specific target groups. One story was told in the context of the project called 'ProStudies' that offered propaedeutic workshops in academic writing and the organization of learning. This project built on the prior project 'Self-made Students' in which the target group were "students who studied as first in their family, who have a migrant background, or enter university with alternative entrance qualifications" (UK_doc_47/5). With the help of advice, coaching and workshops the students were supported during their first year of studies. Thus, the predecessor project had a strong focus on student diversity, defining it in particular in terms of socio-demographic characteristics, like academic family background, migrant background and entrance qualifications. The follow-up project 'ProStudies', in turn, did not explicitly focus on specific student groups. According to the involved QPL employees, this was related to the experience that students who did not fit into the target group scheme expressed an interest in participating in the project because they experienced difficulties with academic writing as well. The QPL employees reported how they became aware that students did not need to belong to these so-called 'special risk' student groups to feel challenged by the organization of their learning activities in the first year. Thus, this experience of positive discrimination led to the decision to open the project to all students, regardless of their socio-demographic characteristics. Consequently, the QPL project team deliberately avoided defining specific target groups and emphasizing certain social characteristics over others.

At the HAW Hamburg, there were several stories about best-practice examples told by organizational actors. One story was told in the context of the project 'Teaching-Learning Coaching'. In this story, a group of committed lecturers decided that they wanted to use the planned re-accreditation of their study program to initiate an overall change to their approach to studying and teaching. The professors involved decided to fundamentally redesign the study program by "letting go of the old way and going new, innovative ways" (HAW_ conference_protocol/13). This process was accompanied by an external moderator who knew the lecturers and was familiar with the HAW culture and its structures. She initiated a solution-oriented dialogue between the committed professors that prevented that the professors discuss specific teaching modules. Instead, according to the professors involved, the moderation enabled a paradigm shift to take place, "away from the perspective that 'students first need to know the fundamentals' to 'providing little insights into the field they will also be working in later, [something which] is possible from the first semester onwards'" (HAW_ conference_protocol/19). This led to the development of an alternative curriculum. Such a bottom-up approach was perceived to be much more successful than a top-down approach, like one professor formulated: "if someone from quality management had come to us and told us to develop this in a more competence-oriented way, there would have been much more resistance" (HAW_conference_protocol/23). Due to the close collaboration of dedicated employees, as mentioned before, such best-practice examples and stories about innovative ideas were more easily spread among central and decentral units.

6.1.3 Editing Rules of Logic

At all three universities, editing rules of logic were identified that aimed to frame the idea of student diversity and dealing with student diversity in a rationalistic way. On the level of the QPL initiative's strategy and structure, evaluations of strengths and weaknesses and statistics played a major role in legitimizing definitions of student diversity and the perception of appropriate instruments to deal with it. Concerning the QPL initiative's activities, success stories about QPL single projects were told, whereas 'success' was legitimized based on statistics or personal experiences.

First, the QPL initiative at the University of Hamburg was evaluated by an external evaluation agency after the first round. The recommendations of this agency were adopted on a one-to-one-basis. In other words, the evaluation findings were used as a legitimization to not only change the strategic focus of the QPL initiative, but also the initiative's overall structure and activities. At the University of Hamburg, the analysis of strengths and weaknesses of the external evaluation agency even resulted in an overall change of strategy concerning student diversity, from having a focus on students lacking academic competences to defining 'diversity as a chance'. Other recommendations of the evaluation agency were also incorporated to make the QPL strategy fit better to other strategic developments, including thematic issues like 'sustainability' and 'digitalization'. Concerning the structure level, the recommendations of the evaluation agency also resulted in a changed project structure: the seven clusters of QPL projects that focused mostly on improving students in the transition period were reduced to three clusters that bundled activities along the whole student life cycle. The three clusters in the second round were called 'Preparation', 'Studying' and 'Teaching'. Thereby, the strategic shift of the QPL initiative also impacted the structure and action levels by focusing not solely on students as the main target group who need compensating measures but adding activities that seek to improve the institutional context in which teaching and learning take place.

At the University of Kassel, editing rules of logic were used extensively. For example, an evaluation of strengths and weaknesses served as a background for the QPL proposals of the first round and second round. In the first round, it was argued on the basis of a Bachelor's student survey that students were unsatisfied with the study organization and study support provided by the University of Kassel. The findings of this survey thus laid the basis for declaring the fields of study organization and study support to be the main areas to invest in with the help of the QPL initiative. According to the project documents, the overall aim was to achieve "a complementary allocation of resources to already existing financial resources" (UK_doc_28_/3). Thus, the QPL funding was displayed as an opportunity to complement already existing third-party funding that was mostly spent in areas other than study organization and study support. Further, a lot of emphasis was put on the question how the QPL initiative fits within other strategic approaches in order to present a comprehensive picture. At the structure level, the activities of the QPL initiative were organized in three clusters, called 'Professionalization of Propaedeutics', 'Professionalization of the Didactic Quality of Teaching' and 'Professionalization of Quality Management and Counseling'. These three clusters were again identified based on an evaluation of strengths and weaknesses. Here, the evaluation findings suggested that to improve the quality of teaching, not only students' preparation for higher education needed support, but also the didactic quality of teaching as well as the quality of service units needed to be optimized. On the action level, the single QPL projects at the University of Kassel were again legitimized by findings of the Bachelor' student survey. Further, the 'successes' of these single QPL projects were measured based on students' satisfaction rates. In other words, whether QPL single projects showed an 'effect' was indicated by higher satisfaction rates in the Bachelor' student survey conducted the following year. In preparation for writing the proposal for the second round, the QPL initiative was evaluated again by an external agency in the winter term 2014/15. The evaluation report reached very positive results that were prominently displayed on the QPL initiative websites. As described in the case-specific section, the positive results were legitimized based on the Bachelor' student survey findings that indicated improved satisfaction rates among students. Thus, the improvement in the general satisfaction with the conditions of teaching and studying was displayed as a direct effect of the QPL initiative. In this sense, statistics played a prominent role for legitimizing the university's approach to deal with student diversity.

At the HAW Hamburg, the strategic outline of the QPL initiative was based on study program analyses that used student surveys to identify certain 'hot spots' within the faculties that the QPL initiative should put its focus on: advising and accompanying students, the conception of study programs and the training of lecturers. Further, based on the findings of the student survey, a number of faculty-wide central themes were identified that were to be taken into consideration in the context of the QPL initiative as well. According to the QPL proposal, these evaluation findings resulted in the first round in a project structure that consisted of four university-wide projects and four faculty projects. In the second round, this structure changed towards only implementing university-wide projects. This structural change was legitimized by the faculty projects having been proven successful so that they were expanded to other faculties, becoming thereby university-wide projects as well.

The 'success' of these projects, however, was not clearly related to data and evaluations but based on personal observations and experiences made by the involved organizational actors. Thus, when a project or an idea turned out to be a 'success' from the perspective of organizational actors working in these projects, this idea was used as a best-practice example to make it known to other faculties or study programs. These success stories were told in order to find allies to implement this idea in other contexts as well. The knowledge about push- and pull factors that were important for the 'success' of these innovations was secured and spread by the previously mentioned group of committed employees. Thereby, the projects were continuously developed further, new aspects were added, while aspects that were perceived as being not successful, were eliminated.

6.1.4 Summary

Based on the concept of 'translation', the travel of the idea of student diversity was portrayed in different institutional contexts. The notion of editing rules helps to understand how this idea has been re-embedded on a symbolic and linguistic level. However, this approach goes even further by explaining how linguistics correspond to concrete actions, being more or less coupled with each other. Thereby, this part indicates how the idea of student diversity was translated not only on a strategy level but also on the levels of structure and action in the context of the QPL initiative. The study was able to identify three different types of editing rules (see Table 6.1).[38] First, the respective interpretations were connected to the local context where a fit was reconstructed between the edited idea and the universities' educational mission, its profile, but also other funding programs (i.e., editing rules concerning context). Second, dealing with student diversity was embedded into a wider storyline, using dramatic linguistic turns and giving ideas specific labels (i.e., editing rules concerning formulation). Third, arguments for certain perspectives and activities were reformulated in rationalistic terms, referring to evaluations and statistics that support universities' actions to deal with student diversity (i.e., editing rules concerning logic).

---

[38] For an extended version of the summarized findings on editing rules identified at the three case studies, see Table 6.A in the online appendix.

Table 6.1 Summarized Findings: Editing Rules Identified at the Three Levels of Strategy, Structure and Action

	Strategy	**Structure**	**Action**
Editing rules of context	mission, history, type of institution, size and profile	tradition, prior existing structures and experiences, size and existing networks	tradition, prior existing structures and experiences, size and existing networks
Editing rules of formulation	conflict with other institutional demands, dramatization, current challenges, symbols and language, interpretative patterns	symbols and language, best-practice examples, sustainability	best-practice examples, sustainability
Editing rules of logic	evaluation of strengths and weaknesses, study program analyses/statistics, other strategic papers	evaluation of strengths and weaknesses, study program analyses/statistics, other strategic papers	evaluation of strengths and weaknesses, statistics, personal experiences

6.2 Retelling the Narrative of Student Diversity — The Importance of the Local Context

The findings presented above provide an answer to the research question how German universities respond to student diversity in the context of the QPL initiative by showing how the translation of the idea of student diversity is guided by editing rules that arise from the local context. Since local contexts differ, the findings of editing rules also indicate how German universities respond very differently to the demand of dealing with student diversity.

To provide an answer to the research question how these variations in organizational responses can be explained, this study follows the narrative-oriented Scandinavian research tradition (Czarniawska 2008). Accordingly, the study suggests that as experiences with student diversity are narrated, they tend to be framed and presented in a familiar way that is commonly accepted and as such makes sense to the audience in the organization (Sahlin/Wedlin 2008). Thus, organizational actors tell about their experiences with student diversity by referring to familiar templates, classifications and examples. These templates, classifications and examples form the framework that direct and restrict translation. However, the framework is not the same everywhere, it differs between local contexts. In other words, certain templates, classifications and examples might be well-known and accepted at one university, while at another university they are unknown or even dismissed (Sahlin/Wedlin 2017).

Thus, there are certain aspects of the local context that direct the translation and lead to local variations in translating student diversity. Based on the previous literature review (see Chapter 3.6.), the present study distinguishes between institutional characteristics and dominant diversity paradigms as important aspects of the local contexts that direct translation processes. First, structural and cultural characteristics of the respective universities are expected to play an important role for the way student diversity is defined and in which organizational responses to student diversity are perceived as appropriate in the local context (see Chapter 3.6.1.). Examples for institutional characteristics are the university's profile, traditions, or size. Second, universities differ considerably in the way they approach the topic of student diversity, depending on the diversity paradigms that are dominant in the local context. Based on the work by Gaisch/Aichinger/Preymann (2017), the present study distinguishes five diversity paradigms that have been identified in the context of higher education on the organizational level (see Chapter 3.6.2.). These diversity paradigms differ, for example, according to the way organizational actors define student diversity (e.g., educational biography), how student diversity is valued in the organizational context (e.g., diversity as a problem) and how organizations respond to student diversity on the strategy, structure and action level.

In order to identify these aspects of the local context, the following subchapters will introduce the 'overarching narratives' of student diversity as told by the three universities in the context of the QPL initiative. Within these narratives, framing can be attributed not only to institutional characteristics of the respective university but also to organizational actors' interpretations of different underlying diversity paradigms. At the same time, the findings show how in many cases the newly introduced language and models did have an impact on how practices were introduced and presented. Thus, different understandings of student diversity were enacted on the strategy, structure and action level, while these levels were more or less tightly coupled with each other.

6.2.1 University of Hamburg

At the University of Hamburg, the QPL initiative of the first funding round had the title 'Bridges to the University — Pathways to Academia'. The QPL initiative *Universitätskolleg* was implemented following the idea to install a sort of cross-faculty pre-college that students visit in their first year of studies to prepare them for research-oriented studies and compensate for the lack of academic competences. Student diversity was defined in terms of academic competences that students lack at the beginning of their studies. In the second round, the title of the QPL initiative changed to 'Diversity as a Chance', indicating a perspectival shift on the topic of student diversity, but without concretely elucidating what is meant by this phrase.

The QPL initiative's strategy was strongly impacted by the university's research profile and its mission statement of 'Education through Science and Scholarship'. The guiding principle of the University of Hamburg is to educate students in an academically-oriented or research-oriented way. In order to be educated in a research-oriented way, students must have certain academic competences. In this context, the data materials highlight the critique that students lack these academic competences when they enter higher education. The 'culprits' are mostly the schools: they are accused in the interviews to not prepare their pupils sufficiently for higher education. The *Universitätskolleg*, thus, was supposed to compensate for this inadequate preparation by supporting students in their development of academic competences. The university's strong research orientation also resulted in an imbalance regarding the university's two main tasks of research and teaching. In other words, teaching was not regarded to be as important as research by the academics of the university. One participant of a workshop described this imbalance with the words "teaching is like nightshift, no one wants to do it"

(UHH_workshop_protocol/4). The emphasis on research was intensified by the university's application for the Excellence Initiative that focused on supporting excellent research. This application can be understood as a signal to organizational members that research still plays a much more important role than teaching. Within the application for the Excellence Initiative, the university intended to build a research profile towards becoming a 'University for a Sustainable Future'. For the second round of the QPL program, the strategic focus on student diversity shifted to align the QPL initiative with the sustainability objective. This means, dealing with student diversity was integrated within the university-wide sustainability strategy, referring to the responsibility the university has "in a changed educational and academic world" (UHH_doc_2/3). The shift of perspective concerning student diversity was legitimized out of a fear of the *Universitätskolleg* being perceived as a 'repair shop' due to the QPL initiative's focus on the lack of academic competences. Such a focus was perceived as conflicting with the university's aim to become an excellent research university. Consequently, for the second round, the phrase 'Diversity as a Chance' was used to signal a positive validation of student diversity. However, in the data materials, there is no specification of what is meant by this phrase, resulting in rather vague statements about student diversity on the strategy level.

On the structure level, the QPL initiative of the University of Hamburg was characterized by the enormous size of the initiative, incorporating 45 single QPL projects in the first round. This size made documentation and channels for the exchange of information even more important. A service unit was responsible for a vast amount of publications in the context of the QPL initiative. Persons working in the single QPL projects were regularly asked by this service unit to document their current project status. Despite the high degree of documentation, there was not much exchange of experiences among the projects, which can be attributed to the sheer size of the initiative, traditionally little experience with cross-faculty interaction and interdisciplinary collaborations. The *Universitätskolleg* was the first cross-faculty institution for teaching and learning at the University of Hamburg. In the beginning, the academics from the traditionally highly autonomous and powerful faculties met this new institution with great skepticism, since the *Universitätskolleg* held decision-making-powers and financial resources that they supposedly rather would have liked to have for themselves as they were convinced they knew best what to do. In order to improve the acceptance towards the QPL initiative among those academics, the QPL leadership team chose to emphasize throughout, how the QPL initiative was not involved in 'third-party development' or 'external control'. Instead, they highlighted how this institution developed measures in close cooperation with the faculties. Thus, despite its character as an institution functioning across all faculties, it seems to be important to underline the decision-making independence for the faculties and their academics in determining the types and designs of the measures to be developed under the auspices of the initiative. Further, it is emphasized throughout the documents and interviews that the QPL initiative was merely an experimental phase or a pilot run for how such a cross-faculty institution might work. This points out how careful the QPL leadership team was in picturing the future of the QPL initiative since they knew how fragile the existence of this institution was. Thus, the major innovation and challenge for the university were to install such a central institution against the skepticism of the faculties. Overall, the *Universitätskolleg* resembled a hybrid unit that, however, perceived itself 'only' as a central platform or a think-tank for activities that were organized by the faculties themselves. However, due to the external agency's recommendations, the structure of the *Universitätskolleg* changed substantially in the second round of the QPL initiative. Not only did the number of projects change, but the structural anchoring of the projects was also altered. In the first round, most of the 45 projects were realized within the faculties and central service units. In the second round, however, the six remaining projects were implemented by the *Universitätskolleg* directly. Consequently, the personnel working in the projects was also employed centrally. This new structure of personnel was accompanied by an extension of administrative support.

On the action level, a broad range of activities could be identified in the QPL initiative. Each differed according to the definition of student diversity and the perception of appropriate ways of dealing with it. However, although what was regarded as the appropriate way of dealing with student diversity varied, there was a consensus about the uniqueness of the faculties with regard to their own functional logics of teaching and learning. As mentioned before, it was apparent that academics in faculties supposedly knew best what kind of measures were needed to suit the needs of their faculty and their students. However, such a faculty-focused approach made it difficult to stimulate a university-wide discussion about the topic of student diversity and how to deal with it as perceived by QPL management. Further, the relatively few contacts among faculties and the large size of the QPL initiative limited spillover effects of single QPL projects to other faculties. Consequently, single measures petered out, although there were voices that would have liked to combine them towards a more process-oriented general concept for improving studying and teaching. However, these voices mostly came from central units and not from decentral faculties. Besides, there were huge differences among the academic staff in the faculties with respect to the commitment to the activities of the *Universitätskolleg*. According to the project documents, academics from the MIN Faculty and the Faculty of Humanities were more involved than others because they were responsible for a much higher number of QPL projects. This can be traced back to the very dedicated Deans of Studies who had already been responsible for many projects and clusters in the first phase of the QPL initiative and who backed the activities enormously. This is also the reason why these two faculties were more involved in projects of the second phase of the QPL initiative. This is in particular remarkable since these two faculties were often displayed as characterized by oppositional disciplinary cultures. Consequently, faculty leadership and its commitment to the QPL initiative seemed to play an important role for the involvement in project activities.

Overall, there was a broad spectrum of activities in the *Universitätskolleg* dealing with student diversity. Most of these activities focused on students as their main target group. For example, at the University of Hamburg, activities like extra-curricular courses (e.g., crash courses, preparatory courses) or writing workshops (e.g., academic writing tutorials or seminars held by professional writing coaches) aimed *to improve the student*. Here, the underlying assumption was that students did not meet the study requirements that were expected of them from the institution. Thus, the central problem was the student's lack of study-specific knowledge. The appropriate solution was consequently to offer extra-curricular measures to compensate for the lack of study-specific knowledge so that students met the desired study requirements at the beginning of their studies. Activities like student orientation and online self-assessments, advisory services for specific target groups (e.g., online advice services, mentoring programs) and tutoring and mentoring programs, in turn, aimed *to improve the fit between the student and institution*. These activities were based on the assumption that the main issue at hand was the lack of fit between the individual student and the respective institution. In order to deal with student diversity, students needed to be informed about the institution's expectations, just as the institutional setting had to adjust to the (changed) needs and requirements of the student population. Finally, activities like didactic training (e.g., teaching laboratory), aimed *to improve the institution*. Here, the institutional setting in which studying and teaching take place was perceived as the central problem because it was not adequate to meet the needs of a diverse student population. Consequently, the appropriate way to deal with this component of student diversity was to adapt the institutional setting accordingly.

Concerning the impact of institutional characteristics, the research findings indicate that the university's research profile, its academically oriented mission and current developments like the university's application for the Excellence Initiative have substantially influenced the definition of student diversity on the strategy level (see Figure 6.1). On the structure level, institutional characteristics like the lack of prior experiences with a cross-faculty institution, the tradition of highly autonomous and powerful faculties and the sheer size of the QPL initiative played a marginal role for the way structures to deal with student diversity were implemented. In this context, the lack of structural anchoring of QPL management and the *Universitätskolleg* made discussions held in the institution as a whole about student diversity difficult. On the action level, the dominance of faculties and the belief that academics knew best how to deal with student diversity resulted in the development of multiple measures that were realized within the faculties or central service units.

From the point of view of the diversity paradigms introduced by Gaisch/Aichinger/Preymann (2017), one can observe on the strategy level of analysis how the shift from a perspective of homogenization to one of heterogenization took place. Starting with a deficit-based perspective, student diversity was defined in terms of the lack of academic competences among students. Such a perspective was perceived as a threat to the university's striving for excellence. Consequently, the QPL initiative was perceived as a way of preparing students for their way into university by providing activities that could compensate for these deficits. This bears clear parallels to the *resistance diversity paradigm* (Dass/Parker 1999). According to this diversity paradigm, widening participation is encountered with skepticism because student diversity is perceived as opposed to 'elite education'. Consequently, the aim of the organization is to preserve the exclusive status quo of the dominant, homogeneous majority.

For the second round, the diversity definition was completely turned around with the change of the QPL initiative's title to 'Diversity as a Chance'. In the data material, it was emphasized that it is the university's social responsibility to deal with student diversity. This resembles the logic of the *responsibility and sensibility diversity paradigm* (Schulz 2009) that understands diversity as an important educational mission for universities, next to research and teaching. According to this diversity paradigm, dealing with student diversity should be considered as an important contribution to society to build and secure (human) resources in a sustainable way. However, at the University of Hamburg, the shift from a homogenization perspective that perceives diversity as a threat to a heterogenization perspective that values diversity as a social responsibility seems to be only political rhetoric. On the strategy level, the phrase 'Diversity as a Chance' is used but without specifying what exactly is meant by this phrase. On the structure level, a unit is missing that could coordinate activities and is responsible for the exchange of experiences made among organizational members. In fact, the coordinating unit at the University of Hamburg was very much involved in documentation activities, but it was difficult for them to promote an exchange of experiences and reduce the distance among faculties and break with faculty-focused traditions without structural linkages to other units of the university. On the action level, multiple measures were developed but without any coherent underlying strategy for how to deal with student diversity. Most of the single QPL projects concentrated on homogenizing activities to adapt them to the norm expectation of the 'traditional' student. Consequently, these activities forced students to a one-sided adaptation to the institution and its prevalent cultural norms and attitudes.

Figure 6.1   The Story of Student Diversity in the Context of the QPL Initiative at the University of Hamburg

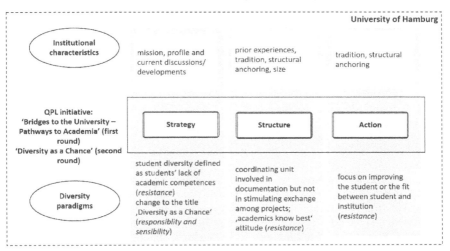

Note. The figure illustrates the impact of institutional characteristics and diversity paradigms on the translation of student diversity in the context of the QPL initiative at the University of Hamburg. Source: Own illustration.

6.2.2 *University of Kassel*

At the University of Kassel, the title of the QPL initiative in both rounds was 'Growth and Quality — Professionalization of Studying and Teaching'. In the data materials, the QPL initiative was displayed as a response to the challenges posed by increasing student numbers and a growing diversity of students' study requirements, while the support structures in studying and teaching had not been able to keep pace with this growth. Student diversity was defined here in terms of different study requirements that result from students' heterogeneous entrance qualifications with which they enter university.

The QPL initiative's strategy was strongly impacted by the university's mission, its history and profile, but also recent developments or challenges. In the QPL strategy of both rounds, widening participation played — next to increasing participation — a crucial role. Widening participation was defined here in terms of a traditionally broadened access for students entering higher

179

education via alternative access routes. This broadened access was legitimized by organizational actors based on the university's historical roots as a *Gesamthochschule* that allowed access to students arriving with different entrance qualifications. Here, the university emphasized its guiding principle to "enable and ensure the full access to education without social, gender-related, ethnic or national selection" (UK_doc_42/1). At the same time, the university understood itself as an important contributor to regional development, which was displayed as the reason why the university has traditionally welcomed a broad spectrum of first-year students and avoided early selective measures. This background — together with the fact that there are no competing universities of applied sciences nearby — resulted in a different student composition in terms of entrance qualifications. Dealing with this different student composition was presented as a challenge for the university, although organizational actors at the same time emphasized the university's social responsibility to include persons entering university via alternative entrance qualifications. Here, a narrative about the precarious situation of the University of Kassel was constructed, which highlighted the confrontation with an incredible number of external challenges. Consequently, it was told in repetitive and dramatic ways how drastic the increase in student number was and how shocked organizational actors were by the diverse study and learning requirements of first-year students. In this narrative, the university was displayed as a sort of fire extinguisher, trying bravely to extinguish the constant fires flaming up, although it was badly equipped in terms of finances and personnel and received almost no external support, which further aggravated the situation. Thus, a threatening scenario was constructed in which the University of Kassel was under extreme and constant pressure due to external forces, in particular in the form of the demand to increase and widen participation. Since at the same time the university had only limited financial and personal resources, organizational actors saw the scope of action as highly restricted. The right way to deal with this threatening scenario was seen in 'filling the gaps'. In other words, the QPL funding was perceived as filling the missing funding opportunities to improve the quality of studying and teaching without lowering academic standards.

The QPL initiative's structure was influenced by the structural anchoring of the QPL initiative and recent developments or challenges. Central administration of the QPL initiative was in the hands of the Department for Development Planning. This department is responsible for academic controlling, which means that it coordinates the collection and processing of university-related statistical information and data (e.g., rankings, evaluations). These remits of the department shaped the QPL initiative's structure in that the establishment of the QPL initiative was very data-driven. For example, the structure of the QPL initiative was legitimized on the basis of a SWOT analysis that indicated the need to professionalize propaedeutics, the didactic quality of teaching and the quality management and advisory services. This resulted in a project structure consisting of three clusters that in total subsumed eighteen single QPL projects. Further, the QPL management team was occupied with developing 'success' indicators for the QPL activities and measuring the 'success' of single QPL projects on a regular basis, based on evaluation questionnaires and statistical information. Finally, the QPL management team was mostly responsible for the allocation of personnel resources to the faculties and service units in which the single QPL projects were realized. Here, the previously mentioned logic of 'filling the gaps' could be found again because the QPL funding was mostly spent on supporting already existing projects and organizational structures. Almost all funding was used for personnel and creating additional job positions to support the daily business of studying and teaching that were perceived as severely underfinanced. According to an involved QPL manager, it was a conscious decision to concentrate on already existing projects and structures and not 'waste' resources by building up parallel organizational structures. One disadvantage of this was that the QPL management team was not involved much in documentation efforts or in stimulating the exchange of experiences among single QPL projects, since such communicative-oriented tasks were not part of the core business of the Department for Development Planning. Consequently, the degree of interaction and communication about experiences made in the projects can be described as relatively small.

The activities in the QPL initiative were oriented towards three target groups, namely students, lecturers and administrative and support staff. In other words, it can be said that in the context of the QPL initiative dealing with student diversity was not only conceived as the responsibility of students but also considered the institutional setting in which studying and teaching took place. The activities of the first cluster were to contribute to a professionalization of propaedeutics. Here, it can be distinguished between activities that aimed to improve the student and activities that aimed to improve the fit between the student and the institution. Propaedeutic activities that aimed *to improve the student* defined student diversity in terms of a lack of certain academic competences. This lack of academic competences was identified in comparison to a certain academic standard that was more or less obvious for the students. Students who lacked these competences were requested to participate in compensatory extra-curricular activities. Other propaedeutic activities focused on the social integration of first-year students with the aim *to improve the fit between the student and the institution.* For example, via tutoring or mentoring programs experienced students accompanied new students on their way into their studies. Other propaedeutic activities aimed to improve self-information and self-reflection on the part of the students. These activities were inspired by student-centered teaching approaches, a principle that had been held high in several strategic papers of the University of Kassel. According to this principle, students should be acknowledged as autonomous learners. Consequently, 'good' teaching was considered to be something more than the pure imparting of knowledge and encouraged students to learn independently and autonomously.

Propaedeutic activities in the first cluster focused on the student as the main target group. Activities in the second and third clusters, however, aimed *to improve the institutional setting* in which studying and teaching took place. More precisely, activities of the second cluster focused on the professionalization of the didactic quality of teaching. These activities aimed to improve lecturers' teaching competences and stimulated lecturers to develop research-related or practice-oriented teaching approaches. Other activities explored how blended learning concepts or e-exams could be integrated into the teaching settings. Activities of the third cluster, in turn, focused on the professionalization of quality management and counseling and included mostly the provision of additional personnel resources. The intention here was to fill these positions with experts. Further, these persons should free lecturers from having to do those administrative-oriented tasks that normally do not belong to their job description.

Overall, on the action level, dealing with student diversity built on differing teaching approaches, from interpreting student diversity in terms of a lack of certain presumed competences that needed to be compensated by means of several extra-curricular activities to translating student diversity in terms of individual characteristics or living situations that needed special consideration and individual solutions by means of consultation and accompanying support. As mentioned before, most of the single QPL projects built on already existing projects that had been funded before with third-party funding from other sources. QPL employees raised some critical points by lamenting the lack of any long-term plan for dealing with the topic of student diversity or how these actions could be financed and supported as permanent tasks. This always resonates with the question of what happens to the urgently needed positions after the funding period ends.

Concerning the impact of institutional characteristics, the research findings indicate that the definition of student diversity on the strategy level was clearly affected by the university's historical roots as a *Gesamthochschule*, its regionally oriented profile and current challenges arising from the lack of funding (see Figure 6.2). On the structure level, the structural anchoring of the QPL initiative in the Department of Development Planning played a huge role for the way structures to deal with student diversity were implemented. This department was not so much involved in stimulating communication and collaboration among the single QPL projects, but rather pursued a very data-driven approach to documentation. Further, the financial situation played an important role in that the QPL funding was used to 'fill the gaps' of already existing projects and organizational structures. Finally, on the level of activities, data and statistics played a crucial role again. Here, the findings of the SWOT analysis led to the understanding that in order to deal appropriately with student diversity, activities within the QPL initiative should not only focus on improving students' competences but also on improving the institutional setting in which studying and teaching take place. Further, the data-driven approach of the responsible Department for Development Planning led to a massive emphasis on the identification of 'success' indicators that legitimized certain activities as 'successful' in dealing with student diversity.

Referring to the diversity paradigms by Gaisch/Aichinger/Preymann (2017), the study identifies elements of two different diversity paradigms at the University of Kassel. Both paradigms follow a heterogeneous perspective due to the tradition and self-understanding as a university that enables widened and fair access. In this context, the *anti-discrimination and fairness diversity paradigm* (Thomas/Ely 1996) became most apparent. As mentioned before, this has its roots in the historical foundation as a *Gesamthochschule*, which can be seen as a moral experiment to enable equal opportunities in the field of education. Consequently, the data materials show that much emphasis was put on social permeability and the dismissal of discrimination based on socio-demographic characteristics and entrance qualifications. However, such an approach bears the danger of categorical thinking in that certain characteristics are attributed to diversity categories. This happened in one project that started with a strong focus on students with a migrant background, assuming that they experienced certain challenges in the field of learning management. However, this project was eventually opened to all students as many outside of the initial target group claimed an interest in these issues as well. Further, the university's orientation towards students with vocational qualifications and their strong orientation towards key figures and statistics show some elements of the *market access diversity paradigm* (ibid.). For example, due to the university's strong orientation towards the needs of the regional labor market, organizational actors perceive the university as a booster for local industry and structural regional growth, which is regarded as a competitive advantage in the face of scarce resources.

Figure 6.2   The Story of Student Diversity in the Context of the QPL Initiative at the University of Kassel

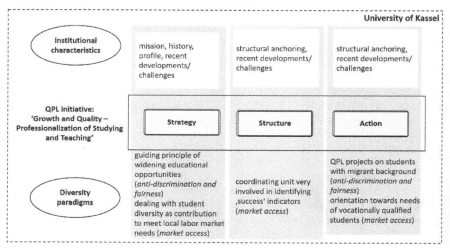

Note. The figure illustrates the impact of institutional characteristics and diversity paradigms on the translation of student diversity in the context of the QPL initiative at the University of Hamburg. Source: Own illustration.

6.2.3 HAW Hamburg

The title of the QPL initiative of the HAW Hamburg was in both rounds 'Pilot Teaching. Dialogue-oriented Quality Development in Studies and Teaching'. The QPL initiative was developed with the aim to establish a dialogue-oriented quality culture that promotes the development of innovative and competence-oriented teaching and learning scenarios. Student diversity was defined in terms of individual competences with which students entered higher education and that should be acknowledged in studying and teaching.

The QPL initiative's strategy was strongly influenced by the university's teaching profile, which can be attributed to the fact that the HAW Hamburg is a university of applied sciences. This type of higher education institution regards teaching as their main educational task and professors have a higher teaching load than their colleagues at universities. Further, at universities, teaching duties are often transferred to non-professorial teaching staff to give professors more time to do research. At universities of applied sciences, however, this teaching staff does not exist, so that the teaching load is actually carried out by the professors themselves. As indicated in the interviews and the university documents, this emphasis on teaching results in a much more intensive discussion about how to provide a high quality of teaching and what constitutes 'good' teaching among academic staff. The HAW Hamburg defined 'good' teaching in the context of the QPL initiative in terms of competence-oriented teaching. The guiding principle of competence orientation was pushed by the Vice President for Studies and Teaching and her vision to turn the HAW Hamburg into a learning organization that facilitates continuous learning for its members. This vision emphasizes the competences with which students enter university and those they should have acquired before graduating. Such a perspective can be seen as directly oppositional to a deficit orientation, which focuses on what students lack in comparison to a certain assumed academic standard. Consequently, student diversity is defined at the HAW Hamburg in terms of an individual learner personality, according to which students learn differently and the university — or more specifically the lecturer — has the task to develop teaching further to do justice to the diverse ways students are learning and studying. At the same time, students are asked to take responsibility for their own learning processes. In the data materials, the university shows its responsibility to establish teaching and learning scenarios that acknowledge and deliberately use the differences in students' competences. This responsibility was particularly emphasized against the institutional background as a university of applied sciences with its specific student composition in terms of entrance qualifications, socio-demographic characteristics and living situation.

The QPL initiative's structure was influenced by already existing networks and projects as well as the structural anchoring of the QPL initiative. In the first round, the QPL initiative comprised four university-wide projects and four faculty projects and in the second round, five university-wide projects. First, the basic structure of the QPL initiative was legitimized on the basis of empirical findings and statistics. Such a data-oriented emphasis can be explained by the fact that the QPL initiative was located in the Evaluation, Quality Management and Accreditation Unit. Second, prior experiences of organizational members played an important role for the structure of the QPL initiative because most of the projects were based on prior third-party funded projects. Persons working in these projects formed an inner circle of committed academics and administrative staff who were highly involved in activities related to improving studying and teaching at the HAW Hamburg. This inner circle surrounded the Vice President for Studies and Teaching shared her vision of the university as a learning organization whose actions in studying and teaching should be guided by a so-called 'compass' of competence orientation. They perceived themselves as making a change and promoting cultural change within the university, celebrating their approach as innovative, modern and open-minded. Consequently, they appeared as a harmonious group of enthusiastic employees and professors who were convinced that the HAW was a special place in which a dialogue about improving studying and teaching was welcomed. The degree of interaction and communication among persons in the inner circle can be described as high. However, there was only a low amount of documentation, which was particularly a problem in case of personnel fluctuation. Further, communication about dealing with student diversity with organizational members who had no links to this inner circle of committed employees was underdeveloped because formal communicative channels or tools were missing.

On the action level, most QPL projects in the QPL initiative were oriented towards *improving the institutional setting* in which studying and teaching take place. These activities ranged, for example, from the implementation of faculty quality managers to didactic coaching and the professionalization of study program monitoring. With the help of QPL funding, additional administrative staff supported organizational members to join the dialogue about the quality of studying and teaching. Further, this administrative staff identified and supported the spread of 'best-practices' to other study programs, departments, or faculties, particularly when these practices fit the guiding principle of competence orientation. Here, the medium size of the university and the well-established connections among the inner circle of committed administrative and academic staff eased the spread of best-practice examples.

In addition to these measures, the HAW Hamburg had already established a relatively broad spectrum of extra-curricular activities that aimed *to improve students' competences* or the *fit between students and the institution*. These projects were based on different underlying assumptions about student diversity. For example, the viaMINT preparatory courses were based on the assumption that students enter university with differing levels of prior knowledge. The appropriate way to deal with student diversity was seen in identifying possible knowledge gaps and assigning students to online modules to compensate for these gaps. The first-semester tutorials, in turn, were based on the assumption that first-year students differ with regard to their individual abilities, but also their prior experiences and current living situations. The appropriate way to deal with this component of student diversity was seen in providing the students a space to exchange experiences with other students and develop appropriate strategies that fit their individual situation to overcome the challenges in their first year of studies.

Concerning institutional characteristics, the research findings indicate that the definition of student diversity on the strategy level was clearly affected by the teaching profile, its type as a university of applied sciences as well as prior discussions about competence-oriented teaching (see Figure 6.3). On the structure level, the anchoring of the QPL initiative to the unit for evaluation and quality management played a role because the basic structure of the QPL initiative was based on empirical findings. Further, existing networks — such as the inner circle of committed employees and prior projects the single QPL projects were based on — laid the basis for the way structures to deal with student diversity were implemented. Finally, on the action level, the inner circle played a crucial role again because they facilitated the spread of best-practice projects, particularly when these projects fit the overall guiding principle of competence orientation.

Concerning diversity paradigms (Gaisch/Aichinger/Preymann 2017), the stance on student diversity at the HAW Hamburg is highly influenced by their teaching profile and derived from a heterogeneous perspective in which diversity is valued as a resource. Following a competence-oriented definition of student diversity, much emphasis was put on the individual competences with which students enter university and, consequently, how individual the ways of studying and learning can be. Such a perspective has parallels to the *learning and efficacy paradigm* (Thomas/Ely 1996) that focuses strongly on improving competence orientation and student-centered teaching within the university. This paradigm is based on the assumption that learning takes place individually and in different ways. At the HAW Hamburg, the involved actors proposed an openness and flexibility towards the ongoing further development and transformation of studying and teaching. They particularly promoted activities that aimed to support the development of competence-oriented teaching settings. This was displayed as very innovative and it can be interpreted as a direct attempt of interference in the ways professors should teach. This is likely to become a delicate matter because it might be seen as conflicting with the fundamental right of the academic freedom of research and teaching. In this context, it was emphasized by the actors involved that such a competence-oriented perspective is much more prone to become apparent at universities of applied sciences that are characterized by a stronger emphasis on teaching than on research. Further, the smaller size of the university and the good networking among different units, which was mostly due to the inner circle of highly committed employees who are actively pursuing new projects and developed their ideas further along the same guideline, resulted in a relatively tight coupling between the strategy and action level.

Figure 6.3   The Story of Student Diversity in the Context of the QPL Initiative at the HAW Hamburg

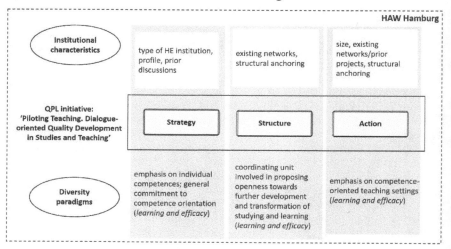

Note. The figure illustrates the impact of institutional characteristics and diversity paradigms on the translation of student diversity in the context of the QPL initiative at the University of Hamburg. Source: Own illustration.

6.2.4   Summary

This chapter recounted the 'overarching narratives' of student diversity that could be identified at the three universities in the context of their respective QPL initiatives. In these narratives, the idea of student diversity was framed against the background of the respective local contexts so that it made sense to the story-tellers and their local audiences at the universities. Thus, the local context played a crucial role for the way the idea of student diversity was translated within the levels of strategy, structure and action of the universities' QPL initiatives. Comparing the narratives of student diversity at the three case study universities, it emerges that organizational actors did not only relate the idea of student diversity to institutional characteristics (e.g., profile, type of institution, mission, size) but also to diversity paradigms that seemed to be dominant in the respective local contexts. Since the three universities differ in their institutional characteristics and dominant diversity paradigms, local variations of organizational responses to student diversity can be explained by the importance of the local context for translation processes. It is the local context that frames the narratives about student diversity at the three case study universities. The next chapter will turn to the final research question and aims to identify organizational practices to deal with student diversity at the three universities in the context of the QPL initiative.

6.3 Definitions and Organizational Practices to Deal with Student Diversity

Special interest should be put on answering the question how dealing with student diversity was materialized on the level of concrete actions. A closer look at the action level reveals the different understandings of student diversity, leading to the selection of different target groups as appropriate candidates for certain practices deemed appropriate to deal with the aforementioned aspects of student diversity.

The group discussions conducted at all three universities appear as particularly useful for answering this question because the group discussions made interpretative patterns detectable that linked the definitions of student diversity to different ways of dealing with student diversity (Glaser/Strauss 1967; Keller 2009). This analytical perspective was guided by the question of how the term 'student diversity' was understood in the context of the single QPL projects. Accordingly, in the group discussions, persons working in those QPL projects were asked how they understood the term 'student diversity' in the context of their projects and to what extent they perceived their QPL projects as appropriate ways of dealing with it.

Depending on the single QPL project's context, the analysis of the group discussion shows that the definitions of student diversity as well as attitudes about appropriate ways of dealing with student diversity differ. To develop an understanding of the conditions under which these differing definitions emerge and how these definitions are connected to different ways of dealing with student diversity, the 'coding paradigm' was used (Corbin/Strauss 1990). The coding paradigm offers a guide for the focused analysis of central phenomena in order to examine their characteristics as well as their relation to other concepts and categories on the basis of data material, an approach that is called axial coding (Böhm 1994). As explained in more detail in Chapter 4.6., the coding paradigm helps to detect the relationships between the central categories (e.g., *definitions* of student diversity, underlying *assumptions* about student diversity, attributed *causes* for student diversity, *contexts* in which student diversity is defined accordingly, *strategies* to deal with student diversity and the respective *consequences* resulting from the way student diversity is dealt with). Such a perspective on the data is needed to detect relations between concepts and categories and relate them on a more abstract level (Vollstedt/Rezat 2019). These relations are detected by constant comparison of coded data material that results in the identification of interpretative patterns that link translations of student diversity with concrete organizational practices. These organizational practices are not only found within subjects, but rather represent collective interpretative patterns that organizational members share.

The following part introduces seven interpretative patterns and their corresponding organizational practices. At the end, a table will summarize the seven identified organizational practices and the contexts in which they appear.

6.3.1 Prior Knowledge: Deficit Compensation

The first example stems from a person working in the project viaMINT at the HAW Hamburg, an online learning environment in which first-year students could fill their knowledge gaps with the help of online modules. Student diversity was interpreted in the context of the project in the following way:

> The diversity is very clearly given among first-year students. Especially within mathematics the kinds of prior knowledge they arrive with here differ markedly from each other. By means of this first knowledge test, the individual obviously learns, 'where are my individual weaknesses that I need to compensate for?' And here we give justice to diversity in that the individual recommendations that are made via the system become clearly visible on the personal online desk. The one person with a lot of prior knowledge is required to do less rework. The one who lacks a lot of prior knowledge, of course, has to rework a little bit more. That's the one thing: visibility of the differences in prior knowledge via the test (HAW_gd/306).

In this quote, student diversity was translated as representing different levels of prior knowledge in mathematics. This can be interpreted as a rather narrow perspective on the *phenomenon* of student diversity. The *cause* for this phenomenon was attributed to divergent educational biographies and school-leaving certifications of first-year students. Based on the *assumption* that there is a certain performance standard that should be present at the beginning of studies, it was regarded as an appropriate *strategy* to identify and give students feedback on their individual weaknesses in comparison to this standard and to provide appropriate learning offers. As a *consequence*, the deficits on the part of students were expected to be compensated by participating in these measures. This was interpreted as a very individual-oriented approach because every person received a personal recommendation based on their test results which areas to improve to reach the expected performance standard. The *context* of this text passage was the project viaMINT at the HAW Hamburg that included online learning modules for mathematics, physics and informatics for the Faculty of Technology and Informatics as an addition to regular bridging courses. First-year students could identify their knowledge gaps on the basis of an online self-assessment and received recommendations for certain online modules to take. The aim of the measure was *subject-specific adjustment* because prior knowledge of students was to be refreshed and gaps compensated so that first-year students were able to follow the basic lectures. Students could decide for themselves whether or not to take part in this offer, so it can be described as extra-curricular. However, there were also integrative tendencies to be seen due to the tight connection of online modules with the pre-courses offered at the HAW Hamburg. Further, the content of the online modules was matched to the content of the basic lectures and lecturers tended to recommend the online modules to first-year students in their lectures.

The interpretative pattern 'prior knowledge' can be found in similar contexts that share certain characteristics. For example, this interpretative pattern is most apparent in contexts in which measures are offered at the beginning of studies or in the first semester. Second, these measures are discipline-specific and, thus, mostly organized by the faculties or departments themselves. Consequently, they have a rather narrow focus on subject-specific challenges. Third, most of these measures are extra-curricular, but partly integrated into the study programs. This integration can be more or less formally determined. For example, a similar interpretative pattern can be found in the context of the mathematical bridging course at the Faculty of Electrical Engineering and Computer Science at the University of Kassel. Here, student diversity was seen "very clearly in their differing prior mathematical education" (UK_gd/231). Here, the cause for the differing levels of prior mathematical knowledge was even more explicitly tied to the school-leaving entrance qualifications of students, as it was described by the person working in this project:

> You can of course roughly distinguish the causes for this. By now a majority enters the study program with a subject-based entrance qualification and not with a general higher education entrance qualification. And you can clearly see this in the results of the mathematical tests (UK_gd/233).

Thus, the school-leaving certificates were associated with different levels of mathematical qualifications. This was legitimized by statistics, referring to the results of the mathematical test that proved the differences in knowledge. All students within the faculty were obligated to participate in the mathematical test that queried basic mathematical school knowledge. Students who failed this test were mandatorily required to participate in the bridging course. Thus, the *assumption* was that students should be equipped with a predetermined set of mathematical knowledge at the beginning of their studies. This predetermined set was oriented towards the prior education in mathematics that students had received with their general higher education entrance qualification or the *Abitur*. In other words, students with *Abitur* were defined as the norm group, although it was noted at the same time that this norm group did not represent the majority any longer. Another observation in this context was the more general critique of the *Abitur* as no longer serving as an indicator for certain mathematical competences, as indicated in the following quote by a person working in this project:

> Overall, we can observe at the moment that the general performance has declined. Thus, if I compare the cohort of the winter semester 10/11 with that of the winter semester 16/17, you can see very clearly that those people with Abitur also performed much worse than six years ago (UK_gd/233).

This deficit-oriented argumentation was to be found in the areas of mathematics and the natural sciences at all three universities. Often personal observation could be backed by statistics, like in this case the comparison of results of the same mathematical test among different cohorts. The cause for this was often ascribed to changes in the secondary school system, although there was some awareness that this might also be attributed to differing generational perspectives.[39]

Interestingly, a similar interpretative pattern was also to be found in the context of the Language Advancement Coaching at the University of Hamburg and the project 'Foreign Language Requirements for Studying' at the University of Kassel. Here, student diversity was defined in terms of the heterogeneous foreign language skills with which students entered their study courses. Against a previously defined standard of foreign language proficiency and language levels, a lack of language competences could be identified. At the University of Kassel, students who had not achieved a certain grade in the test were recommended to participate in additional courses. The lack of competences was attributed to the school or language institutions they had attended prior and which seemingly had not prepared students adequately for their foreign language studies. In this context, it was also criticized that the language certificates with which students entered university could no longer be seen as a reliable indicator for the competences the certificate-holder possessed, as described by a person working in this project:

> We observe that many language certificates are no longer sufficient or the holders do not fulfill the entrance criteria in the area of language; that is something that we see more frequently. And with the language proficiency test, I have this in black and white (UK_gd/244).

Here again, a standard test and statistics were used to legitimize a personal observation: certain certificates no longer served as indicators for a minimum standard of competences. The appropriate way of dealing with this sort of

---

[39] Zacher (2018) refers to the very old phenomenon of the devaluation of a younger generation by an older generation. This devaluation has its roots in a psychological mechanism that is related to the fear of losing status: the group with a higher status does not want to lose its position of power and be replaced by a younger, more diverse group.

student diversity was again seen in, first, identifying the discipline-specific deficits the students had in comparison to a pre-defined standard and, second, assigning those students to certain compensatory measures, like pre-courses, crash courses, bridging courses or tutorials. Although the name of these measures differed, they all aimed at *subject-specific adjustment* to compensate for the subject-specific deficits of students. Accordingly, the corresponding organizational practice can be described as *deficit compensation*. Due to diverse educational biographies, it was assumed that students' prior discipline-specific competences did not meet the required standard at the beginning of studies while being extremely diversified. Therefore, the overall aim was to minimize these differences by creating "more homogeneous learning groups" (UHH_gd/217). For example, in the context of the crash courses in the natural sciences at the University of Hamburg, the aim was consequently "to absorb the different prior knowledge to find a relatively similar level and provide them guidance so that they can understand the regular lectures in, for example, biology or physiology" (UHH_gd/40). Although participation was voluntary compared to the bridging course at the University of Kassel, certain candidates were given recommendations. Those were mainly students who had been out of school for a longer period or had not attended courses in the natural sciences in the upper-secondary school. Thus, here again, the underlying assumption was that the norm group consisted of students who entered universities on the direct way coming from the *Abitur*, where they had gained upper-secondary knowledge in the area of the natural sciences. Students who did not fulfill those criteria were perceived as lacking competences that were needed in order to be able to start their studies successfully.

6.3.2 Individual Learner Personality: Learning Community

An alternative interpretative pattern could be found in the context of first semester tutorials as they were offered at the HAW Hamburg. Here, a person working in this project defined student diversity in the following ways:

> Well, I think it is about this individual learning personality that includes different aspects. The social diversity, then the psychological, where also aspects of motivation play a role, then the performance diversity, the disciplinary diversity. But also, what are the framework conditions, right? Thus, do I need to work a lot? Or do I need to work less? What about the routes of my journey? All these aspects impact how learning is working out or the way it has to go. In the context of the tutorial, we want to stimulate reflection in order to evaluate oneself: What are my framework conditions? Where do I stand? What are my challenges? In order to find, gather and discuss possible solutions together with the group. I think, there is no right or wrong studying, but there are always ways of supportive and preventive studying. And to look and see, everyone has to find their own way, you can try out different things. And we also have experienced tutors that can talk about their own way and show

> how they are different and how they have gone different ways to show them how diverse this range of studying can be (HAW_gd/309).

According to this quote, student diversity was translated in terms of an individual learning personality that consists of several social, psychological and organizational aspects listed here. Consequently, the definition of student diversity was diversified, rather than narrowly focused on one single aspect, like it was the case for the first interpretative pattern. Thus, the *phenomenon* of interest was defined as individual learning personality. The *cause* for this was seen in individual abilities that differed, but also various living and study situations that had an impact on how and under what kind of circumstances learning can take place. Here, the underlying *assumption* was that studying and learning can occur in different ways. In the *context* of the first semester tutorials, the *strategy* was to offer students an open environment for self-reflection and social exchange with the *consequence* that they were able to find their individual learning paths. They were to experience how diverse students and their ways of studying can be by reflecting on their own status and exchanging experiences with other students. These first-semester tutorials were offered by a central service unit in cooperation with the faculties. First-year students could visit the tutorials that are supervised by more advanced students from the same study program. Although participation is voluntary, some of the tutorials could be perceived as partially integrated because they have a fixed position in the students' schedule for the first week of their studies. The tutorials, consisting of a maximum of 20 students, were offered once per week over the whole first semester. The range of topics discussed within the tutorials was very broad and adapted according to the individual needs and requests of the students (e.g., getting to know each other and the university, individual study planning, organization of learning, exam preparation, or financing studies). Consequently, the overall aim included not only *institutional orientation* and *competence development*, but also *social integration*.

This interpretative pattern can be found at the other three universities as well, in particular in the context of similar measures, like the first-semester tutorials at the University of Hamburg and the study pilots at the University of Kassel.

The first-semester tutorial at the University of Hamburg was quite similar to those of the HAW Hamburg, as it was designed to support students in developing their own individual strategies to deal with the specific requirements they were confronted with. Accordingly, student diversity was defined in terms of an individual learning personality due to the various experiences, backgrounds and living situations students were in. The first-semester tutorial helped to provide an informal atmosphere in which students were encouraged to self-reflect and identify the study objectives they wished to fulfill. Further, new students were accompanied by tutors on their way to find appropriate strategies to help them reach these objectives. The tutorials were again voluntary and extra-curricular, but they were organized within the involved faculties and study programs. This also meant that students and tutors of one group always belonged to the same study program.

The project 'Study Pilots' at the University Kassel, in turn, was a peer-to-peer-program in which a first-year student was matched with a more advanced student from the same study program. The strategy was similar as it assumed that new students would profit from the experience of more advanced students and that this exchange would stimulate self-reflection about their role as students. The peers met individually on a regular basis during the first semester, while there are also events for meeting other students and tutors from the project. In both cases, the spectrum of discussed topics was very broad, depending on individual needs and requests, including questions concerning study and learning organization, exam preparation, but also career prospects. The idea behind this was for new students to realize that facing challenges, although often experienced individually, is very common during the first year of studies. The overall aim was to reflect and discuss possible solutions and hear from more advanced students how they had overcome these challenges. Accordingly, the overall organizational practice can be described as establishing a *learning community* in which students in their mentoring groups are accompanied by tutors or mentors. These mentors were in most cases more advanced students who had already gained the experience of dealing with first-year challenges. This community, which often lasted the whole first semester, allowed the discussion of a relatively broad range that mostly aimed to stimulate *competence development* and provide *institutional orientation*. Besides, due to the group situation that offered students the opportunity to discuss current challenges, exchange experiences and thereby develop their own learning paths, *social integration* was also one of the main objectives of these measures.

6.3.3 Special Target Groups: Starting Aid

A third interpretative pattern could be found in the context of the International Office at the HAW Hamburg. It offered a broad range of different measures explicitly for international students. A person working in the International Office described the role of diversity for their workplace in the following way:

> Due to the reason that we work with international students, diversity plays a huge role because of the intercultural aspect. In the beginning, the main issue is that we want to convey to our students is that it might be a little bit different here. We also try to, for example, connect local students and international students through our program, so that they can learn from each other how it can be different (HAW_gd/307).

As indicated by this quote, the central *phenomenon* of interest was defined in terms of their special status as international students. Consequently, the *cause* for their special status was seen in their foreign nationality, prior experiences and educational biography that differed from those of German students. Because of them being new to the German higher education system and the lack of social contacts, the underlying *assumption* was that they had a specific need for social contacts and orientation. In the *context* of projects that were explicitly targeted at international students, such cross-disciplinary requirements were fulfilled with a whole set of different measures. These included, as illustrated by the following example, buddy programs, international welcome days and international guides. As described by a person working in the International Office:

> These are all measures that shall support the students to make friends and to get into the university, these are so to say the cross-disciplinary aspects. Thus, we do not offer anything discipline-specific because this is the task of our colleagues, we do not have the competences for that. But we support them in social aspects, by making first contacts with their buddy. We try to match the new students with so-called buddies so that they have a contact person on-site, a mentor they can contact because often they know nobody. And that gives them a good feeling because they know: Okay, there is someone I can turn to. That is the WeBuddy program. We have also an International Welcome Week in which different events are offered that all aim to bring people together, encourage cultural exchange and bring them together in a group so that they have someone they can turn to later on. Sometimes they even meet their fellow students in this context, so that they can begin their studies more comfortably. […] And the international guides, they offer low-threshold support. Those are student tutors who help them finding accommodation and dealing with local authorities (HAW_gd/35).

Thus, the appropriate *strategy* for dealing with this sort of student diversity was seen in providing international students with a broad spectrum of target group-specific support. The *consequence* of this strategy was to ease the students' entrance into the university.

This interpretative pattern could be found in the context of other measures aiming at international students at all three universities. In most cases, these measures were offered by a central service unit that provided these services to all international students at the university, despite their disciplinary backgrounds. These measures either began before their studies or with the start of their studies, at the latest in the first week of lectures. Although the concrete design of measures could differ, it mostly included buddy programs and International Welcome Weeks that both aimed at *social integration* and *institutional orientation*.

However, this interpretative pattern could also be found in the project 'Study Orientation for Working Persons without School-based Entrance Qualification' at the University of Hamburg. Here, diversity was again defined in terms of socio-demographic characteristics with a focus on students without school-based entrance qualifications as another specific target group, as it was described by a person working in the project:

> In our case, our target group has a heterogeneous educational biography. They have not visited an upper-secondary school. They are older and often they are at a different point in their life. Thus, they might already have a family, usually they do not live with their parents anymore and also do not want to move into student dormitories. Just in these aspects they are heterogeneous. And of course, they have junior high school experiences. And then they only know their vocational school and in a lot of vocational schools, the school-time is seen as a necessary evil because your identity comes from your craft or vocation. Here you learn a lot and from time to time you have to visit the vocational school. This is totally different (UHH_gd/220).

In this quotation, the QPL employee described in detail how this target group was different compared to 'normal' students. These differences were seen in their educational biography and experience as well as in their living or study situations. Overall, the *phenomenon* of interest can be described as the seeking out of specific target groups. It is assumed that these target groups had very specific needs and requirements due to their different educational biography and starting conditions. The appropriate *strategy* was seen in helping students who were supposed to be inexperienced with the university system to get started and make the beginning easier by fostering *social integration*. Here again, students were brought together to initiate first social contacts and exchange experiences and ways of dealing with the challenges of this new phase. Consequently, the organizational practice can best be described as *starting aid*. In the context of these measures, the exchange of experiences among special target groups was stimulated by a broad spectrum of different offers organized by central service units at the beginning of studies. The QPL employees emphasized that these measures concentrated on the beginning of studies because they should only provide support until students had established their own contacts within their study programs. This support was directed towards *social integration* and *institutional orientation* by offering different support opportunities that students could take advantage of while assuming that these specific target groups were in particular need of support.

6.3.4 *Learner, Writer and Student Types: Practice Space*

The next interpretative pattern could be found in the context of academic writing workshops at the University of Hamburg. One person working in the project described the importance of different types of writers and learners that they observed in their daily work:

> Well, in the practical work, it has been proven as helpful to acknowledge that people — and this can be judged as good or bad — approach texts differently. There are strategic planners who are first starting with outlining a structure. And often it is

taught that this is the best way of doing things: first, you need to make a plan. And then you execute this plan. But there are people who are unable to work this way. They are totally blocked when they need to do a plan first. They rather start writing everything down directly. And, in between, there is a wide range of different types. And in our courses, we say, "for you, this method might be useful, because it makes up for something you are not so trained in so far or it fits quite well with something you are good at." And that is also the point, there is no one size fits all story. This is particularly true for academic writing (UHH_gd/214).

Accordingly, student diversity was translated as different types of writers and learners that should be acknowledged. This perspective concentrated on individual competences in the area of learning, studying and writing. However, the *causes* for these differences in individual competences are in parts related to social aspects as well, such as age, native language, educational biographies and living situations. The underlying *assumption* was two-fold. On the one hand, it acknowledged that there is no one right way of writing, studying and learning, but students have different preferences and styles to acquire knowledge. On the other hand, there are still certain discipline-specific requirements concerning academic writing that function as templates for what students should be capable of. Here, it was emphasized that for all students academic writing can be a challenge because "they need to acquaint themselves with a totally new use of language" (UHH_gd/212) that they had not been confronted with before in their educational biography. Nevertheless, the persons working in this project also observed differences in recognizing the so-called 'hidden curriculum':

There are people who get the hang of [the hidden curriculum] quite fast and can relate to it: "Ok, this is important and this is important." Other people who have the same material at their disposal, are not able to connect this information. This might be related to prior knowledge because they have a specific educational background but I think there is also another category that I cannot specify. For some people it is just easier to comprehend such systems than for others (UHH_gd/213).

Here again, the *phenomenon* of interest was defined in terms of types of individual competences that might be related to social aspects, like educational biography and background. Consequently, the *strategy* was two-fold as well: First, students were shown different methods and techniques for working on and writing academic texts. Within the *context* of academic writing workshops, they were given the opportunity to get to know and try these different methods with the consequence of finding the personally most fitting way of writing and studying. Second, because the discipline-specific requirements concerning academic writing were not always transparent for the students, it was clarified what these requirements are, as it is described by a person working in the project:

Explicating the expectations or the things that we imply or suggest, for example, that our students sit down and work autonomously, that they read the course books,

> that they know they have to behave a certain way in the lectures, you need to prepare and revise the lectures, you need to prepare for the exams and so forth. Those are aspects we all often expect from them, but they are never or seldom communicated in a way for students to consider them as such (UHH_gd/243).

Thus, the second strategy was the transparency of requirements and expectations concerning studying and learning with the *consequence* that students professionalized their academic language competences.

In the case of the University of Hamburg, the academic writing workshops were guided by academic writing coaches who were located in the faculties. Since the respective disciplines are particular in their requirements and conditions for academic writing, it was regarded as the appropriate way to provide discipline-specific courses (e.g., academic writing workshops for cultural history). These courses were offered as extra-curricular activities, but sometimes they were partially integrated into the curriculum in terms of teaching collaborations between lecturers and writing coaches. The overall aim of these courses was *competence development*.

The same interpretative pattern can be found in the context of other propaedeutic workshops, for example, the measure 'German as an Academic Language' at the University of Kassel. Here, student diversity was defined in terms of academic writing skills while it was assumed that "an inappropriate use of academic language, also by students who are native speakers, makes it difficult to participate in academic discourse and successful studying" (UK_doc_17/17). At first sight, this quote seems to entail a stronger deficit-oriented focus compared to the text passages about the academic writing workshops of the University of Hamburg: Students used language in a sense that was perceived as inadequate for partaking in academic discourse, which was, in turn, seen as disadvantageous for studying successfully. Nevertheless, this interpretative pattern acknowledged that the use of academic language was a rather new experience for all students. The conditions they started out with or prior knowledge might have differed due to their educational biographies to begin with, but overall, the academic system with its specific use of academic language (which again differs substantially among disciplines) was new territory for most of the students. In other words, there was no underlying assumption that there is a certain standard in terms of competences that students should possess before they began with their studies. Rather, it was assumed that there are certain (discipline-specific) requirements and guidelines concerning the use of academic language that are new to students and, therefore, should be made transparent. Further, it was acknowledged that there are different ways of studying and writing. Students should be provided with the appropriate space to try these out and find the most fitting way. In the context of the academic writing workshops at the University of Kassel, students got to know the characteristic features of writing in a scientific context, they learned the different steps in the writing process, how to work with academic texts, they reflected on their own writing practice and tried out different techniques and methods. The courses were organized by a central service unit, but they cooperated closely with the study programs as they also developed advanced courses — besides basic courses — for academic writing within the specific disciplines (e.g., academic writing for engineers).

A quite similar interpretative pattern could also be found in the context of other extra-curricular workshops that were concerned with topics like learning strategies, preparation for exams and prohibiting procrastination. These workshops were organized by central service units, e.g., the Service Center Teaching at the University of Kassel or the Central Student Counseling at the HAW Hamburg. Here, the phenomenon of interest comprised the different student and learner types originating in certain individual and social differences. It was acknowledged that students had differing learning experiences which influenced the way the individual student tried to acquire knowledge. Nevertheless, the study experience was a new experience for almost all students and previous learning styles might not fulfill the requirements of the new academic system. With the help of these workshops, students were stimulated to reflect on their own studying and learning behavior and to get to know useful techniques and methods appropriate for the academic context. By experimenting with their own toolbox of techniques and methods, students could professionalize their cross-disciplinary academic competences. Thus, all these workshops aimed at strengthening students in their academic competences rather than compensating for deficits.

Overall, the organizational correlation for this interpretative pattern can be described as the creation of *practice space*. Within the context of extra-curricular workshops, students were given the opportunity to learn and try out different methods and techniques, while simultaneously getting to know the requirements and expectations of academic studies. This practice space took place in group settings, but in comparison to projects providing learning guidance, this approach relied on the leadership of experts. Those were mostly recruited from QPL personnel who were trained in their specific fields of expertise. Although the different ways of studying, learning and writing were acknowledged, the overall aim was nevertheless to strengthen the academic competence of the individual. Therefore, the narrow focus of these measures was on *competence development*.

Similarities in the ways student diversity was defined and the kind of approaches that were seen as appropriate could also be found in the context of study portfolios. For example, at the University of Kassel, a study portfolio was developed that supported students in the documentation and reflection of their own learning successes and organization of studies. It was ordered by document files, including checklists and information materials for different building blocks (e.g., 'My Start at the University'). Some study programs even integrated it in lectures in order to support independent learning and self-reflection. Further, at the University of Hamburg, a study portfolio was used as an additional tool for the first-semester tutorials at the Faculty of Education. It accompanied students in reflecting on their study habits and objectives. At the HAW Hamburg, in turn, a website offered worksheets for students to work on them autonomously. They comprised self-reflective tools in the areas of self-management, learning strategies, methods for decision making, but also mental well-being that students could download and fill out. All these measures acknowledged the differences in studying and learning. The appropriate strategy was to stimulate self-reflection on studying and learning behavior, expand the repertoire of techniques and methods to better organize studying and, thereby, strengthen the competences in the area of studying and learning. In contrast to workshops, study portfolios are self-learning tools. They rely on the assumption that students are capable of developing these competences autonomously by providing them some additional working materials to inspire self-reflection. However, what the study was able to identify in the context of the examples here is that students often wished to discuss their results of self-reflection with experts in this area, as it was described by a person working in the study portfolio project at the University of Kassel:

> The only thing that students give feedback about is, "I want to do this together with someone" and preferably not with someone coming from my student group but someone who has a little bit of expertise (UK_gd /212).

The persons working in study portfolio projects observed that not all students get along with working on these materials by themselves without any feedback given to them. This is in line with the underlying assumption that students learn and study differently. For some students, the additional working materials provided useful stimulation to autonomously develop their repertoire of techniques and methods further. Other students, in turn, needed social exchange and feedback on their learning experiences. Embedding study portfolios into a socially interactive situation, in the best case with an expert, in order to direct self-reflection might for these students be a more efficient way to strengthen their competences. Therefore, these measures can be categorized into the same organizational practice of providing a *practice space* for students in which they are stimulated to reflect on their studying and learning behavior and expand their toolbox of techniques and methods with the overall aim to strengthen academic competences.

6.3.5 *Individual Problems and Needs: Individual Assistance*

The next interpretative pattern could be found in the context of advising. The coaching services for learning and exams at the University of Kassel, for example, focused on individual aspects of student diversity. This was described by a person working in the project in the following way:

> From the perspective of my project, I observe a huge diversity in how students cope with stress, challenges, performance situations, failure, despair or frustration. Students or pupils who enter university have made different experiences with this. People who had always been good at school and then suddenly for the first time fail an exam, and fail this exam again in the second attempt, who have never experienced such a situation, can be devastated. Yet others have not experienced anything else than that. Those people have a different problem, maybe low academic self-esteem. But these are the differences. And this requires of course individual support. ... Thus, for example, for some people it is good to remember that what is needed within the study programs is the same thing as in sports. Some people are really goal-oriented and tolerate frustration in sports but not in their studies. And they only need to see that this might be similar. Other people need a different approach (UK_gd /228).

As indicated by this quote, this interpretative pattern followed the assumption that students deal with challenges differently, depending on their prior experiences. Consequently, the *phenomenon* of interest comprised the individual problems and needs of students that had their *origin* in prior (educational) experiences. These prior experiences influenced the highly individual ways they responded to new situations. The underlying *assumption* suggested that consequently, an individual-oriented approach was necessary. Further, students were seen as competent learners who knew best "where the shoe pinches them", but "in situations in which they got stuck" (UK_gd /12), a professional was needed to help students get back on their feet. In the context of psychological counseling, the appropriate *strategy* was seen in accompanying students in reflecting their own behavior when dealing with challenges. Together counselors and students identified strategies to handle these new situations and challenges. The *consequence* of this measure was that students expanded their repertoire of cross-disciplinary competences and found appropriate solutions to handle challenging situations.

This interpretative pattern could also be detected in the context of other specific consultation services, such as the academic writing services at the University of Kassel and the University of Hamburg, but also the Student Counseling Office at the HAW Hamburg. All these measures shared several characteristics, for example, they were offered by central service units, they were extra-curricular and students used these offers voluntarily. In most cases, students had concrete questions or concerns, for example, they were nervous before exams, they were writing their first academic paper, or they needed tips for better time management. Overall, the measures aimed at *competence development* in that students were to acquire the necessary competences to find solutions to challenging situations. The consultation was guided by professionals who were trained in their specific areas. Advising took place in face-to-face appointments between professionals and students. The number of appointments depended on individual needs and could range from one to five appointments. Sometimes, advisors referred students to other counseling services, for example, psychological ones.

Individual situations, problems and needs could be very specific. So often, the first step was to gain an understanding of the situation at hand, as it was described by a person working in the Academic Writing Advisory Services at the University of Kassel in the following way:

> Well, it varies enormously what other responsibilities the students have besides their studies. Thus, students who have to work a lot to be able to finance their studies need a different form of consultation than students who principally have time all day to do something for university. Or those who have a child or have to care for relatives or something like that. And a lot of students come to me and ask me about tips for time management. And my first question is: "How much time do you have?" And there is a broad spectrum from "Sure, I have time, I have kept my schedule free for the next four weeks" to "I have to do this and this and five other things that always need to be given priority" (UK_gd /229).

As indicated by this quote, the time available to students could vary enormously, depending on their living situations and obligations besides their studies. Consequently, the appropriate way of dealing with this aspect of student diversity was seen in a student-centered approach with a focus on identifying the individual situation, resources in terms of competences and time and aims to find the individually best solution.

Sometimes students were not aware of how specific their situation was. So here the first aim was to make students aware of their individual situation, as it was described by a person working for the Student Counseling Office at the HAW Hamburg:

> Well, I think the focus is very much on working out the individual situation in the context of the Student Counseling Office and to make people aware of where they stand with their requirements. For example, it is often the case that we really try to show people their double burden that they have not have noticed themselves. Instead, they say: "Yes, of course I have to finance my studies, this is why I have to work!" Yeah, sure. But studying is designed for people who can concentrate on their studies full-time. Therefore, they need to adapt their studies accordingly. Thus, we are often in the position that we need to help these persons to orient themselves on multiple axes of diversity and to gain an understanding of where they are in their individual situation and condition (HAW_gd/317).

Thus, the task of the employees of central service units was to make people aware of the extent of their diversity or, in other words, how they diverged from the 'ideal of a normal student' for whom study structures were designed. This is interesting in that diversity was accepted as a reality. Nevertheless, due to the rules and regulations of study programs that were (and continue to be) oriented towards the 'normal student' (although not existing anymore), the appropriate way of dealing with this form of student diversity was not seen in making structural changes, but in advising students in developing their own study plans that fit their individual situation. As employees of a central service unit, this was the most power they had. However, the employees also tried to minimize the negative connotations students often associated with deviations from their regular study plans. Often, it is still perceived as a failure to not be able to finish a study program in the prescribed time period.

The corresponding organizational practice could be classified as *individual assistance*. Within this approach, the overall aim was to help students overcome certain challenging situations and to find fitting solutions to their problems through individual consultation. This advising often took place in challenging situations, although this was not necessarily always the case. Often, challenges had accumulated in such a way that the student sought help to overcome them. At times measures even had to defuse an emergency situation. Help was provided by experts who were trained in their specific field of expertise. But in comparison to the practice space, this organizational practice put the focus on helping students individually instead of creating a group situation. This was related to the fact that the students' individual problems and needs were at the center of interest.

6.3.6 Mismatch Between Student and Study Program: Orientation and Guidance

Online self-assessments provided another interpretational pattern, for example, the HAW Navigator at the HAW Hamburg. This tool included online self-assessments (in the following abbreviated as OSAs) for the study programs of the HAW Hamburg. These OSAs should enable potential students to deal intensively with the requirements of the study programs and the corresponding vocational fields. This test should facilitate orientation and decision-making with respect to the choice of a study program that would match personal interests, motivations and aims. Consequently, the *phenomenon* of interest that emerged at this point was the mismatch between potential students and study programs. The origin for this was seen in the multiple interests, motivations, aims and competences potential students brought with them. Under the *assumption* that students needed more information about the study programs, the *strategy* was two-fold. On the one hand, transparency on the part of the institution about contents, requirements and future prospects of the study programs was increased. On the other hand, it stimulated self-reflection in students on the ways these contents, requirements and future prospects fit their interests, motivations, requirements and study aims. The *consequence* of this was that students became more capable of making well-informed choices in their studies and the fit between student and institution increased.

In the case of the HAW Hamburg, OSAs were partially integrated into the curriculum. Potential students were obligated to use the HAW Navigator before applying for a study program. Further, it was recommended to complement the test results with a personal consultation with the Student Counseling Office. Similar measures could also be observed at the University of Hamburg. Here, several OSAs have been developed for specific study programs, for example in Law and Business Economics. Again, these tests aimed to support potential students in their study choice by testing whether their interests and skills matched with the requirements of the study programs. Further, OSAs provided information about curricular content and expectations. For example, in the case of Law, the OSA included tests and reflective questions that offered potential students to reflect on their own competences and motivations for studying. Further, the test included information on the study location Hamburg, the university, the faculty, but also about study organization and study culture as well as the corresponding vocational field. Thus, again, the strategy was two-fold, stimulating self-reflection on the part of students and improving transparency on the part of the institution. Within medicine, however, the focus was somewhat different: Here, the emphasis was put on developing an empirically valid instrument for assessing the abilities necessary for studying medicine among potential students. Thus, while the other projects acknowledged that students needed to be informed about the contents and requirements of the study programs, the approach in medicine focused on identifying qualified candidates according to previously determined and empirically valid indicators rather than relying on self-selection on the part of the students. This was legitimized by the fact that traditionally the number of applicants is much higher than the number of available places to study.

These activities show certain common characteristics: They all provided online tools that the students could use autonomously, although participation could be mandatory. They all aimed at improving the fit between student and institution by providing *institutional orientation*. Consequently, the corresponding organizational practice can be described as *orientation and guidance*, developed by central service units in close collaboration with faculties. Often these measures come with the side effect that they result in intense discussions within faculties about the aims and objectives of studying, which is often seen as a productive advantage.

6.3.7 *Performance of Students: Alternative Paths of Studying and Learning*

The next interpretative pattern differs from those before because it concerns a shift in perspective with respect to student diversity which takes place among lecturers and other persons working in study programs. This pattern could be found in the context of projects that included changes in curricular structures and teaching developments. One example was provided by the project 'Teaching Laboratory' at the University of Hamburg. Here, lecturers from the MIN Faculty were able to apply for financial resources to develop and implement new teaching concepts. It was observed among the participating lecturers that being able to spend more time on improving teaching and innovatively conveying content often resulted in a changed mindset. The following story was told by a person working in a teaching project:

> There was one teaching project in physics. The point was that students were not well prepared for the lectures. Before class, they were assigned written material to read. But barely any of them actually did. Then, the teacher started to develop some small tests. Then new tools were added, there were videos and interactive scripts or quizzes. And it turned out that no one made use of everything but they chose selectively. Some of them preferred to read. Others liked to watch a video, and others used scripts. But for all of them their level of expertise improved. It is like this: One offer alone is not sufficient because people are always different (UHH_gd/209).

As indicated in this quote, some lecturers began to gradually rethink their assumptions and attitudes — not only on student diversity but also on the complexity and reciprocity of teaching and learning processes. In the beginning, the project implied that students did not finish assigned readings and were inadequately prepared for the lessons. This is associated with a deficit-oriented way of looking at students and student diversity. Over time, lecturers gained an awareness of different types of learners and the idea that teaching should take these different types into account. Thus, the underlying logic changed from assuming that the appropriate way of dealing with student diversity was to confront students with only one traditional way of mediating content, towards a broadened perspective on how teaching and learning could also be adapted by offering alternative learning routes.

A similar observation could be detected in the context of the project 'Extended Beginning of Studies' at the HAW Hamburg. Here, the project was initiated by academic staff under the assumption that first-year students lacked subject-specific requirements, which is an indicator of a deficit-oriented perspective. This led to the development of an extended beginning of studies which entailed an extension of the regular duration of studies from seven to eight semesters. However, over time it became clear that students' prior knowledge, living situations and framework conditions were heterogeneous, yet the study structures were still oriented towards students who had no other obligations than studying and entered university directly after the *Abitur*. This did not sufficiently reflect reality. The academic staff of the study program observed that students were pressuring themselves to fulfill the requirements of the regular study program, while not reflecting on the specificity of their individual situation. Thus, found it necessary to provide students the freedom to design their studies based on their individual requirements:

> and these individual requirements can be: I work next to my studies. Or I lack prior knowledge. Or I am an Olympic champion. Or I need to care for relatives. Because this is something [project assistant] has always told us: "Do not display them as dorks!" Meaning, they are not that good. Of course, they need to realize, "I am lacking certain competences", but more importantly it is about studying on the basis of different requirements, not studying for persons with difficulties (HAW_gd/132).

As indicated by this quote by an academic, this change of perspective did not come naturally to them, but it was suggested by an administrative person working in the project along with them. This person insisted on displaying the alternative study program as a great opportunity for students who realized that their individual situation conflicted with the regular study program. This was to avoid a deficit-oriented perspective that might also scare students away. In this context, the change of perspective was also seen as a strategy to attract students to the project of the extended beginning of studies because it was observed by project staff that students were afraid of being cast in a negative light as not capable of academic studies.

Overall, the *phenomenon* of interest was in all cases the performance of students. This performance was often displayed as being subpar and legitimized based on test results, high dropout quotas or the insufficient use of learning materials. Those responsible for study programs noticed a need for change and tried to understand the origins of this poor performance. Here, a shift emerged: At first, it was *assumed* that students posed the main problem as they needed to adapt to the requirements of the study program. Instead, the awareness grew that it was the institution that posed the main problem since its study structures were not suitable for the current student population. Thus, while accepting a heterogeneous student composition as the reality, the *cause* for this was seen in the different individual competences, requirements and living situations that impacted the way studying could take place. Consequently, the appropriate *strategy* was to adjust the institutional structures while increasing flexibility and diversification. The *consequence* was that students were given the opportunity to find their own learning and studying paths that were compatible with their personal situation. This was best described in the following quote by a person involved in a related project:

> We want to help students to find their own way, to find their own study plan. They should not have to say "I need to do the whole repertoire", but decide on the basis of their own prior knowledge, their own conditions, their own living situation, how many lectures they can take. And within the program we want to show the opportunities they have to extend the duration of studies, in terms of the courses they need to do and in what kind of order (HAW_gd /16).

Thus, the aim of these measures was that students reflected on their personal situation, their individual preferences and requirements to see how institutional structures needed to be adjusted to their situation to provide a useful fit.

These measures shared several characteristics. They all included curricular changes, although these changes could be more or less substantial. In the case of the Teaching Laboratory, only single lectures were adapted by diversifying the different channels of learning (e.g., videos, scripts, quizzes). In the case of the extended beginning of studies, however, the curricular structure of a whole study program was adapted to allow for study structures to become more flexible and provide students with free time slots. These could then be filled with activities tailored to individual contexts (e.g., bridging courses, working, sports). Nevertheless, all these measures aimed at teaching development. Consequently, the corresponding organizational practice can be described as developing alternative paths of studying and learning. Based on the assumption that the problem was not (only) related to the individual but also to the institutional structures that conflicted with the individual framework conditions for studying and learning, the appropriate way of dealing with this sort of student diversity was seen in enabling students to study and learn via alternative ways by developing innovative teaching concepts or introducing more flexible study structures. All these measures were located within study programs and they were mostly initiated by a specific group of actors who were concerned with the (until then absent) success of their programs. This was also the starting point for the project 'Curricula Development and Coaching' at the HAW Hamburg. Here, a group of dedicated lecturers decided to use the re-accreditation of their study program for a fundamental redesign by "letting go of the old way and going new, innovative ways" (HAW_conference_protocol/13). The background for this development was extremely high dropout rates and low numbers of applicants. Accompanied by an external moderator, a paradigm shift took place that acknowledged that students can also experience first practical insights, even if they might not yet fully master the necessary knowledge. At first, the lecturers were skeptical of the moderator's approach, but they realized how efficient her way of moderating the discussion was because she did not allow a discussion that prioritized single modules. They recognized the problem-based learning approach as the best fitting option for their objectives. This led to crucial structural changes in the set-up of the study program: in the first semesters, teaching and learning were now centered around a specific topic to which the different subjects contributed the necessary knowledge.

Often this perspectival change is only the beginning for a broad range of further developments and transformations in study and teaching structures while resulting in a certain openness for innovative new approaches. With this perspectival change, academic staff and other involved persons realized how much potential still went unused. An interesting example could be observed at the Faculty of Humanities at the University of Hamburg. Here, the QPL projects within the faculty resulted in the introduction of elective modules after the realization that their own diversity as a faculty should be used as a resource:

> And in the context of our projects, we have also learned that we as a faculty represent a great diversity and we do not need to shamefully hide this fact, but we should understand this as a chance. And in this context, we worked on representing this diversity in our curricular structures. Thus, we introduced to our bachelor's study programs a discipline-specific space for elective modules that provides the freedom to do individual things, create individual studying paths (UHH_gd/232).

Thus, intense analysis of the topic of diversity and how to support students as a faculty led to the realization that the range of disciplines and subjects within the faculty was diverse. They realized that this should be used positively, providing students the individual freedom to try out certain modules that did not belong to their study program.

6.3.8 Summary

Overall, this study was able to identify seven different organizational practices at three universities that made specific contributions to deal with student diversity. These organizational practices differed not only with regard to their definition of student diversity but also according to the organizational contexts in which they appeared. For example, the organizational practice of *starting aid* was always organized by central service units, whereas the organizational practice of *deficit compensation* was developed by faculties. The organizational practice of establishing a *learning community*, in turn, was organized by central service units in close collaboration with study programs. Besides, some organizational practices were offered as extra-curricular activities (e.g., *the creation of practice space*), whereas other organizational practices were integrated into study structures (e.g., *alternative paths of studying and learning*). Further, organizational practices could be differentiated according to whether they took place in a group setting (e.g., *learning community*), a face-to-face-setting (e.g., *individual assistance*) or were used autonomously by students as online tools (e.g., *orientation and guidance*) (see Table 6.2).

Overall, the study was able to detect almost all organizational practices at all three universities discussed in this context as case studies. In other words, no differences in the appearance of organizational practices were found among the three universities. However, in some disciplines, certain organizational practices could be found more often than in other disciplines. For example, the *deficit compensation approach* was more common among STEM disciplines or linguistic disciplines throughout the studied institutions. The *learning community approach* and the *practice space approach*, in turn, were more often organized by central service units in cooperation with humanities departments or educational disciplines.

However, some small differences among the universities could still be identified. At the University of Hamburg, for example, the sheer number of different projects and units involved allowed the realization of a broad variety of organizational practices, ranging from *deficit compensation* over *starting aid* to pointing out *alternative paths of studying and learning*. In this case differences in the organizational practices used in projects were largely intra-organizational, depending on who was responsible for the organization of respective QPL activities. For example, the MIN Faculty was much more involved in activities following a *deficit compensation logic*, while the Faculty of Education organized projects influenced by the *learning community approach*. The University of Kassel, in turn, placed a narrower and more selective focus on approaches towards student diversity because one central service unit, the Teaching Service Center, was highly involved in QPL activities. This resulted in a focus on QPL projects following a *practice space logic*, but other organizational practices could also be found, such as the *deficit compensation approach* and the *individual assistance approach*. The QPL activities of the HAW Hamburg were varied as well, but projects following the *orientation and guidance logic* and the *alternative paths of studying and learning logic* were strongly emphasized. These projects were perceived as innovative and contributing to a cultural change towards a competence-oriented form of teaching and learning that was in accordance with their strong teaching profile.

Nevertheless, it should be emphasized that these organizational practices are ordered along ideal-typical differentiations and some measures might show some overlapping. The different organizational practice logics found in the study portfolios (UKassel, UHamburg) are one example. The study portfolios were designed to stimulate reflection on learning and study behavior. At first glance, such an objective entails elements of a *learning community logic*. However, since students were invited to use these study portfolios autonomously, the social interactive character concerning the exchange of study and learning experiences was missing. Further, study portfolios bore some similarities to *orientation and guidance practices* because these practices included online tools for self-reflection. However, the focus of the orientation and guidance approach was put on *institutional orientation* where measures were directed at supporting students to make well-informed study decisions. Study portfolios, in turn, had a stronger focus on *competence orientation* for students who were already enrolled in a study program. These measures provided students with an opportunity to try out different methods and techniques for writing, learning and studying — accordingly, they seemed to align best with the *practice space approach*.

Second, it should be acknowledged that this typology of organizational practices does not cover all measures that have been developed at the three universities in the context of their QPL initiatives. Special attention was given to projects that were directed at students, particularly those at the beginning of their studies. In other words, the research focused on activities that — in line with the QPL funding program's call for proposals — concentrated on first-year study programs that "acknowledge the heterogeneous student composition" (BMBF 2010: 2). Consequently, some projects at the three universities were not considered for analysis of organizational practices, for example, projects in the field of quality management, study program monitoring or university didactics.

Group discussions were the most important data source for the analysis of underlying interpretative patterns. They allowed a more detailed examination of statements about student diversity and the perception of appropriate ways of dealing with it by persons working in the QPL projects. Project descriptions on websites and project reports, in turn, were more likely to serve the institutions' public image by suggesting how the organization and its projects should be recognized. This also means that for some measures a more detailed analysis of underlying interpretative patterns was not possible because they were not represented in the group discussions. This includes, for example, the Student Engagement project at the University of Hamburg or the Mentoring in Vocational Transition project at the HAW Hamburg. These projects were not included in the group discussions because they did not focus explicitly on first-year study programs. However, since dealing with student diversity was often not solely restricted to the first year of studies, these projects might be interesting for future research.

Finally, one should be cautious when transferring these findings to other university contexts. It is indeed a possibility that similar projects at other universities will not correspond to the previously described organizational practices. For example: other universities have also begun to introduce more flexible study structures by extending the beginning of studies. Yet it might be the case that the argumentation for such a measure is more strongly driven by a *deficit compensation logic* than by the idea to develop *alternative paths for studying and learning*. In this case, the main phenomenon of interest would be defined in terms of the lack of prior subject-specific knowledge which needs to be compensated by thinning out regular study plans and filling the emerging free time slots with preparatory courses and tutorials.

Table 6.2 Summarized Findings: Definitions of Student Diversity and Organizational Practices

Organizational practices	Student diversity definition	Context — Aim of measures	Examples of measures	Further characteristics
Deficit compensation	Prior knowledge	Subject-specific adjustment	- Online bridging courses (HAW Hamburg) - Crash courses natural sciences (UHamburg) - Foreign language requirements for studying (UKassel)	- Organized within faculties/departments - Partly integrated into curriculum - Prior/at the beginning of studies - Group setting/leadership by project assistant
Learning community	Individual learning personality	Competence orientation, institutional orientation, social integration	- First semester tutorials (HAW Hamburg, UHamburg) - Buddy programs (Study Pilots) (UKassel)	- Organized by central service units, in collaboration with study programs - Extra-curricular - At the beginning of studies - Group setting/leadership by advanced student/tutor
Starting aid	Specific target groups	Institutional orientation, social integration	- Offers of the International Office (HAW Hamburg) - Study orientation for vocationally qualified persons (UHamburg)	- Organized by central service units - Extra-curricular - Prior/at the beginning of studies - Mostly group settings
Practice space	Learner, writer and student types	Competence orientation	- Academic writing workshops (UHamburg) - Workshops concerning studying and learning (UKassel, HAW) - Study portfolios, worksheets (all)	- Organized by central service units, some in collaboration with faculties - Extra-curricular - Whole student-life-cycle - Group setting/leadership by project assistant

Table 6.2 Summarized Findings: Definitions of Student Diversity and Organizational Practices (continued)

Organizational practices	Student diversity definition	Context Aim of measures	Examples of measures	Further characteristics
Individual assistance	Individual problems and needs	Competence orientation	- Coaching for learning and exam preparation (UKassel) - Academic writing consultation (UKassel, UHamburg) - Consultation by student counseling office (HAW Hamburg)	- Organized by central service units - Extra-curricular - Whole student-life-cycle - Face-to-face-setting with project assistant/consultant
Orientation and guidance	Mismatch between student and student program	Institutional orientation	- Online self-assessment for study orientation (HAW Hamburg, UHamburg) - Subject-specific online self-assessments (UKassel)	- Developed by central service units in close collaboration with faculties or by themselves - Party integrated into curriculum - Before application - Online-tool, often combined with individual consultation
Alternative paths of studying and learning	Students' performance	Teaching development	- Teaching laboratory (UHamburg) - Extended beginning of studies (HAW Hamburg) - Curricula development and coaching (HAW Hamburg)	- Developed by faculties - Fully integrated into curriculum - Teaching concepts/flexible study structures - Whole student-life-cycle

7 Conclusion and Discussion

This chapter concludes this study by reflecting on how the results of this study provide answers to the initial research questions. In addition, the chapter entails an assessment of the usefulness of the methodological approach for answering these research questions and it identifies questions for further research and its implications for policy and practice. This study has shown that German universities have responded very differently to the institutional demand of widening participation. Depending on the local contexts, universities' interpretations of the idea of student diversity resulted in heterogeneous definitions of student diversity and heterogeneous organizational practices to deal with student diversity.

7.1 Answers to Research Questions

The central research question for this study was:

How do German universities respond to student diversity in the context of the widening participation policy agenda? How can variations in organizational responses at German universities be explained?

In order to address the overall research problem, four sub-questions guided the research process and data analysis:
- Research Question 1: *What perspectives on student diversity can be identified in the political discourse on widening participation?*
- Research Question 2: *How do German universities respond to student diversity in the context of the QPL initiative?*
- Research Question 3: *How can variations in organizational responses to student diversity be explained?*
- Research Question 4: *Which organizational practices dealing with student diversity can be identified?*

Concerning the first sub-question, student diversity is conceptualized "as a story of ideas turning into actions in ever new localities" (Czarniawska/Joerges 1996: 13) that travels around in the field of (academic) organizations and is manifested within the political discourse through reforms and program initiatives. Here, the study focused on the identification of the political discourse that underlies the widening participation agenda (Archer 2007; Boch Waldorff 2013) since it was expected to transport certain beliefs about what constitutes the role of (higher education) organizations with regard to student diversity. Thereby, the study concentrated on the construction of the political discourse by the most important and influential political stakeholders in the organizational field (BMBF, KMK, Science Council). Such a policy analysis served as a frame of reference for the analysis of the organizational responses, i.e., how the idea of student diversity was translated within the organizational context.

The political discourse analysis (see Chapter 2.4.2.) revealed that the political discourse on widening participation contains two dominant perspectives which perceive widening participation either as a means to bring about social justice or to secure the pool of skilled labor. According to the first perspective, the underrepresentation of certain social groups due to underlying structural barriers is perceived to be the central problem. Here, universities are displayed as promoters of educational equality with the purpose of increasing educational opportunities for these groups that are mostly defined in terms of certain socio-demographic characteristics or their specific living situations (*social justice perspective*). The second perspective sees demographic change and the shortage of skilled labor due to a lack of attractiveness of higher education for certain groups as the central problem. Since universities are perceived as important providers of professionals, the purpose of higher education is to promote the so-far untapped potential of knowledge and talent. In particular, this potential is seen in vocationally qualified persons (*economic competitiveness perspective*).

These findings from the analysis of the German political discourse support previous studies from other countries on how the widening participation discourse is dominated by economic as well as social justice imperatives (Archer 2007; Davies 2003) and how initiatives for widening access to higher education are influenced by different underlying norms (Goastellec 2008). Thus, although these findings come as no surprise when looking at similar studies in the context of other countries, it is indeed interesting that the exact same two perspectives have been proven dominant in the German context as well. Particularly against the background of trends like Globalization and Europeanization (Goastellec 2012, 2008), this might be interpreted as a sign of how national policy agendas are becoming more alike or how they are influenced by the "European project of social justice" (Goastellec 2012: 503). Findings from these studies indicate how the European Union, with the help of its soft instrument of public policy, encourages its members (and other non-European countries) to recognize diversity as an important issue in higher education. The European Union encourages to adopt diversity definitions in a way that corresponds with a certain European (and democratic) frame for the interpretation of the world (ibid.). In this context, Sahlin-Andersson (1996) also points to the importance of international editing organizations, like the OECD and how they frame ideas in a certain way.

At the same time, it is also suprising that only these two perspectives have been identified as dominant in the widening participation political discourse.

As mentioned before in Chapter 3.6.2., research on diversity management has identified at least five diversity paradigms that can be distinguished according to their definition of diversity, their validation of diversity and their underlying logic of response to corresponding reactions on the strategy, structure and action levels (Gaisch/Aichinger/Preymann 2017). Similarities can indeed be found between the *fairness and anti-discrimination diversity paradigm* and the *social justice perspective*. Both focus on socio-demographic characteristics in their definition of diversity and share the same underlying logic of social permeability and the need to fight against discrimination and unequal treatment. The *market access diversity paradigm* and the *economic competitiveness perspective* also have similar characteristics. Among their reasons for diversity, activities are the focus on educational biography, vocationally qualified persons and the underlying dominant logic of contributing to economic growth in the face of a lack of highly skilled labor. However, the document analysis of the political discourse did not reveal any evidence of *resistance, learning and efficacy* and *responsibility and sensibility diversity paradigms* (ibid.). There might be several reasons for this.

First, these diversity paradigms have been identified on the organizational level of universities and not on the macro-level of political discourse. As Boxenbaum/Strandgaard Pedersen (2009) mention, the further distanced the observer is from the phenomenon of interest, the more details and complexities get lost. Since the political discourse analysis was carried out on a more abstract level than the organizational level, this might be the reason for not having been able to identify characteristics of the other three paradigms in the German political discourse.

Second, since the main focus of this study lies on the identification of translation processes of the institutional demand of student diversity on the organizational level, it was decided to limit the document analysis of the political discourse to a certain timeframe. This decision was also based on the fact that previous authors have already provided detailed historical descriptions of past policy processes concerning the topic of student diversity and widening participation (Hanft 2015; Wild/Esdar 2014; Wildt 1985). Consequently, the document analysis covers only a specific, limited period of time from 2006 to 2016. Before that, the political discourse on widening participation might have been influenced by other logics and paradigms that were dominant back then due to certain social, cultural, political, legal or economic trends within the general environment of organizations that affected political discussions, debates and decisions (Bess/Dee 2012; Clark 1983). Apparently, the two most dominant contemporary approaches are displayed in terms of a market orientation and a social justice orientation.

Third, the document analysis does not only involve a temporal limit, but it is also restricted to the main circle of political stakeholders who influence the German policy discourse on widening participation, including the BMBF, the

KMK and the Science Council. However, many other stakeholders are contributing to the discourse on widening participation. It was decided to only include this limited set of stakeholders because the main research interest lies in the perspectives on student diversity to be found in the political discourse. But universities are confronted with a very complex environment, in which suppliers, customers, competitors, regulatory agencies and special interest groups all influence how student diversity is defined and what role universities should have in dealing with this topic (Bess/Dee 2012).

As universities are scientific institutions, they are also influenced by the way the topic of student diversity and widening participation is discussed within the academic discourse among researchers in the fields of pedagogy, didactics, politics, sociology and so forth. Thus, researchers and the academic discourses they recreate are also important for the analysis of the overall discourse on widening participation. Consequently, all these other stakeholder groups have an impact on widening participation discourse in a much wider sense. It might be an interesting field for future research to extend the analysis from the political discourse towards a more holistic in-depth analysis of the widening participation discourse where more emphasis is put on identifying the different stakeholders and debates that all influence how student diversity is defined and what universities should do about it. An interesting perspective might also be provided by examining how widening participation is displayed in the media, as it was examined, for example, in the context of nuclear power and the energy turnaround (Bohn/Walgenbach 2017).

The second research question is based on the theoretical perspective that on the local level, ideas are not just translated in a symbolic manner. Instead, they have long-lasting effects by being adopted into organizational practice (Sahlin/Wedlin 2008). The distinction between verbal accounts and actual practices can be traced back to the classical distinction made by Brunsson (1989) between the three organizational outputs of talk, decision and action. Consequently, the present study was not only interested in the way universities translate the external demand rhetorically (i.e., on the strategy level) or make ceremonial decisions (i.e., on the structure level), but also in the ways these translations affect their daily routines and activities (i.e., the action level). The QPL funding program was selected as an example for the external demand of student diversity. Since the study was interested in examining variations in organizational responses of universities, three universities that participated in this funding program and differ according to type of institution, location and institutional profile were selected as case studies.

To provide an answer to the second sub-question, this study examined how the idea of student diversity was translated in the context of the universities' QPL initiatives on the levels of strategy, structure and action. The strategy level refers to information on the QPL initiative's strategy, motives, aims and purposes. The structure level refers to the structure of the QPL initiative, including the institutional anchoring, its components and involved faculties or departments. On the action level, the analysis identified the single projects within the QPL initiatives that dealt with student diversity (e.g., bridging courses, academic writing workshops).

To explain how the idea of student diversity was translated in the context of the QPL initiative, the theoretical concept of editing rules (Sahlin-Andersson 1996) proved to be useful. Editing rules enable and restrict how actors translate circulating ideas and make them fit to the local context (Sahlin/Wedlin 2008). These rules arise from the local context and emerge as implicit rules to be followed during the process of (re)telling the stories of editing. This study was able to identify all three rules of framing ideas according to context, logic and formulation.

First, the translations were connected to the local context in order to create a fit between the edited idea and certain local characteristics. On the strategy level, all universities connected the institutional demand of student diversity with their mission and profile. For example, the QPL strategy at the University of Kassel was directly related to the traditionally broadened access to university for certain non-traditional students which is deeply embedded within this university's history. The university originated from a *Gesamthochschule* that enabled students to complete consecutive academic degrees before the Bachelor's and Master's degree structure was introduced in Germany. The principle of widening educational opportunities was seen as the reason behind the enormous growth in student numbers and the growing diversity. This in turn provided the background for the QPL strategy to extend the support structures in studying and teaching.

On the levels of structure and action, prior experiences, structures and networks played an important role, but also the size and institutional anchoring of the QPL initiative. For example, at the HAW Hamburg, the medium size of the university and a group of committed employees with a clear vision for future prospects enabled the exchange of ideas and approaches to dealing with student diversity.

Second, universities embedded dealing with student diversity into a wider storyline, using dramatic vocabulary by giving ideas specific labels. The University of Hamburg for example provided an interesting case of how the translated idea of student diversity was perceived as conflicting with another institutional demand, namely excellence. Guided by the university's mission statement and its strong research profile, student diversity was understood in terms of academic competences necessary for academic studies. Such a perspective was highly deficit-oriented, assuming that students were not well equipped for their start into the university world. The QPL initiative was used for installing a sort of pre-college, subsuming measures preparing students for studies at the university. The corresponding title of the initiative was 'Bridges to the University — Pathways to Academia'. After the first round, the university management involved in the QPL initiative realized that the initiative's strong focus on eliminating deficits ran the risk of reputational loss. Thus, the strategic focus was seen as problematic since it conflicted with the aim of becoming excellent. This had its origins in the context of the Excellence Initiative, a different funding program the university applied for during that time. Consequently, they changed the title to 'Diversity as a Chance', although it remained open what was to be understood under this term.

On the levels of structure and action, success stories concerning best-practice examples were emphasized at all three universities. For example, at the HAW Hamburg, one story described the changed opinions of lecturers about how a curriculum should look like. With the help of an external moderator, their perspective changed from thinking that students needed to learn fundamentals first to the view that providing practical insights was possible from the very beginning. Due to the close collaboration of committed employees at this university, best-practice examples were easily spread among involved faculties and service units at the HAW Hamburg.

Finally, the study was able to identify editing rules concerning logic at all three universities and on all three levels. Here, organizational actors framed their arguments for certain perspectives and activities to deal with student diversity in rationalistic terms, referring to evaluations and statistics. For example, organizational actors referred to evaluations of strength and weaknesses, other strategic papers, statistics and personal experiences to legitimize definitions of student diversity and organizational practices to deal with it. This was most obvious at the University of Kassel, where data and statistics played a significant role in the context of the QPL initiative. For example, the results of an external evaluation agency were displayed prominently on the QPL website, indicating the successes of the single QPL projects of the first round. These data were used to legitimize the continuation of these projects in the second round. On the strategy level, the main areas that QPL funding was invested in were identified based on an evaluation of strengths and weaknesses. Further, the university management involved in the QPL initiative emphasized how important it was that the QPL strategy fit in with other strategic papers of the university and how they complemented each other. On the structure level, the QPL initiative's single projects were grouped according to three clusters on the basis of an evaluation of strengths and weaknesses. On the level of action, persons involved in the QPL projects used satisfaction rates of students to indicate the success of measures.

The concept of editing rules emphasizes the act of interpretation in which that is steered by certain institutional beliefs and norms (Boxenbaum/Jonsson 2008). Here, ideas that enter a certain local context are framed in a familiar way to facilitate sense-making among other organizational members (Czarniawska 2005; Weick 1995). However, the results of the present study are not able to answer the question of the role of agency in the translation process. According to Sahlin-Andersson (1996), editing rules represent "implicit principles of action rather than deliberate tools of strategizing" (p. 85). In other words, the translation occurs when an idea presents a pragmatic solution to a certain organizational problem. Yet other authors have argued that different interpretations provide certain strategic opportunities and that actors have a certain freedom to choose a certain way of translating an idea within a local context. Consequently, actors might be more likely to give attention to frames of interpretation that correspond with their own interests (Boxenbaum/Strandgaard Pedersen 2009). For example, Boxenbaum's (2006) study about the translation of diversity management practices in Danish firms showed that actors were aware of the strategic power of interpretation and that they negotiated certain interpretations that guided organizational practices according to their own preferences. A similar observation was made in the present study in the case of the HAW Hamburg. Here, the Vice President for Studies and Teaching put forward a competence-oriented definition of student diversity that supported her vision of the university as a learning organization. This perspective reflects a more agentic line of inquiry within the translation literature in Scandinavian institutionalism and follows a logic similar to that of international literature on institutional entrepreneurship and institutional work (Lawrence/Suddaby/Leca 2009; Boxenbaum/Strandgaard Pedersen 2009). Future research should put special emphasis on the role of agency in translation processes as the present study did not include this as an explicit focus; rather it was a by-product of the findings. Nevertheless, this study contributes to one of the most central debates on agency vs. embeddedness in institutional theory (Sahlin/Wedlin 2017).

Overall, the study was able to identify significant variations in the ways the idea of student diversity was translated in the context of the QPL initiatives at the three universities. However, what is being transferred from one local context to another is not the idea per se, but rather materializations of the idea (Czarniawska/Joerges 1996). To explain these variations and, thereby, answer the third sub-question, the study follows Scandinavian scholars who have argued that these materializations can best be identified in edited narratives that are told in the organizations (Czarniawska 2009). The study was able to identify the 'overarching narratives' on dealing with student diversity that are told at the three examined universities. These narratives provided a useful framework for analyzing how the idea of student diversity was re-embedded in the local context (ibid.). This not only affected the rhetorical level but also involved how rhetorical responses were more or less coupled with concrete actions (Brunsson 1989).

Overall, the findings from the overarching narratives on student diversity support theoretical assumptions that the act of interpretation is guided by institutional beliefs and norms that derive from the local context (Boxenbaum/Jonsson 2008). The present results are in line with those of prior studies that have noted the importance of institutional characteristics as explaining factors for local variations of organizational responses (Kirkpatrick et al. 2013; Greenbank 2006). The present thesis even went beyond previous studies by adding the concept of diversity paradigms as an additional explanatory factor for local variations (Gaisch/Aichinger/Preymann 2017). This concept was helpful to explain why organizational members at German universities interpret student diversity so differently and arrive at widely different conclusions in response to student diversity.

The most interesting finding to emerge from the analysis is that two aspects seem to be important for the degree of coupling between the QPL initiative's strategy, structure and action, namely a *strategic guiding principle* concerning student diversity that connects the three levels and the *structural anchoring* of the QPL initiative within the structures of a university. The finding of the strategic guiding principle supports previous studies that suggest universities need holistic institutional approaches for studying and teaching to acknowledge the diverse needs of today's student population (Gorard/Smith 2006; Kift/Nelson/Clarke 2010; Knauf 2016). Such a strategic guiding principle, however, needs to be communicated among all organizational members and units involved to make sure that it influences organizational responses on the strategy level as well as on the structure and action level. This is where the structural anchoring of the QPL initiative comes into place. The present findings suggest that a QPL initiative that is embedded within existing university structures has a tighter coupling between the three levels. Coupling is even intensified when the unit in which the QPL initiative is integrated is well connected to other central and decentral units of the university. These internal networks are crucial for establishing communication channels and opportunities for the exchange of experiences of involved organizational members and, thereby, for contributing to a tight coupling of strategies, structures and activities to deal with student diversity. Here, QPL management can use these communication channels to distribute their frames for interpreting student diversity that fit with the overall strategic guiding principle.

This study assumes that the idea of student diversity travels from the macro-level of the widening participation agenda to the organizational level of German universities. This leads to the question whether the identified perspectives on student diversity within the political discourse on widening participation can be retrieved in the context of the QPL initiatives of the three studied German universities. As mentioned before, the document analysis of policy documents revealed a *social justice perspective* and an *economic competitiveness perspective* on widening participation. These two perspectives show similarities with the *fairness and anti-discrimination diversity paradigm* and, respectively, the *market access diversity paradigm* that have been identified as dominant for the translation of the idea of student diversity in the context of the University of Kassel's QPL initiative. Interestingly, as indicated in the overarching narrative, this university perceived itself as highly challenged by external demands and, at the same time, badly equipped with sufficient resources to deal with these demands adequately. Thus, the data material indicates how organizational actors at the University of Kassel feel a strong pressure triggered by the political agenda to deal with student diversity. The findings suggest that the University has adopted the inconsistent values and norms embedded in the widening participation agenda and, by linking them to its institutional characteristics, made them their own. At the other two universities, however, other demands deriving from internal expectations (i.e., excellence, competence orientation) seem to have a more profound impact on the translation of the idea of student diversity in the context of their QPL initiatives.

The fourth sub-question made the concrete actions to deal with student diversity the focus of attention. Here, the present study emphasized how dealing with student diversity is manifested on the level of concrete organizational practices. This micro-focus on the action level was of special interest because this level is commonly ignored by institutional theory studies. Often, the main interest follows the strategic responses of organizations, while assuming that the strategy level is decoupled from actual practices (Meyer/Rowan 1977). However, in line with Scandinavian institutionalism, this study argues that in the long run, the diffused idea of student diversity has an impact on organizational performance. Based on a university didactics literature review of organizational responses, the concrete activities within the QPL initiatives at the three universities were analyzed. The group discussions with persons involved in QPL projects at the three universities were used as data sources. Group discussions were perceived as particularly useful since it was possible to identify certain interpretative patterns that linked definitions of student diversity to different ways of dealing with this topic. For data analysis, the coding paradigm (Corbin/Strauss 1990) was applied to develop an understanding of the conditions under which the phenomenon of interest (i.e., student diversity) emerges and how this phenomenon is connected to causes, strategies, conditions, consequences and context. This led to the identification of seven interpretative patterns that correspond to organizational practices to deal with student diversity.

Overall, almost all organizational practices could be found at all three universities. They all made specific contributions to deal with student diversity as they not only differed in their definitions of student diversity but also in terms of the contextual conditions in which they appeared. These contextual conditions varied according to types of measures, aims and other contextual characteristics (e.g., organized by central service units or developed within the faculties). For example, the *deficit compensation approach* was mostly to be found among measures that aimed at *subject-specific adjustment*, while defining student diversity according to students' prior knowledge. These measures were organized within faculties or departments and partly integrated with regard to content. They were organized prior to or at the very beginning of studies in a group setting and under the leadership of a QPL employee or lecturer. The *learning community approach*, in turn, could be found among measures that had a broader focus on competence orientation as well as on *institutional orientation* and *social integration*. Also, the definition of student diversity was broader as these projects defined student diversity in terms of an individual learning personality composed of a diverse set of individual, social and organizational diversity components. These measures were organized by central service units in collaboration with the study programs. The measures were offered in the form of extra-curricular group settings under the leadership of advanced students. Usually, they took place at the beginning of studies and lasted the whole semester. Besides these two opposing practices, a series of other organizational practices could be found at the three universities.

Comparing the identified organizational practices at the three universities, only small differences could be detected with regard to the dominance of certain kinds of organizational practice. For example, due to the extensive size of the QPL initiative as a whole and the large number of single QPL projects under the umbrella of the *Universitätskolleg*, all types of organizational practices could be found at the University of Hamburg. At the University of Kassel, in turn, the study identified a certain focus on measures following the logic of *practice space*. Many single QPL projects were organized by one central service unit, although other approaches were to be found, too. The QPL activities of the HAW Hamburg were strongly influenced by their teaching profile and competence orientation that resulted in an emphasis on organizational practices following the *orientation and guidance logic* and the *alternative paths of studying and learning logic*.

Overall, this study found diverse sets of organizational practices to deal with student diversity at the examined universities. In this sense, this study contradicts the claim made by some authors that German universities meet the demand of student diversity only on a rhetorical basis ((Kehm 2000; Hanft 2015). Instead, the present findings confirm other studies that suggest that universities have begun to develop multiple measures to deal with student diversity (Leicht-Scholten 2011). However, whether these measures are united by a coherent underlying strategy is questionable. This study found mixed evidence. Even if an underlying strategy and corresponding practices to deal with student diversity were detected (e.g., competence orientation), the same university also offered other organizational practices that were based on very different understandings of student diversity (e.g., deficit orientation). The different underlying rationales of organizational practices to deal with student diversity within one and the same local context seem at first sight contradictory. It was somewhat surprising that involved organizational members did not seem to recognize the contradictory logics of their organizational practices. Instead, they framed the organizational practices in such a way that it made sense to them to offer a broad spectrum of different measures. Consulting practice-oriented literature, such an approach might be actually more appropriate in the face of the heterogeneous needs and interests of students who enter universities (Bosse et al. 2019). In other words, a heterogeneous student body might require universities to offer a plurality of different organizational practices to support them according to their individual needs and requirements. The most important finding concerning organizational practices might be that there is no 'one size fits all' solution to deal with student diversity and universities have begun to realize this.

However, one unanticipated finding was that the study found no significant differences in the occurrence of organizational practices between the three case study universities. Almost all organizational practices that were identified were apparent at all three case study universities. As discussed in the theory chapter, institutional theory is based on the assumption that organizations within the same organizational field become more alike because these organizations are confronted with similar institutional demands. Due to isomorphic pressures they then tend to respond to these demands in a similar way to preserve their legitimacy and, thus, secure their survival (Meyer/Rowan 1977). Scandinavian scholars, in turn, emphasize that institutional demands are translated to make them fit the respective local context, which results in local variations and, thus, increasing heterogeneity of organizations within the same organizational field (Sahlin/Wedlin 2008; Czarniawska/Joerges 1996). Here, the study shows mixed findings. On the one hand, the study supports Scandinavian studies by showing the importance of the local context for translation processes. The findings suggest that the examined universities interpret student diversity very differently, resulting in local variations of the idea of student diversity in the context of their QPL initiatives. On the other hand, looking at the QPL single projects as the level of universities' actual daily practices of studying and teaching, the findings suggest that the universities have developed a similarly broad spectrum of different organizational practices to deal with student diversity. Thus, it can be interpreted that on the action level, we can see homogenizing tendencies among the examined universities.

However, these results must be interpreted with caution because of the limited set of examined universities. There might also be different explanations for this observation. For example, it might be possible that universities become more alike on the level of organizational practices to deal with student diversity because organizational members involved in student diversity practices exchange their experiences with similarly involved persons from other universities. As mentioned before, since universities are 'professional organizations', organizational members are often better connected to persons from their discipline working at other higher education institutions than with organizational members from other disciplines working at the same university (Clark 1983). These connections ease the spread of experiences and projects among organizations. This is particularly true for the action level of the QPL initiative because most of the single QPL projects are bottom-up initiatives developed by committed academics. Thus, it is possible that some of these project ideas have been 'copied' by academics because they had heard from their colleagues at other universities about their 'new and innovative' way of dealing with student diversity and wanted to try out whether this practice 'worked' for them, too. However, the study did not examine in detail the provenance of project ideas, suggesting a promising field for future research.

7.2 Main Contribution of the Study

This study was able to fulfill its four study objectives:
1. To identify dominant perspectives on student diversity in the German political discourse on widening participation.
2. To retell the narrative of how the idea of student diversity is translated at three German universities in the context of the QPL initiative.
3. To indicate how these translations relate to institutional characteristics and dominant diversity paradigms deriving from the local contexts of German universities.
4. To identify organizational practices to deal with student diversity at German universities.

This study contributes to research on social inequalities in higher education in several ways. First, the findings from the analysis of the political discourse within the German context support previous studies from other countries on the way the widening participation discourse is dominated by economic as well as social justice imperatives (Archer 2007; Davies 2003) and how initiatives for widening access to higher education are influenced by different underlying norms (Goastellec 2008). However, these studies mostly focus on the changing practices of admission procedures on the macro-level of national policies (Clancy/Goastellec 2007). This study argues that access, participation and success can be regarded as different "degrees of social inclusion" (Gidley et al. 2010: 123), in which access represents only the first step. It broadens the scope by looking at changes in access criteria as well as the ways in which German universities support underrepresented student groups throughout the student life cycle and thus contribute to a sustainable change in study and teaching.

Second, this study calls for more qualitative-oriented research designs that comprise not only the macro-level of national policies but also consider institutional differences on the organizational level to capture the different meanings given to widening participation. Such methodology is particularly useful in the context of soft steering instruments due to their non-binding character, which leaves universities with a large scope for action (Boch Waldorff 2013). Due to their widespread application in the field of German higher education and the increasing amount of financial resources they entail, future research on the role of soft steering instruments is crucial.

Third, the study shows how the translation framework provides a useful analytical tool for studying both the macro-level of national policies and the organizational level of universities. The findings suggest that the translation process of the 'traveling idea' of student diversity was guided by underlying rationales that build a frame of reference for how universities should respond to this demand (Czarniawska/Joerges 1996). Whether these more general rationales were enacted, however, depended on the prevalent assumptions and beliefs embedded in the local context. These assumptions and beliefs differed according to certain institutional characteristics as well as diversity paradigms that were dominant within the local context. The importance of the local context is based on the central notion of Scandinavian institutionalism that ideas do not travel in a vacuum but instead are actively translated in the context of other ideas, traditions and institutions (ibid.). Processes of imitation, thus, do not result in passive copying, but instead "things change as they are moved" (Sahlin/Wedlin 2017: 106).

Consequently, the study shows the potentials of concepts from Scandinavian institutionalism for theoretically explaining heterogeneous organizational responses to the external demand of student diversity. Based on the concept of translation (Czarniawska/Joerges 1996), the travel of the idea of student diversity was portrayed in different local contexts. The notion of editing rules (Sahlin-Andersson 1996) helps to understand how this idea was re-embedded on a symbolic and linguistic level. However, this thesis is also able to indicate how the idea of student diversity was translated on the levels of structure and action in the context of the QPL initiative. Consequently, this study provides explanations of how rhetoric corresponds to concrete actions, while the levels of strategy, structure and action are more or less coupled with each other.

Fourth, this study illustrates how the concept of editing rules can be applied in the context of (German) universities. To date, this concept has been most commonly examined in the context of currently popular management ideas (Sahlin-Andersson 1996; Czarniawska/Joerges 1996). This study shows how editing rules can also be found at work in German universities, where through editing an idea is made more explicit, although its focus, content and meaning might change. In other words, this study applied the concept of editing rules to a non-management idea like 'student diversity' that travels between contexts, although this does not necessarily mean that the corresponding given meanings remain the same. Further, activities might remain similar in varying local contexts, but they derive from different ideological or programmatic notions (Sahlin-Andersson 1996; Sahlin/Wedlin 2017). This is what this study was able to detect with regard to the question of what types of organizational practices can be identified to deal with student diversity.

The aim of this study was to highlight the potential of Scandinavian institutionalism for higher education research in general and the German higher education landscape in particular. First, to acknowledge institutional complexity and the dynamics of the higher education landscape, more in-depth approaches on the organizational level can provide nuanced insights into the ways universities make sense of external pressures and re-interpret them in their local contexts (Greenwood et al. 2011). This focus on organizational heterogeneity complements existing research on institutional isomorphism on a more aggregated level of analysis. Second, Scandinavian institutionalism adds richness to our understanding of the role of 'soft actors', who edit and translate the circulating ideas (Sahlin/Wedlin 2017). At the same time, this process of editing is always embedded within the local context that entails underlying rationales enabling and restricting how actors translate circulating ideas and fit them to the local context (Sahlin/Wedlin 2008).

7.3 Limitations

Concerning the chosen conceptual framework, this thesis investigated the phenomenon of 'student diversity' in the context of German higher education. As mentioned before, this term subsumes a rather ambiguous conglomeration of different value-laden expectations, beliefs and logics (Buß 2010; Watson 2006). Choosing such a vague term distinguishes this research from previous studies conducted from a Scandinavian institutionalist perspective (Waeraas/Nielsen 2016). The latter mostly investigated currently popular management ideas that are represented through concrete techniques, models or templates. In these studies, these models (e.g., total quality management) traveled from one context to another and were adapted, modified or reshaped, while taking on new forms of meaning during their travel (Sahlin/Wedlin 2008). Since these management ideas were materialized as concrete models or templates, studies were able to compare the 'original' template with the local version of this template along certain defined criteria. In the case of the present study, the 'original' idea of student diversity was missing because there was no 'original' template. Instead, it was decided that a literature review on the concept of student diversity in German higher education should serve as a template for this study (see Chapter 2). An alternative template was provided by the analysis of the German political discourse on widening participation.

Further, student diversity does not have a management background. Rather, the term 'diversity' subsumes different perspectives, ranging from biological or technological to sociological, pedagogical or psychological logics.

However, it was a conscious decision to keep the perspective on student diversity broad, open and vague and have organizational members at the examined universities choose their interpretation. After all, the original observation that led to the idea of this study was that people associated a wide range of diverse connotations with the term of student diversity. Nevertheless, the conceptual openness of the phenomenon under investigation was a challenge to the present study as the notion of student diversity intersected with many other related topics (e.g., inclusion, internationalization). Considering all these possible interpretations pushed the limits of what was feasible to examine in this study. Consequently, I had to neglect some of the diversity-related issues because each of these topics would have required a study of its own.

Further, the main focus of the present study was on translation processes within universities in the context of government policies and programs. Therefore, an analysis of the political discourse on widening participation provided the necessary background for examining organizational responses to the political demand to deal with student diversity. As mentioned before, it was decided to limit the analysis to the output of the most important political stakeholders, although many other stakeholder groups influence the discussion on widening participation. Therefore, it might be possible that organizational responses of German universities have been influenced by other discourses (e.g., media discourse, academic discourse) and stakeholder groups (e.g., higher education scholars, representatives of economy, parents, students) that have not been considered in this study.

In addition, the analysis of both the political discourse on widening participation and on organizational responses of German universities in the context of the QPL initiative was limited to a certain timeframe and a specific empirical setting. There are particular trajectories of developments, trends, history and traditions that are specific to the empirical context and limit the generalizability of the findings of this study. Further, this study chose the QPL funding program as one example for a soft steering instrument that intends to stimulate universities to deal with student diversity in the German higher education context. As mentioned before, this funding program was chosen because it aimed to contribute to a more general improvement of the quality of studying and teaching within regular Bachelor's and Master's study programs against the background of a postulated increasingly heterogeneous student body. Such an openness leaves universities with a high degree of autonomy to choose to connect their QPL initiatives with the topic of widening participation. The selection of alternative examples for widening participation programs in the German higher education context might have led to alternative translations of the idea of student diversity. Consequently, a different focus on organizational practices to deal with this student diversity might have offered itself. For example, as mentioned before, the BMBF funding program ANKOM supports university projects that focus on the recognition of prior learning for vocationally qualified persons without school-based entrance qualification and on the introduction of flexible study programs for employed students. Such a funding program has a much narrower focus on one specific underrepresented student group, which also limits the scope of actions for certain organizational practices on the part of universities.

Further, organizational responses of German universities to student diversity within the QPL funding program were examined in the context of three case studies. These three case studies differed not only in several structural and cultural characteristics but also with respect to the QPL initiatives, their strategies, structures and included single QPL projects. Therefore, to generalize these findings and apply them to other universities and their QPL initiatives will not be possible and would contradict the central notion of this study. However, the importance of the local context for translation processes is a general aspect for understanding local variations in universities' responses to student diversity. From that perspective, the findings of this study can be generalized for other universities in Germany. Nevertheless, additional research is needed to verify the findings in other local contexts, while also accounting for the impact of institutional characteristics besides the type of institution, location and institutional profile.

Further, in interpretative research, it is crucial to reflect on the specific conditions under which the study took place. This research was highly practice-oriented. I met regularly with QPL employees working at the three universities to present preliminary findings, discuss what they meant and what could be done with them to stimulate organizational change. In this context, I organized workshops and didactic trainings for organizational members of those universities to raise awareness for student support and student diversity. Therefore, it should be noted that the research was part of the phenomenon under investigation, triggering a change of perspectives and understandings of student diversity in organizational members who held key positions within the QPL initiative.

Since these elements of self-ethnography were part of the research design, it was particularly important to reflect how it was possible to maintain the necessary distance to the research object (Wilkesmann 2019). Here, GT methodology was perceived as particularly useful: not only did data collection and analysis go hand in hand, but research findings were also constantly written down and revised in reflection of theoretical assumptions. Further, the presentation of research findings in various formats (e.g., conferences, publications, reports, presentations to university units) and addressed to different target groups (e.g., researchers from various disciplines, academic and administrative staff from case study universities and other doctoral students) were perceived as particularly helpful to lower the probability of self-objectification. Overall, to ensure the high quality of the qualitative research process, appropriate qualitative evaluation criteria were met, including subject comprehensibility, triangulation and a reflection on the role of the researcher (see Chapter 4.7.).

7.4 Avenues for Future Research

The aim of this study was to show the potentials of Scandinavian institutionalism for analyzing both the macro-level of national policies and the organizational level of higher education institutions. Further, the study advocates for more in-depth qualitative approaches on the micro-level to account for the institutional complexity of institutional pressures and organizational responses of higher education institutions.

On the macro-level, more process-oriented research is necessary that takes the formation and development of the widening participation agenda into consideration, including an in-depth analysis of the multiple political stakeholders on the national and global level. As mentioned before, future research should take the complex environment of universities into account, encompassing (apart from the state) the different suppliers, customers, competitors, regulatory agencies and special interest groups that all circulate ideas like student diversity (Bess/Dee 2012). Those who circulate these ideas have been called carriers (Sahlin/Wedlin 2008). For example, Berger/Berger/Kellner (1973) distinguish between 'primary carriers' and 'secondary carriers' of the idea of modernization. Primary carriers of modernization are seen in technical production and the bureaucratic state and spread certain ideas relating to the fundaments of modern society. Secondary carriers, however, serve as transmitting agencies for the ideas and ideology that come from the primary carriers. A similar distinction was made by Meyer (1996) who distinguishes the 'others' from 'actors': Actors are described as people who pursue their own interests and are held responsible for their actions. Others, in turn, perceive themselves as neutral mediators, although they are involved in activities that impact the way ideas are circulated and translated (Sahlin/Wedlin 2008). These 'others' can be single persons, organizations, or groups that each influence activities since they discuss, interpret and judge some ideas to be 'good' while ignoring others. These theoretical concepts in combination with a network analysis might provide a beneficial opportunity to identify different actors, organizations and groups and their influence on the widening participation discourse.

Further, the thesis follows the Scandinavian research tradition of discussing case studies of individual organizations where the main interest lies in how organizations adopt new ideas (Boxenbaum/Strandgaard Pedersen 2009). In subsequent studies, though, interest has turned to understand where these ideas come from and how they are produced and circulated (Sahlin/Wedlin 2008). Here, future research should investigate the travel routes from the macro-level of organizational fields to the organizational level of universities. Czarniawska (2008: 93) emphasizes that ideas or practices that travel around the world first have to become dis-embedded and then re-embedded in another place. She uses a gardening metaphor for this process, arguing that "the plant growing at a new place is never identical to the one that started traveling". The question in this context is whether there existed an 'original' idea of student diversity and where it had begun to spread. Diversity can be seen as an idea that has become a 'fashion' (Røvik 2011; Abrahamson 1996) that follows determinate cycles of imitation. Thus, the meaning given to diversity changes according to time and place. As indicated in the literature review in Chapter 2, the term 'diversity' had already been popular in the 1960s and 1970s, but the main focus within the debates and discourses at that time was on diversity aspects like gender, race and disability (Buß 2010). Further, while the US diversity debates were heavily influenced by the civil rights movement which fought for equal rights for black persons to enter higher education, interest in the German diversity discourse turned to unequal access to higher education for women and persons with non-academic family backgrounds (Wild/Esdar 2014). Here, future research on the travel routes of the idea of student diversity might include a more in-depth longitudinal analysis of historical processes and the changing meaning of the idea through time and space.

Overall, the study shows the high potential of Scandinavian Institutionalism for explaining variations in organizational responses of German universities to the demand of student diversity. At the same time, the findings suggest for future research that a combination of concepts from Scandinavian institutionalism with other related concepts from institutional theory might be conducive to mapping the complexities of organizational responses to institutional demands on the individual level of each university. For example, to understand the organizational response of the University of Hamburg to student diversity, literature on institutional complexity might provide interesting additional insights (Greenwood et al. 2011). According to this literature, organizations engage within organizational fields that have become increasingly ambiguous and complex, often entailing mutually incompatible institutional pressures which result in conflicting behavioral prescriptions. Organizations in certain organizational fields are more likely to be confronted with institutional complexity than others, for example in health and educational sectors, because these sectors entail a diverse and broad spectrum of occupations whose practices and behaviors are influenced by different underlying logics (Berg Johansen/Boch Waldorff 2017). Further, the intensity of experiencing institutional complexity differs according to organizations' characteristics as well as their positions within an environmental field. In other words, their structure, governance and identity can make an organization more sensitive to certain logics and less to others (Greenwood et al. 2011). Here, the University of Hamburg's strong research profile, as well as its position as one of the biggest research-oriented universities in Germany, might provide an explanation as to why their orientation towards academia and science plays such a significant role for their way of defining and dealing with student diversity.

Since organizations experience institutional complexity differently, their responses might also differ. However, dealing with complexity represents a difficult task for organizations since they depend on social legitimacy for their survival (Bohn/Walgenbach 2017). According to the literature, organizations use different strategies to deal with this complexity. For example, in their study on the energy-turnaround debate in Germany and the responses of atomic power plant operators, Bohn and Walgenbach (2017) show how organizations refuse, connect and play off conflicting institutional demands. In situations where organizations are confronted with two competing demands, they tend to play these institutional demands off against each other. This might have been the case at the University of Hamburg as well. The institutional demand to deal with student diversity was perceived by the university as conflicting with the second institutional demand of becoming excellent. The literature on institutional complexity and institutional logics might provide an interesting field for further research on how different response strategies are used by organizations.

In the case of the University of Kassel, resource dependency theory might provide a useful theoretical addition for explaining its response to student diversity (Pfeffer/Salancik 1978). Resource dependency theory claims that organizations depend on their environments for resources that are essential for their survival. The dependency on external entities varies based on two aspects: how critical or important the resource is to the organization and how scarce the resource is, i.e., to what extent there are alternative sources in the environment (ibid.). In this context, organizations have two related objectives: they want to acquire control over resources that minimize their dependence on other organizations and they want to gain control over resources that maximize the dependence of other organizations on them. This is achieved by a wide range of active choice behaviors that organizations exercise either "to manipulate external dependencies or exert influence over the allocation or source of critical resource" (Oliver 1991: 148).

Thus, organizations are displayed as embedded in their social interactions. To understand the impact of external pressures, it is crucial to examine the external control and dependencies as well as internal power and control relations. However, this perspective assumes that it is not sufficient to examine the 'objective' resource dependencies and interdependencies. Rather, it is important to investigate the way organizations perceive their environments and their behavior to control and prevent dependencies (Gornitzka 1999). Here, resource dependence theorists emphasize the necessity of organizations to adapt to environmental uncertainty, the ways they cope with problematic interdependencies and how they actively manage and control resource acquisition (Oliver 1991). Consequently, this strand of theory is interested in the varieties of strategies that organizations undertake to alter the situation they find themselves in, in contrast to institutional theorists that predict (passive) compliance to environmental demands (Pfeffer/Salancik 1978). In the case of the University of Kassel, for example, the research findings indicate that the environment contains scarce and valued resources that the organization needed to survive. At the same time, the organization experienced the dilemma that they did not know how to gain control over resource acquisition, which contributed to the feeling of powerlessness. For future research, a more in-depth analysis of the strategic responses of the University of Kassel through the additional lenses of resource dependency theory might provide interesting insights.

At the HAW Hamburg, in turn, interesting insights for explaining organizational responses to student diversity might be derived from the field of organizational learning as well as from research on skilled actors. First, as already noted by Dee/Leisyte (2016), certain structural and cultural characteristics of universities hamper learning at the organizational level, while they are often described as difficult to change. However, against the background of recent governmental trends and changes in knowledge production processes, alternative working modes and steering forms are promoted. For example, Senge (1990) developed the concept of the learning organization which provides an ideal version of a reflective organization that responds to environmental needs in a flexible and innovative way. In the case of the HAW Hamburg, the Vice President for Studies and Teaching followed exactly Senge's concept when she described her vision for the university as a learning organization that is capable of continuous organizational change, celebrating her approach as 'innovative', 'modern' and 'open-minded'. For future research, it can be helpful to examine in more detail to what extent the HAW Hamburg has already become a learning organization and what kinds of characteristics or factors have encouraged this process.

Second, the role of committed academics and administrative staff might also be explained by literature on skilled actors or institutional entrepreneurs (Fligstein 1997). This literature is based on a critique of institutional theory and its (traditionally) limited role for action and actors. According to Fligstein (1997), action is the result of a certain type of social skill that institutional entrepreneurs have. Here, some social actors are more successful in accomplishing desired social outcomes than others. Social skill is defined as "the ability to motivate cooperation in other actors by providing those actors with common meanings and identities in which actions can be undertaken and justified" (ibid.: 398). In other words, skilled actors have the ability to engage others in collective action that is vital to the construction and reproduction of local social orders by providing identities and cultural frames to motivate them (Fligstein 2001). They are better at inducing cooperation because they are more capable of making sense of a particular situation and producing shared meaning for others. Such a concept of social skill has its origins in symbolic interaction. Instead of assuming that their behavior is driven solely by self-interest or by fixed goals, the concept assumes that skilled actors focus on evolving collective ends. In the case of the HAW Hamburg, the Vice President for Studies and Teaching and her inner circle of committed employees provided interesting examples for socially skilled actors, while they framed 'stories' that helped to elicit cooperation from people at the university that seemed to fit their own identity and interests (ibid.). For future research, it might be interesting to reveal the concrete tactics that were used by the socially skilled actors here as listed by Fligstein (1997), who included key aspects such as agenda-setting, framing action, or aggregating interests and see under which conditions they were exercised.

In this context, a more extensive research on the power positions of editors (Sahlin-Andersson 1996) within organizations can provide an interesting insight into the ways of certain organizational actors to frame the translation process more or less extensively. Future research might provide insights into the role of editors and their power positions within the organization by including network analyses. Here, the question remains which possibilities local actors have to control the translation process within the organization.

Combinations of Scandinavian institutionalism with other theoretical constructs, especially with practically-oriented literature, have a certain tradition to grasp the complexities of continuously changing and dynamic organizations (Boxenbaum/Strandgaard Pedersen 2009). However, it should be noted that the above described theoretical constructs of institutional complexity, resource dependency and learning organization can not on their own explain the organizational responses observed here at all three universities. Here, Scandinavian institutionalism proved to be a useful framework to understand how the idea of student diversity travels among local contexts of German universities, how it is translated and leads to different ways of dealing with student diversity.

7.5 Implications for Policy and Practice

This final section is concerned with the implications for policy and practice that can be derived from the present study. The study has shown that the widening participation discourse is dominated by two main perspectives that are often used in an intertwined way and which perceive widening participation either as a means to bring about social justice or to secure the pool of skilled labor. The documents of the main political actors often reflect very different and, at times, opposing positions and perspectives that result in overly complex, value-laden expectations as to how universities should respond to student diversity and which often refrain from defining 'diversity'. On the one hand, it is beneficial that universities are given so much freedom to interpret this demand according to what fits best with their local context. On the other hand, in some cases it might be necessary to steer the discussions about student diversity in a more productive and active way by confronting organizations with alternative interpretative frames that might also be of relevance for them and that had been ignored before. This can, for example, be observed in the context of diversity audits conducted by the *Stifterverband* that seek to help universities to develop and implement diversity strategies. These diversity audits are designed to trigger a more holistic way of looking at the topic of 'diversity' for the respective university, while processes of organizational change are accompanied scientifically. Consequently, this study assumes that political stakeholders should reflect more on their own interests and interpretations: What are the underlying rationales in the political discourse on student diversity? Is it about reducing dropout rates and improving retention quotas in order to improve the country's status in international comparisons concerning the equality of access to higher education (Holmegaard/Madsen/Ulriksen 2017)? Or is it about exploiting the potential of talent that has not been exhausted yet to deal with the increasing demand for skilled labor?

This study shows how the political discourse on widening participation demands universities to be prepared for a student body with increasingly heterogeneous demands and requirements. Since the role of universities towards students is changing in the long run and in so many ways, it should be clear to policy makers that this requires a considerable effort on the part of universities in terms of personnel and financial resources (Leicht-Scholten 2011). It is highly questionable whether the soft steering instruments like third-party funding that are so commonly used in this policy area really contribute to the development of sustainable approaches to deal with student diversity because their scope of action is always limited to a certain timeframe. This also means that the locally diverse expertise that personnel employed through third-party funding has accumulated in projects to deal with student diversity often vanishes once the funding ceases. Here, funding mechanisms are needed that support universities in their widening participation efforts in a more sustainable and longitudinal way.

Further, this study has shown how diversity consists of a complex mosaic of aspects and how heterogeneous the group of non-traditional students is. They experience different social, cultural and institutional challenges that result from a complex interplay between structural framework conditions of the higher education system and the individual competences, interests and motivations with which they enter higher education (Bosse 2015). Consequently, this study calls for more research that acknowledges the complexity of student diversity to get away from stereotypical images of non-traditional students. Likewise, and in accordance with the complexity of the phenomenon of interest, the organizational responses to the demand of student diversity also reveal a complex and heterogeneous picture. Here, this study shows how important a closer look at the organizational level is to identify differences and organizational practices that go beyond simplified descriptions of measures that either aim to homogenize student groups or accept heterogeneity. This study demonstrated how qualitative, process-oriented methods in particular allow digging deep into the diversity of the empirical material.

In addition, organizational actors within universities should be aware of the power they have in choosing certain interpretations of the idea of student diversity over others. It can be beneficial, though, to stimulate discussions among different organizational units, including different faculties as well as central service units, in order to expand the existing interpretative patterns of student diversity and to find the most appropriate ones for the respective local context. Further, the study points out that neither exclusively top-down nor bottom-up approaches to deal with student diversity have proven successful. The important point seems to be the balance between these two levels and their suitability for local contexts. Thus, what is needed is a holistic institutional approach that acknowledges the institutional characteristics as well as dominant diversity paradigms, but also takes the interdependency of top-down and bottom-up approaches to deal with student diversity into account.

References

Abrahamson, Eric (1996): Management fashion. In: Academy of Management Review 21, 1, S. 254–285.

Abrahamson, Eric (2006): Global ideas: How ideas, objects, and practices travel in the global economy. Barbara Czarniawska and Guje Sevón, eds. In: Administrative Science Quarterly 51, 3, S. 512–514.

Altheide, David L./Johnson, John M. (2011): Reflections on interpretive adequacy in qualitative research. In: Denzin, N. K./Lincoln, Y. S. (Hrsg.): The SAGE handbook of qualitative research. Thousand Oaks, London, New Delhi, Singapore: Sage Publications, S. 581–594.

Altvater, Peter/Bauer, Ivonne/Gilch, Harald (2007): Organisationsentwicklung in Hochschulen. Dokumentation. HIS: Forum Hochschule. Hannover: HIS.

Archer, Louise (2007): Diversity, equality and higher education. A critical reflection on the ab/uses of equity discourse within widening participation. In: Teaching in Higher Education 12, 5, S. 635–653.

Arnold, Patricia/Kolbinger, Martin Lu (2012): USuS - Untersuchung Studienverläufe und Studienerfolg: Wie Studium gelingt (Verbundprojekt). Identifizierung der Faktoren gelingenden Lernens unter Bologna-Bedingungen mit dem Ziel der Entwicklung und Erprobung von Fördersystemen auf hochschuldidaktischer und organisatorischer Ebene. München.

Auferkorte-Michaelis, Nicole/Linde, Frank (Hrsg.) (2018): Diversität lernen und lehren – ein Hochschulbuch. Opladen, Berlin, Toronto: Verlag Barbara Budrich.

Auferkorte-Michaelis, Nicole/Linde, Frank/Großi, Christopher (2018): Forschung über Diversität und Diversitätsforschung an Hochschulen. In: Auferkorte-Michaelis, N./Linde, F. (Hrsg.): Diversität lernen und lehren – ein Hochschulbuch. Opladen, Berlin, Toronto: Verlag Barbara Budrich, S. 99–115.

Autorengruppe Bildungsberichterstattung (2016): Bildung in Deutschland 2016. Ein indikatorgestützter Bericht mit einer Analyse zu Bildung und Migration.

Autorengruppe Bildungsberichterstattung (2018): Bildung in Deutschland 2018. Ein indikatorengestützter Bericht mit einer Analyse zu Wirkungen und Erträgen von Bildung.

Baethge, M. (2007): Das deutsche Bildungs-Schisma: Welche Probleme ein vorindustrielles Bildungssystem in einer nachindustriellen Gesellschaft hat. SOFI-Mitteilungen.

Baldridge, J. Victor (1971): Models of university governance: Bureaucratic, collegial, and political. Research and Development Memorandum, Issue 7: Stanford Center for Research and Development in Teaching.

Bandura, A. (1977): Self-efficacy: Toward a unifying theory of behavioral change. In: Psychological Review 84, 2, S. 191–215.

Banscherus, Ulf/Himpele, Klemens/Staack, Sonja (2011): Die soziale Dimension: Der blinde Fleck im Bologna-Prozess. In: Die Hochschule 1, S. 142–154.

Banscherus, Ulf/Kamm, Caroline/Otto, Alexander (2015): Information, Beratung und Unterstützung von nicht-traditionellen Studierenden. Angebote der Hochschulen und deren Bewertung durch die Zielgruppe. In: Hanft, A./Zawacki-Richter, O./Gierke, W. B. (Hrsg.): Herausforderung Heterogenität beim Übergang in die Hochschule. Münster, New York: Waxmann, S. 81–96.

Banscherus, Ulf/Pickert, Anne (2013): Unterstützungsangebote für nicht-traditionelle Studierende. Stand und Perspektiven. Thematischer Bericht der wissenschaftlichen Begleitung.

Barbour, Rosaline S. (2014): Analysing focus groups. In: Flick, U. (Hrsg.): The SAGE handbook of qualitative data analysis. London, Thousand Oaks, Singapore: SAGE, S. 313–326.

Battilana, Julie/D'Aunno, Thomas (2009): Institutional work and the paradox of embedded agency. In: Lawrence, T. B./Suddaby, R./Leca, B. (Hrsg.): Institutional work. Actors and agency in institutional studies of organizations. New York: Cambridge University Press, S. 31–58.

Becher, Tony/Trowler, Paul (2001): Academic tribes and territories. Intellectual enquiry and the culture of disciplines. 2nd ed. Philadelphia, PA: Open University Press.

Bellen, Britta/Tiesler, Jens (2015): "Perspektive Ingenieur" - Informationsportal zum Studieneinstieg für beruflich Qualifizierte in ingenieurwissenschaftliche Studiengänge. In: Freitag, W. K. et al. (Hrsg.): Übergänge gestalten. Durchlässigkeit zwischen beruflicher und hochschulischer Bildung erhöhen. Münster: Waxmann, S. 117–132.

Bensimon, Estela M./Neumann, Anna/Birnbaum, Robert (1989): Making sense of administrative leadership: The `L´ word in higher education. ASHE ERIC Higher Education Report, Band 1. Washington, DC: ERIC.

Berg Johansen, Christina/Boch Waldorff, Susanne (2017): What are institutional logics - and where is the perspective taking us? In: Krücken, G. et al. (Hrsg.): New themes in institutional analysis. Topics and issues from European research. Cheltenham: Edward Elgar, S. 51–76.

Berger, Peter L./Berger, B./Kellner, H. (1973): The homeless mind: Modernization and consciousness. New York: Random House.

Berger, Peter L./Luckmann, Thomas (1966): The social construction of reality. A treatise in the sociology of knowledge. London: Penguin Books.

Bergquist, William H. (1992): The four cultures of the academy. Washington, DC: ERIC.

Bernstein, Basil (1977): Beiträge zu einer Theorie des pädagogischen Prozesses. Frankfurt am Main: Suhrkamp.

Berthold, Christian/Leichsenring, Hannah (Hrsg.) (2012): Diversity Report. Der Gesamtbericht (A1 - D3). Gütersloh: CHE Consult GmbH.

Bess, James L./Dee, Jay R. (2012): Understanding college and university organization. Theories for effective policy and practice. Volume I - The State of the System. Sterling: Stylus Publishing LLC.

Birnbaum, Robert (1988): How colleges work: The cybernetics of academic organization and leadership. San Francisco: Jossey-Bass.

Bleiklie, Ivar/Enders, Jürgen/Lepori, Benedetto (2015): Organizations as penetrated hierarchies: Environmental pressures and control in professional organizations. In: Organization Studies 36, 7, S. 873–896.

Bleiklie, Ivar/Kogan, Maurice (2007): Organization and governance of universities. In: Higher Education Policy 20, 4, S. 477–493.

Bleiklie, Ivar/Marton, S./Hanney, S. (1995): Policy Arenas, Network and Higher Education Reforms. The Cases of England, Sweden and Norway. Bergen: LOS-senteret Notat 9540.

Bleiklie, Ivar/Michelsen, Svein (2013): Comparing HE policies in Europe. In: Higher Education 65, 1, S. 113–133.

BMBF (2009): Verwaltungsvereinbarung zwischen Bund und Ländern gemäß Artikel 91 b Abs. 1 Nr. 2 des Grundgesetzes über den Hochschulpakt 2020 (zweite Programmphase).

BMBF (2010): Richtlinien zur Umsetzung des gemeinsamen Programms des Bundes und der Länder für bessere Studienbedingungen und mehr Qualität in der Lehre.

BMBF (2013): Aufstieg durch Bildung. Bilanz und Perspektiven für Deutschland.

BMBF (2014): Hochschulen öffnen sich neuen Zielgruppen.

BMBF (2015): Aufstieg durch Bildung. https://www.bmbf.de/de/aufstieg-durch-bildung-1240.html [Zugriff: 31.01.2021].

BMBF (2017): Qualitätspakt Lehre. https://www.bmbf.de/de/qualitaetspakt-lehre-524.html.

BMBF (2020a): Begleitforschung zum Qualitätspakt Lehre. https://www.qualitaetspakt-lehre.de/de/begleitforschung-zum-qualitatspakt-lehre-1677.php.

BMBF (2020b): Startseite - Qualitätspakt Lehre. https://www.qualitaetspakt-lehre.de/.

Boch Waldorff, Susanne (2013): What is the meaning of public sector health? Translating discourse into new organizational practices. In: Journal of Change Management 13, 3, S. 283–307.

Bogner, Alexander/Littig, Beate/Menz, W. (Hrsg.) (2009): Interviewing experts. Research methods series. London: Palgrave Macmillan.

Böhm, Andreas (1994): Grounded Theory - wie aus Texten Modelle und Theorien gemacht werden. In: Böhm, A./Mengel, A./Muhr, T. (Hrsg.): Texte verstehen. Konzepte, Methoden, Werkzeuge. Schriften zur Informationswissenschaft, Bd. 14. Konstanz: Universitätsverlag Konstanz, S. 121–140.

Bohn, Stephan/Walgenbach, Peter (2017): Refusing, connecting, and playing off conflicting institutional demands: a longitudinal study on the organizational handling of the end of nuclear power, climate protection, and the energy turnaround in Germany. In: Krücken, G. et al. (Hrsg.): New themes in institutional analysis. Topics and issues from European research. Cheltenham: Edward Elgar, S. 162–193.

Bohnsack, Ralf (2003): Rekonstruktive Sozialforschung. Einführung in qualitative Methoden. 5. Auflage. Opladen: Leske & Budrich.

Bohnsack, Ralf (2004): Group discussion and focus groups. In: Flick, U./von Kardoff, E./Steinke, I. (Hrsg.): A companion to qualitative research. London, Thousand Oaks, New Delhi: Sage Publications, S. 214–221.
Bohnsack, Ralf (2013): Gruppendiskussion. In: Flick, U./von Kardoff, E./Steinke, I. (Hrsg.): Qualitative Forschung. Ein Handbuch. 10. Auflage. Hamburg: Rowohlt Taschenbuch Verlag, S. 369–383.
Bosse, Elke (2015): Exploring the role of student diversity for the first-year experience. In: ZFHE 10, 4, S. 45–66.
Bosse, Elke (2018): Studienrelevante Heterogenität erkunden: Erhebung und Analyse von critical incidents. In: Auferkorte-Michaelis, N./Linde, F. (Hrsg.): Diversität lernen und lehren – ein Hochschulbuch. Opladen, Berlin, Toronto: Verlag Barbara Budrich, S. 116–134.
Bosse, Elke et al. (2019): Gelingendes Studieren in der Studieneingangsphase. Ergebnisse und Anregungen für die Praxis aus der Begleitforschung zum Qualitätspakt Lehre im Projekt StuFHe.
Bosse, Elke/Mergner, Julia (2019): Besser einsteigen - Analyse von Anforderungen und Gestaltungsmöglichkeiten der Studieneingangsphase. In: Berendt, B. (Hrsg.): Neues Handbuch Hochschullehre. Teil F. Beratung und Betreuung. Studieneingangsphase. Berlin: DUZ Verlags- und Medienhaus, S. 71–102.
Bourdieu, Pierre (1992): Ökonomisches, kulturelles und soziales Kapital. In: Bourdieu, P. (Hrsg.): Die verborgenen Mechanismen der Macht. Hamburg, S. 49–75.
Bowl, Marion (2001): Experiencing the barriers. Non-traditional students entering higher education. In: Research Papers in Education 16, 2, S. 141–160.
Boxenbaum, Eva (2006): Lost in translation. The making of Danish diversity management. In: American Behavioral Scientist 49, 7, S. 939–948.
Boxenbaum, Eva/Jonsson, Stefan (2008): Isomorphism, diffusion and decoupling. In: Greenwood, R. et al. (Hrsg.): The SAGE handbook of organizational institutionalism. Los Angeles, London: SAGE, S. 78–98.
Boxenbaum, Eva/Jonsson, Stefan (2017): Isomorphism, diffusion and decoupling: Concept evolution and theoretical challenges. In: Greenwood, R. et al. (Hrsg.): The SAGE handbook of organizational institutionalism: Sage Publications, S. 79–104.
Boxenbaum, Eva/Strandgaard Pedersen, Jesper (2009): Scandinavian institutionalism - a case of institutional work. In: Lawrence, T. B./Suddaby, R./Leca, B. (Hrsg.): Institutional work. Actors and agency in institutional studies of organizations. New York: Cambridge University Press, S. 178–204.
Braun, Dietmar/Merrien, F. X. (1999): Towards a new model of governance for universities? A comparative view. London: Jessica Kingsley.
Brunner, Stefanie et al. (2015): Blended counselling: Konzeption eines Online-Beratungsportals für beruflich qualifizierte Studieninteressierte. In: Freitag, W. K. et al. (Hrsg.): Übergänge gestalten. Durchlässigkeit zwischen beruflicher und hochschulischer Bildung erhöhen. Münster: Waxmann, S. 31–48.
Brunsson, Nils (1986): Organizing for inconsistencies: On organizational conflict, depression and hypocrisy as substitutes for action. In: Scandinavian Journal of Management Studies 2, 3-4, S. 165–185.

Brunsson, Nils (1989): The organization of hypocrisy. Talk decisions and actions in organizations. Chichester: Wiley.

Brunsson, Nils/Olsen, Johan P. (1993): The reforming organization. London, New York: Routledge.

Brunsson, Nils/Sahlin-Andersson, Kerstin (2000): Constructing organizations: The example of public sector reform. In: Organization Studies 21, 4, S. 721–746.

Bülow-Schramm, Margret (2016): Expansion, Differenzierung und Selektion im Hochschulsystem: DIe Illusion der heterogenen Hochschule. Zum Widerspruch von Heterogenität und Homogenität. In: Lange-Vester, A./Sander, T. (Hrsg.): Soziale Ungleichheiten, Milieus und Habitus im Hochschulstudium. Weinheim: Beltz Juventa, S. 49–69.

Burrell, Gibson/Morgan, Gareth (1979): Sociological paradigms and organisational analysis. Elements of the eociology of corporate life. Hants, Burlington: Ashgate Publishing Company.

Buß, Imke (2010): Diversity management in deutschen Hochschulen. Die Auswirkungen von Diversität auf Bildungsprozesse. In: Jent, N./Günther, V./Krause, F. (Hrsg.): Zur Verbreitung von Diversity Management. München, Mering: Rainer Hampp Verlag, S. 117–197.

Buß, Imke/Erbsland, M./Rahn, P. (2018): Eine Einführung in die Öffnung von Hochschulen: Impulse zur Weiterentwicklung von Studienangeboten. In: Buß, I. et al. (Hrsg.): Öffnung von Hochschulen. Impulse zur Weiterentwicklung von Studienangeboten. Wiesbaden: Springer VS, S. 11–29.

Charmaz, Kathy (2011): Grounded theory methods in social justice research. In: Denzin, N. K./Lincoln, Y. S. (Hrsg.): The SAGE handbook of qualitative research. Thousand Oaks, London, New Delhi, Singapore: Sage Publications, S. 359–380.

Cho, Ji Young/Lee, Eun Hee (2014): Reducing confusion about grounded theory and qualitative content analysis: Similarities and differences. In: The Qualitative Report 19, 32, S. 1–20.

Clancy, Patrick/Goastellec, Gaële (2007): Exploring access and equity in higher education: Policy and performance in a comparative perspective. In: Higher Education Quarterly 61, 2, S. 136–154.

Clark, Burton R. (1972): The organizational saga in higher education. In: Administrative Science Quarterly 17, 2, S. 178–184.

Clark, Burton R. (1983): The higher education system. Academic organization in cross-national perspective. Berkeley, Los Angeles, London: University of California Press.

Cohen, Michael D./March, James G. (1974): Leadership and ambiguity: The American college president.

Cohen, Michael D./March, James G./Olsen, Johan P. (1972): A garbage can model of organizational choice. In: Administrative Science Quarterly 17, 1, S. 1–25.

Corbin, Juliet/Strauss, Anselm (1990): Grounded theory research: Procedures, canons, and evaluative criteria. In: Qualitative Sociology 13, 1, S. 3–21.

Czarniawska, Barbara (1992): Exploring complex organizations. A cultural perspective. Newbury Park: Sage Publications.

Czarniawska, Barbara (1998): A narrative approach to organization studies. Qualitative Research Methods, Volume 43. Thousand Oaks: Sage Publications.

Czarniawska, Barbara (2000): The Uses of Narrative in Organization Research. GRI Report.
Czarniawska, Barbara (2005): Karl Weick. Concepts, style and reflection. In: The Sociological Review 53, S. 267–278.
Czarniawska, Barbara (2008): A theory of organizing. Cheltenham, Northampton: Edward Elgar.
Czarniawska, Barbara (2009): Emerging institutions: Pyramids or anthills? In: Organization Studies 30, 4, S. 423–441.
Czarniawska, Barbara (2010): The uses of narratology in social and policy studies. In: Critical Policy Studies 4, 1, S. 58–76.
Czarniawska, Barbara/Joerges, Bernward (1996): Travels of ideas. In: Czarniawska, B./Sevón, G. (Hrsg.): Translating organizational change. Berlin, New York: de Gruyter, S. 13–48.
Czarniawska, Barbara/Sevón, Guje (1996a): Introduction. In: Czarniawska, B./Sevón, G. (Hrsg.): Translating organizational change. Berlin, New York: de Gruyter, S. 1–12.
Czarniawska, Barbara/Sevón, Guje (Hrsg.) (1996b): Translating organizational change. Berlin, New York: de Gruyter.
Dahrendorf, Ralf (1966): Bildung ist Bürgerrecht. Hamburg: Nannen-Verlag.
Dass, Pashotam/Parker, Barbara (1999): Strategies for managing human resource diversity. From resistance to learning. In: The Academy of Management Executive 13, 2, S. 68–80.
Davies, Pat (2003): Widening participation and the European Union: Direct action — indirect policy? In: European Journal of Education 38, 1, S. 99–116.
de Boer, Harry/Enders, Jürgen/Schimank, Uwe (2007): On the way towards new public management? The governance of university systems in England, the Netherlands, Austria, and Germany. In: Jansen, D. (Hrsg.): New forms of governance in research organizations: Dordrecht, S. 137–154.
de Boer, Harry/Enders, Jürgen/Schimank, Uwe (2008): Comparing higher education governance systems in four European countries. In: Soguel, N. C./Jaccard, P. (Hrsg.): Governance and performance of education systems. Wiesbaden: Springer VS, S. 35–54.
Dee, Jay R. (2016): Universities, teaching, and learning. In: Leisyte, L./Wilkesmann, U. (Hrsg.): Organizing academic work in higher education. Teaching, learning, and identities. London, New York: Routledge, S. 13–32.
Dee, Jay R./Leisyte, Liudvika (2016): Organizational learning in higher education institutions: Theories, frameworks, and a potential research agenda. In: Paulsen, M. B. (Hrsg.): Higher education: Handbook of theory and research, Band 31. [Cham]: Springer.
Deming, W. Edwards (1986): Out of the crisis. Cambridge: MIT Press.
Denzin, Norman K. (1970): The research act. Chicago: Aldine.
Denzin, Norman K./Lincoln, Yvonna S. (2011): Introduction. The discipline and practice of qualitative resarch. In: Denzin, N. K./Lincoln, Y. S. (Hrsg.): The SAGE handbook of qualitative research. Thousand Oaks, London, New Delhi, Singapore: Sage Publications, S. 1–19.

Deutscher Bundestag (2006): Die Lissabon-Strategie. Ausarbeitung. Wissenschaftliche Dienste.

DFG (2020): DFG Funding Atlas 2018. Key indicators for publicly funded research in Germany.

DiMaggio, Paul J./Powell, Walter W. (1983): The iron cage revisited: Institutional isomorphism and collective rationality in organizational fields. In: American Sociological Review 48, 2, S. 147–160.

Ditzel, Benjamin/Lust, M./Scheytt, Tobias (2016): Das Begleitforschungsprojekt WirQung. In: HAW Hamburg (Hrsg.): Lehre Lotsen 2011 - 2016: Erste Förderphase. Dialogorientierte Qualitätsentwicklung für Lehre und Studium an der Hochschule für Angewandte Wissenschaften Hamburg. Hamburg: HAW Hamburg, S. 106–108.

Djelic, Marie-Laure/Sahlin-Andersson, Kerstin (2006): Transnational governance. Institutional dynamics of regulation. Cambridge: Cambridge University Press.

Döring, Leif (2018): Unterschiede von Studierenden als Herausforderung betrachten. In: Forschung & Lehre 25, 8.

Duden (2019a): Diversität. https://www.duden.de/rechtschreibung/Diversitaet [Zugriff: 09.11.2019].

Duden (2019b): heterogen. https://www.duden.de/rechtschreibung/heterogen [Zugriff: 09.11.2019].

Duong, Sindy/Püttmann, Vitus (2014): Studieren ohne Abitur: Stillstand oder Fortentwicklung? Eine Analyse der aktuellen Rahmenbedingungen und Daten. CHE Arbeitspapier, AP 177. Gütersloh: Centrum für Hochschulentwicklung gGmbH.

Emirbayer, Mustafa/Mische, Ann (1998): What Is agency? In: American Journal of Sociology 103, 4, S. 962–1023.

Enders, Jürgen/de Boer, Harry/Leisyte, Liudvika (2008): On striking the right notes: Shifts in governance and the organisational transformation of universities. In: Amaral, A./Bleiklie, I./Musselin, C. (Hrsg.): From governance to identity. A festschrift for Mary Henkel. Higher Education Dynamics, Band 24. Dordecht: Springer, S. 113–129.

Enders, Jürgen/Teichler, Ulrich (1995): Berufsbild der Lehrenden und Forschenden an Hochschulen: Ergebnisse einer Befragung des wissenschaftlichen Personals an westdeutschen Hochschulen. Bonn: Bundesministerium für Bildung und Wissenschaft.

Euler, Dieter/Seufert, Sabine (2005): Change Management in der Hochschullehre: Die nachhaltige Implementierung von e-Learning-Innovationen. In: ZFHD, 3, 3-15.

Eurydice (2011): Modernisation of higher education in Europe: Funding and the social dimension 2011. Brussels: Eurydice.

Eurydice (2019): The education system in the Federal Republic of Germany 2016/2017. A description of the responsibilities, structures and developments in education policy for the exchange of information in Europe.

Fairclough, N. (1993): Critical discourse analysis and the marketization of public discourse: The universities. In: Discourse & Society 4, 2, S. 133–168.

Feldman, M. S. et al. (2004): Making sense of stories. A rhetorical approach to narrative analysis. In: Journal of Public Administration Research and Theory 14, 2, S. 147–170.

Flick, Uwe (2004): Triangulation in qualitative research. In: Flick, U./von Kardoff, E./Steinke, I. (Hrsg.): A companion to qualitative research. London, Thousand Oaks, New Delhi: Sage Publications, S. 178–183.

Flick, Uwe (2014): Gütekriterien qualitativer Sozialforschung. In: Baur, N./Blasius, J. (Hrsg.): Handbuch Methoden der empirischen Sozialforschung. Wiesbaden: Springer Fachmedien Wiesbaden, 411-423.

Fligstein, Niel (1997): Social Skill and Institutional Theory. In: American Behavioral Scientist 40, 4, S. 397–405.

Fligstein, Niel (2001): Social skill and the theory of fields. In: Sociological Theory 19, 2, S. 105–125.

Flyvbjerg, Bent (2011): Case study. In: Denzin, N. K./Lincoln, Y. S. (Hrsg.): The SAGE handbook of qualitative research. Thousand Oaks, London, New Delhi, Singapore: Sage Publications, S. 301–316.

Foskett, Nick (2002): Marketing imperative or cultural challenge? embedding widening participation in the further education sector. In: Research in Post-Compulsory Education 7, 1, S. 79–95.

Freitag, Walburga Katharina (2012): Zweiter und Dritter Bildungsweg in die Hochschule. Arbeitspapier 253. Bildung und Qualifizierung. Düsseldorf.

Freitag, Walburga Katharina et al. (Hrsg.) (2015): Übergänge gestalten. Durchlässigkeit zwischen beruflicher und hochschulischer Bildung erhöhen. Münster: Waxmann.

Fumasoli, Tatiana/Stensaker, Bjørn (2013): Organizational studies in higher education. A reflection on historical themes and prospective trends. In: Higher Education Policy 26, 4, S. 479–496.

Gaisch, Martina/Aichinger, Regina/Preymann, Silke (2017): Diversitätsparadigmen neu gedacht: Schnittmengen zwischen hochschulischer Vielfalt und unternehmerischer Sinnwelten. Forschungsforum der Österreichischen Fachhochschulen. IMC FH Krems, Österreich.

Geißler, Rainer (2005): Die Metamorphose der Arbeitertochter zum Migrantensohn. Zum Wandel der Chancenstruktur im Bildungssystem nach Schicht, Geschlecht, Ethnie und deren Verknüpfungen. In: Berger, P. A./Kahlert, H. (Hrsg.): Institutionalisierte Ungleichheiten. Wie das Bildungswesen Chancen blockiert. Weinheim: Juventa-Verl., S. 71–100.

Giddens, Anthony (1984): The constitution of society. Outline of the theory of structuration. Berkeley, Los Angeles: University of California Press.

Gidley, Jennifer M. et al. (2010): From Access to Success: An Integrated Approach to Quality Higher Education informed by Social Theory and Practice. In: Higher Education Policy 23, 1, S. 123–147.

Glaser, B./Strauss, Anselm (1967): The discovery of grounded theory. Chicago: Aldine.

Glassman, Robert B. (1973): Persistence and loose coupling in living systems. In: Behavioral Science 18, 2, S. 83–98.

Goastellec, Gaële (2008): Globalization and implementation of an equity norm in higher education: Admission processes and funding framework under scrutiny. In: Peabody Journal of Education 83, 1, S. 71–85.

Goastellec, Gaële (2012): The Europeanisation of the measurement of diversity in education. A soft instrument of public policy. In: Globalisation, Societies and Education 10, 4, S. 493–506.

Gorard, Stephen/Smith, Emma (2006): Review of widening participation research: Addressing the barriers to participation in higher education. A report to HEFCE by the University of York, Higher Education Academy and Institute for Access Studies.

Gornitzka, Åse (1999): Governmental policies and organisational change in higher education. In: Higher Education 38, 1, S. 5–31.

Gornitzka, Åse/Maassen, Peter (2000): The economy, higher education, and European integration: An introduction. In: Higher Education Policy, 13, S. 217–223.

Graham, Claire Louise (2010): Institutional commitment to widening participation: Mission, rhetoric and framing. Unpublished doctoral dissertation: University of Birmingham.

Graham, Claire Louise (2013): Discourses of widening participation in the prospectus documents and websites of six English higher education institutions. In: British Journal of Sociology of Education 34, 1, S. 76–93.

Greenbank, Paul (2006): Widening participation in higher education. An examination of the factors influencing institutional policy. In: Research in Post-Compulsory Education 11, 2, S. 199–215.

Greenbank, Paul (2007): Introducing widening participation policies in higher education. The influence of institutional culture. In: Research in Post-Compulsory Education 12, 2, S. 209–224.

Greenwood, Royston et al. (2008): Introduction. In: Greenwood, R. et al. (Hrsg.): The SAGE handbook of organizational institutionalism. Los Angeles, London: SAGE, S. 1–46.

Greenwood, Royston et al. (2011): Institutional complexity and organizational responses. In: The Academy of Management Annals 5, 1, S. 317–371.

Hall, Richard H./Tolbert, Pamela S. (2005): Organizations. Structures, processes, and outcomes. Upper Saddle River, NJ: Prentice Hall.

Hanft, Anke (2012): Lebenslanges Lernen an Hochschulen - Strukturelle und organisatorische Voraussetzungen. In: Hanft, A./Brinkmann, K. (Hrsg.): Offene Hochschulen. Die Neuausrichtung der Hochschulen auf Lebenslanges Lernen. Münster: Waxmann, S. 13–52.

Hanft, Anke (2015): Heterogene Studierende – homogene Studienstrukturen. In: Hanft, A./Zawacki-Richter, O./Gierke, W. B. (Hrsg.): Herausforderung Heterogenität beim Übergang in die Hochschule. Münster, New York: Waxmann, S. 13–28.

Hanft, Anke/Brinkmann, Katrin (Hrsg.) (2012): Offene Hochschulen. Die Neuausrichtung der Hochschulen auf Lebenslanges Lernen. Münster: Waxmann.

Hanft, Anke/Kretschmer, Stefanie (2014): Studiengestaltung und -organisation für heterogene Studierende. In: Das Hochschulwesen 62, 3, S. 74–80.

Hanft, Anke/Zawacki-Richter, Olaf/Gierke, Willi B. (Hrsg.) (2015): Herausforderung Heterogenität beim Übergang in die Hochschule. Münster, New York: Waxmann.

Harris-Hümmert, Susan/Mitterauer, Lukas/Pohlenz, Philipp (Hrsg.) (2015): Heterogenität der Studierenden: Herausforderung für die Qualitätsentwicklung in

Studium und Lehre, neuer Fokus für die Evaluation? Qualität - Evaluation - Akkreditierung, Band 8. Bielefeld: UVW UniversitätsVerlag Webler.

Hasse, Raimund/Krücken, Georg (1999): Neo-Institutionalismus. Bielefeld: Transcript Verlag.

Hauschildt, Kristina/Vögtle, Eva Maria/Gwosc, Christoph (2018): Social and economic conditions of student life in Europe. Eurostudent VI 2016-2018 | Synopsis of Indicators: W. Bertelsmann Verlag GmbH & Co. KG.

HAW Hamburg (2020): HAW Hamburg A-Z. Organisational units from A-Z. https://www.haw-hamburg.de/en/university/haw-hamburg-a-z/.

Heide-von-Scheven, Bernd/Brauns, Frauke/Beuter, Friederike (2015): Blended guiding und virtuelle Kurse - Studienorientierung für beruflich Qualifizierte an der FH der Diakonie. In: Freitag, W. K. et al. (Hrsg.): Übergänge gestalten. Durchlässigkeit zwischen beruflicher und hochschulischer Bildung erhöhen. Münster: Waxmann, S. 93–116.

Heublein, Ulrich et al. (2017): Zwischen Studienerwartungen und Studienwirklichkeit. Ursachen des Studienabbruchs, beruflicher Verbleib der Studienabbrecherinnen und Studienabbrecher und Entwicklung der Studienabbruchquote an deutschen Hochschulen. Forum Hochschule.

Holland, Natalie et al. (2017): Accessing and assessing appropriate widening participation data. An exploration of how data are used and by whom. In: Studies in Continuing Education 39, 2, S. 214–233.

Holmegaard, Henriette Tolstrup/Madsen, Lene Møller/Ulriksen, Lars (2017): Why should European higher education care about the retention of non-traditional students? In: European Educational Research Journal 16, 1, S. 3–11.

HRK (2008): Für eine Reform der Lehre in den Hochschulen. Mitgliederversammlung der HRK vom 22.04.2008.

Hüther, Otto/Krücken, Georg (2016): Hochschulen. Fragestellungen, Ergebnisse und Perspektiven der sozialwissenschaftlichen Hochschulforschung. Organization & Public Management. Wiesbaden: Springer VS.

Hüther, Otto/Krücken, Georg (2018): Higher education in Germany. Recent developments in an international perspective. Higher Education Dynamics, Band 49. Wiesbaden: Springer.

Jones, Robert/Thomas, Liz (2005): The 2003 UK government higher education white paper. A critical assessment of its implications for the access and widening participation agenda. In: Journal of Education Policy 20, 5, S. 615–630.

Jungblut, Jens/Jungblut, Marc (2016): All different? All equal? Differentiation of universities' mission statements and excellence initiatives in Germany. In: Science and Public Policy 4, 44, 535-545.

Kehm, Barbara M. (2000): Die Funktionserweiterung der Hochschulen durch lebenslanges Lernen. Reaktionen angesichts hochkomplexer Erwartungen. In: Kehm, B. M./Pasternack, P. (Hrsg.): Hochschulentwicklung als Komplexitätsproblem. Fallstudien des Wandels: BELTZ - Deutscher Studien Verlag, S. 122–143.

Kehm, Barbara M. (2010): The German system of accreditation. In: Dill, D. D./Beerkens, M. (Hrsg.): Public policy for academic quality. Analyses of innovative policy instruments. Higher Education Dynamics, Band 30. Dordrecht: Springer, S. 227–248.

Kehm, Barbara M. (2012): Hochschulen als besondere und unvollständige Organisationen? - Neue Theorien zur ‚Organisation Hochschule'. In: Wilkesmann, U./Schmid, C. J. (Hrsg.): Hochschule als Organisation. Wiesbaden: VS Verlag für Sozialwissenschaften, S. 17–25.

Keller, Reiner (2009): Das interpretative Paradigma. In: Brock, D. et al. (Hrsg.): Soziologische Paradigmen nach Talcott Parsons. Eine Einführung. 1. Auflage. Wiesbaden: VS Verlag für Sozialwissenschaften, S. 17–126.

Kerres, Michael/Hanft, Anke/Wilkesmann, Uwe (2012): Implikationen einer konsequenten Öffnung der Hochschule für lebenslanges Lernen - eine Schlussbetrachtung. In: Kerres, M. et al. (Hrsg.): Studium 2020. Positionen und Perspektiven zum lebenslangen Lernen an Hochschulen. Münster: Waxmann, S. 285–290.

Kezar, Adrianna (2014): How colleges change. Understanding, leading and enacting change. New York: Routledge.

Kezar, Adrianna/Eckel, Peter D. (2002): The effect of institutional culture on change strategies in higher education: Universal principles or culturally responsive concepts? In: The Journal of Higher Education 73, 4, S. 435–460.

Kift, Sally (2009): Articulating a transition pedagogy to scaffold and to enhance the first year student learning experience in Australian higher education. Final Report for ALTC Senior Fellowship Program. Queensland: Australian Learning and Teaching Council.

Kift, Sally/Nelson, Karen/Clarke, John (2010): Transition pedagogy: A third generation approach to FYE - A case study of policy and practice for the higher education sector. In: The International Journal of the First Year in Higher Education 1, 1, S. 1–20.

Kirkpatrick, Ian et al. (2013): The translation of hospital management models in European health systems. A framework for comparison. In: British Journal of Management 24, 48-61.

Kleimann, Bernd/Hückstädt, Malte (2018): Auswahlkriterien in Berufungsverfahren: Universitäten und Fachhochschulen im Vergleich. In: Beiträge zur Hochschulforschung 40, 2, 20-46.

Klein, Uta/Daniela, Heitzmann (Hrsg.) (2012): Hochschule und Diversity. Theoretische Zugänge und empirische Bestandsaufnahme. Weinheim, Basel: Beltz Juventa.

Kluge, N. et al. (1981): Gesamthochschule Kassel 1919-1981. Rückblick auf das erste Jahrzehnt, Kassel. Kassel: Stauda.

KMK (2019): The Standing Conference of the Ministers of Education and Cultural Affairs. https://www.kmk.org/kmk/information-in-english/standing-conference.html.

KMK/BMBF (2010): Nationale Strategien zur Sozialen Dimension des Bologna-Prozesses.

KMK/BMBF (2015): Die Umsetzung der Ziele des Bologna-Prozesses 2012-2015. Nationaler Bericht von Kultusministerkonferenz und Bundesministerium für Bildung und Forschung.

Knauf, Helen (2016): Heterogenität – ein umfassendes Projekt für Hochschulen und Hochschulentwicklung. In: Brahm, T./Jenert, T./Euler, D. (Hrsg.): Pädagogische Hochschulentwicklung. Von der Programmatik zur Implementierung. Wiesbaden: Springer VS, S. 325–336.

Kosmützky, Anna (2012): Between mission and market position. Empirical findings on mission statements of German higher education institutions. In: Tertiary Education and Management 18, 1, S. 57–77.

Kosmützky, Anna/Krücken, Georg (2015): Sameness and difference. Analyzing institutional and organizational specificities of universities through mission statements. In: International Studies of Management & Organization 45, 2, S. 137–149.

Kraatz, Matthew S./Zajac, Edward J. (1996): Exploring the limits of the new institutionalism: The causes and consequences of illegitimate organizational change. In: American Sociological Review 61, 5, S. 812–836.

Kreft, Anne-Kathrin/Leichsenring, Hannah (2012): Studienrelevante Diversität in der Lehre. In: Klein, U./Daniela, H. (Hrsg.): Hochschule und Diversity. Theoretische Zugänge und empirische Bestandsaufnahme. Weinheim, Basel: Beltz Juventa, S. 145–163.

Krell, Gertraude (2008): Diversity Management: Chancengleichheit für alle und auch als Wettbewerbsfaktor. In: Krell, G. (Hrsg.): Chancengleichheit durch Personalpolitik. Wiesbaden: Gabler, S. 63–80.

Krücken, Georg/Meier, Frank (2006): Turning the university into an organizational actor. In: Drori, G./Meyer, J. W./Hwang, H. (Hrsg.): Globalization and organization: World society and organizational change. Oxford: Oxford University Press, S. 241–257.

Krücken, Georg/Röbken, Heinke (2009): Neo-institutionalistische Hochschulforschung. In: Koch, S./Schemmann, M. (Hrsg.): Neo-Institutionalismus in der Erziehungswissenschaft: Grundlegende Texte und empirische Studien. Wiesbaden: Springer VS, 326-346.

Kühl, Stefan (2010): Der Sudoku-Effekt. Zu den Gründen und Folgen der Komplexitätssteigerung an den Hochschulen. In: Soziale Systeme 16, 2, S. 444–460.

Ladenthin, Volker (2018): Da läuft etwas ganz schief. In: Forschung & Lehre 25, 8.

Lamb, Peter/Currie, Graeme (2011): Eclipsing adaptation: The translation of the US MBA model in China. In: Management Learning 43, 2, S. 217–230.

Lawrence, Thomas B./Suddaby, Roy/Leca, Bernard (2009): Introduction: Theorizing and studying institutional work. In: Lawrence, T. B./Suddaby, R./Leca, B. (Hrsg.): Institutional work. Actors and agency in institutional studies of organizations. New York: Cambridge University Press, S. 1–27.

Leicht-Scholten, Carmen (2011): Hochschule öffne dich: Wie Vielfalt und Chancengerechtigkeit Hochschulen stärken. In: Öffnung der Hochschule. Chancengerechtigkeit, Diversität, Integration. Dossier, S. 38–43.

Leisyte, Liudvika (2016): Bridging the duality between universities and the academic profession: a tale of protected spaces, strategic gaming, and institutional entrepreneurs. In: Leisyte, L./Wilkesmann, U. (Hrsg.): Organizing academic work in higher education. Teaching, learning, and identities. London, New York: Routledge, S. 55–67.

Leisyte, Liudvika/Enders, Jürgen/de Boer, Harry (2009): The balance between teaching and research in Dutch and English universities in the context of university governance reforms. In: Higher Education 58, 5, S. 619–635.

Levi-Faur, David/Jordana, Jacint (2016): The rise of regulatory capitalism. The global diffusion of a new order. In: The ANNALS of the American Academy of Political and Social Science 598, 1, S. 200–217.

Levy, D. C. (2006): How private higher educations's growth challenges the new institutionalism. In: Meyer, H.-D./Rowan, B. (Hrsg.): The new institutionalism in education. Albany: State University of New York Press, S. 143–162.

Lewis, Ben (2002): Widening participation in higher education: The HEFCE perspective on policy and progress. In: Higher Education Quarterly 56, 2, S. 204–2019.

Lincoln, Yvonna S./Lynham, Susan A./Guba, Egon G. (2011): Paradigmatic controversies, contradictions, and emerging confluences, revisited. In: Denzin, N. K./Lincoln, Y. S. (Hrsg.): The SAGE handbook of qualitative research. Thousand Oaks, London, New Delhi, Singapore: Sage Publications, S. 97–128.

Maguire, Steve/Hardy, Cynthia/Lawrence, Thomas B. (2004): Institutional entrepreneurship in emerging fields: HIV/AIDS treatment advocacy in Canada. In: Academy of Management Journal 47, 5, S. 657–679.

Mampaey, Jelle (2018): Are higher education institutions trapped in conformity? A translation perspective. In: Studies in Higher Education 43, 7, S. 1241–1253.

Mangold, Werner (1960): Gegenstand und Methode des Gruppendiskussionsverfahrens. Frankfurter Beiträge zur Soziologie, Band 9. Frankfurt am Main: Europäische Verlangsanstalt.

Manning, Kathleen (2013): Organizational theory in higher education. New York: Routledge.

March, James G./Olsen, Johan P. (1984): The new institutionalism: Organizational factors in political life. In: The American Political Science Review 78, 3, S. 734–749.

March, James G./Olsen, Johan P. (1989): Rediscovering institutions. The organizational basis of politics. New York, NY: Free Press.

Marginson, Simon (2016): The worldwide trend to high participation higher education. Dynamics of social stratification in inclusive systems. In: Higher Education 72, 4, S. 413–434.

Mazza, Carmelo/Sahlin-Andersson, Kerstin/Pedersen, Jesper Strandgaard (2016): European constructions of an American model. In: Management Learning 36, 4, S. 471–491.

McCaig, Colin (2015): Marketisation and widening participation in English higher education: A critical discourse analysis of institutional access policy documents. In: Higher Education Review 48, 1, S. 6–24.

McCaig, Colin (2018): English higher education: Widening participation and the historical context for system differentiation. In: Bowl, M./McCaig, C./Hughes, J. (Hrsg.): Equality and differentiation in marketised higher education. A new level: Springer International Publishing, S. 51–72.

McCowan, Tristan (2016): Three dimensions of equity of access to higher education. In: Compare: A Journal of Comparative and International Education 46, 4, S. 645–665.

McInnis, Craig (2003): New realities of the student experience: How should universities respond? Conference paper. Financial Review Higher Education Summit. Sydney, Australia.

Meier, Frank (2010): Die gemanagte Universität – Zum Organisationswandel der Hochschule. Working paper. Bremen.

Meier, Frank/Schimank, Uwe (2009): Matthäus schlägt Humboldt? New Public Management und die Einheit von Forschung und Lehre. In: Beiträge zur Hochschulforschung 31, 1, S. 42–61.

Meier, Stefan/Pentzold, Christian (2010): Theoretical sampling als Auswahlstrategie für Online-Inhaltsanalysen. In: Die Online-Inhaltsanalyse, S. 124–143.

Mergner, Julia/Bosse, Elke (2018): Parallelen und Unterschiede im Umgang mit der politischen Forderung nach Öffnung der Hochschulen am Beispiel des Qualitätspakt Lehre. In: Buß, I. et al. (Hrsg.): Öffnung von Hochschulen. Impulse zur Weiterentwicklung von Studienangeboten. Wiesbaden: Springer VS, S. 55–83.

Mergner, Julia/Leisyte, Liudvika/Bosse, Elke (2018): The widening participation agenda in German higher education: Discourses and legitimizing strategies. In: Social Inclusion 6, 4, S. 61–70.

Mergner, Julia/Mishra, Shweta/Orr, Dominic (2017): Changing the mindset: How Germany is trying to combine access and equity. In: Atherton, G. (Hrsg.): Access to higher education. Understanding global inequalities. Palgrave Teaching & Learning. London: Palgrave Macmillan, S. 55–67.

Meuser, Michael/Nagel, Ulrike (2009): The expert interview and changes in knowledge production. In: Bogner, A./Littig, B./Menz, W. (Hrsg.): Interviewing experts. Research methods series. London: Palgrave Macmillan, S. 17–42.

Meyer, John W. (1996): Otherhood: The promulgation and transmission of ideas in the modern organizational environment. In: Czarniawska, B./Sevón, G. (Hrsg.): Translating organizational change. Berlin, New York: de Gruyter, S. 241–252.

Meyer, John W./Rowan, Brian (1977): Institutionalized organizations: Formal structures as myth and ceremony. In: American Journal of Sociology 83, 2, S. 340–363.

Meyer, John W./Scott, W. Richard (1983): Organizational environments: Ritual and rationality. London: SAGE.

Middendorff, Elke et al. (2013): Die wirtschaftliche und soziale Lage der Studierenden in Deutschland 2012. 20. Sozialerhebung des Deutschen Studentenwerks.

Middendorff, Elke (2015): Wachsende Heterogenität unter Studierenden? Empirische Befunde zur Prüfung eines postulierten Trends. In: Banscherus, U. et al. (Hrsg.): Differenzierung im Hochschulsystem. Nationale und internationale Entwicklungen und Herausforderungen. Münster: Waxmann Verlag, S. 261–278.

Middendorff, Elke et al. (2017a): Die wirtschaftliche und soziale Lage der Studierenden in Deutschland 2016 - 21. Sozialerhebung des Deutschen Studentenwerks durchgeführt vom Deutschen Zentrum für Hochschul- und Wissenschaftsforschung. Berlin.

Middendorff, Elke et al. (2017b): The economic and social situation of students in Germany 2016. Summary of the 21st Social Survey of Deutsches Studentenwerk, conducted by the -German Centre for Higher Education Research and Science Studies (DZHW). Berlin.

Mintzberg, Henry (1979): The Structuring of Organizations: Prentice Hall.

Mintzberg, Henry (1983): Power in and around organizations. New Jersey: Prentice Hall, Englewood Cliffs.

Mooraj, Margrit/Wiese, Mina (2013): Vielfalt gestalten und Chancen nutzen. Diversität in Studium und Lehre. Projekt nexus - Konezpte und gute Praxis für Studium und Lehre. nexus Impulse für die Praxis.

Mooraj, Margrit/Zervakis, Peter A. (2014): Der Umgang mit studentischer Heterogenität in Studium und Lehre. Chancen, Herausforderungen, Strategien und gelungene Praxisansätze aus den Hochschulen. In: Zeitschrift für Inklusion.

Morphew, Christopher C./Hartley, Matthew (2006): Mission statements: A thematic analysis of rhetoric across institutional type. In: The Journal of Higher Education 77, 3, S. 456–471.

Morphew, Christopher C./Huisman, Jeroen (2002): Using institutional theory to reframe research on academic drift. In: Higher Education in Europe 27, 4, S. 491–506.

Mörth, Ulrika (2005): Soft law and new modes of EU governance – A democratic problem? Conference paper. Darmstadt.

Mueller, F./Whittle, A. (2011): Translating management ideas: A discursive devices analysis. In: Organization Studies 32, 2, S. 187–210.

Musselin, Christine (2006): Are universities specific organisations? In: Krücken, G./Kosmützky, A./Torka, M. (Hrsg.): Towards a multiversity? Universities between global trends and national traditions. Bielefeld: Transcript Verlag, S. 63–84.

Mussmann, J. G. (1832): Vorlesungen über das Studium der Wissenschaften und Künste auf der Universität. Ein Taschenbuch für angehende Studierende. Halle: Ruff.

Offenberger, Ursula/Nentwich, Julia (2017): Chancengleichheit, Translation und Interpretative Repertoires - die Übersetzung des Bundesprogramms Chancengleichheit an einer Schweizer Universität oder: ein Tanzkurs für Elefanten im Raum. In: Funder, M. (Hrsg.): Neo-Institutionalismus - Revisited: Bilanz und Weiterentwicklungen aus Sicht der Geschlechterforschung. Arbeit, Organisation und Geschlecht in Wirtschaft und Gesellschaft, Band 6. Baden-Baden: Nomos, S. 307–338.

Oliver, Christine (1991): Strategic responses to institutional processes. In: Academy of Management Review 16, 1, S. 145–179.

O'Meara, KerryAnn (2007): Striving for what? Exploring the pursuit of prestige. In: Smart, J. C. (Hrsg.): Higher education: Handbook of theory and research, Band 22. Dordrecht: Springer, S. 121–179.

Orr, Dominic/Gwosc, Christoph/Netz, Nicolai (2011): Social and economic conditions of student life in Europe. Synopsis of indicators | Final report | Eurostudent IV 2008–2011.

Orr, Dominic/Hovdhaugen, Elisabeth (2014): 'Second chance' routes into higher education. Sweden, Norway and Germany compared. In: International Journal of Lifelong Education 33, 1, S. 45–61.
Osborne, Michael (2003a): Increasing or widening participation in higher education? - A European overview. In: European Journal of Education 38, 1, S. 5–24.
Osborne, Michael (2003b): Policy and practice in widening participation. A six country comparative study of access as flexibility. In: International Journal of Lifelong Education 22, 1, S. 43–58.
Palmer, Donald/Biggart, Nicole/Dick, Brian (2008): Is the new institutionalism a theory? In: Greenwood, R. et al. (Hrsg.): The SAGE handbook of organizational institutionalism. Los Angeles, London: SAGE, S. 739–768.
Paradeise, Catherine/Reale, Emanuela/Goastellec, Gaële (2009): A comparative approach to higher education reforms in Western European countries. In: Paradeise, C. et al. (Hrsg.): University governance. Western European comparative perspective. Higher Education Dynamics, Band 25. London: Springer Science + Business Media B.V., S. 197–226.
Pasternack, Peer (2013): Hochschulen in peripherer Metropolregion. Der Fall Mitteldeutschland: SWOT-Analyse. In: Pasternack, P. (Hrsg.): Jenseits der Metropolen. Hochschulen in demografisch herausgeforderten Regionen. Leipzig: Akademische Verlagsanstalt, S. 320–338.
Pasternack, Peer/Kehm, Barbara M. (2000): Angemessen komplex? Zum Verhältnis von Hochschulproblemen und Hochschulreformen. In: Kehm, B. M./Pasternack, P. (Hrsg.): Hochschulentwicklung als Komplexitätsproblem. Fallstudien des Wandels: BELTZ - Deutscher Studien Verlag, S. 13–30.
Pfeffer, Jeffrey/Salancik, Gerald R. (1978): The external control of organizations. A resource dependence perspective. New York: Harper & Row.
Phillips, Nelson/Lawrence, Thomas B./Hardy, Cynthia (2004): Discourse and institutions. In: Academy of Management Review 29, 4, S. 635–652.
Power, Michael (2000): The audit society - second thoughts. In: International Journal of Auditing 4, 1, S. 111–119.
Przyborski, Aglaja/Riegler, Julia (2010): Gruppendiskussion und Fokusgruppe. In: Mey, G./Mruck, K. (Hrsg.): Handbuch Qualitative Forschung in der Psychologie. 1. Auflage. Wiesbaden: VS Verlag für Sozialwissenschaften, S. 436–448.
Przyborski, Aglaja/Wohlrab-Sahr, Monika (2013): Qualitative Sozialforschung. Ein Arbeitsbuch. 4. Auflage. München, München: Oldenbourg Verlag.
Read, B./Archer, A./Leathwood, Carole (2003): Challenging cultures? Student conceptions of 'belonging' and 'isolation' at a post-1992 university. In: Studies in Higher Education 28, 3, S. 261–277.
Richardson, M./Abraham, C./Bond, R. (2012): Psychological correlates of university students' academic performance: A systematic review and meta-analysis. In: Psychological bulletin 138, 2, S. 353–387.
Riddell, Sheila/Weedon, Elisabet/Holford, John (2014): Lifelong learning and higher education in Europe 1995–2011. Widening and/or narrowing access? In: International Journal of Lifelong Education 33, 1, S. 1–6.
Rogers, E.M (2002): Diffusion of preventive innovations. In: Addictive Behaviors, 27, S. 989–993.

Røvik, Kjell Arne (2011): From fashion to virus. An alternative theory of organizations' handling of management ideas. In: Organization Studies 32, 5, S. 631–653.

Røvik, Kjell Arne (2016): Knowledge transfer as translation. Review and elements of an instrumental theory. In: International Journal of Management Reviews 18, 3, S. 290–310.

Röwert, Ronny et al. (2017): Diversität und Studienerfolg. Studienrelevante Heterogenitätsmerkmale an Universitäten und Fachhochschulen und ihr Einfluss auf den Studienerfolg - eine quantitative Untersuchung. CHE Arbeitspapier.

Sahlin, Kerstin/Wedlin, Linda (2008): Circulating ideas: Imitation, translation and editing. In: Greenwood, R. et al. (Hrsg.): The SAGE handbook of organizational institutionalism. Los Angeles, London: SAGE, S. 218–242.

Sahlin, Kerstin/Wedlin, Linda (2017): The imitation and translation of management ideas. In: Greenwood, R. et al. (Hrsg.): The SAGE handbook of organizational institutionalism: Sage Publications, S. 102–127.

Sahlin-Andersson, Kerstin (1996): Imitating by editing success: The construction of organizational fields. In: Czarniawska, B./Sevón, G. (Hrsg.): Translating organizational change. Berlin, New York: de Gruyter, S. 69–92.

Sandhu, Swaran (2014): Public Relations und gesellschaftliche Kommunikation: Legitimation im Diskurs. In: Zerfaß, A./Piwinger, M. (Hrsg.): Handbuch Unternehmenskommunikation. Strategie Management Wertschöpfung. 2. Aufl. Springer NachschlageWissen. Wiesbaden: Springer Gabler, S. 1161–1183.

Schein, Edgar H. (1990): Organizational Culture. In: American Psychologist 45, 2, S. 109–119.

Scheller, Percy et al. (2013): Studienanfängerinnen und Studienanfänger im Wintersemester 2011/12. HIS: Forum Hochschule.

Schimank, Uwe (2009): Germany: A latecomer to new public management. In: Paradeise, C. et al. (Hrsg.): University governance. Western European comparative perspective. Higher Education Dynamics, Band 25. London: Springer Science + Business Media B.V., S. 51–76.

Schmid, Christian J. (2016): Die soziale Organisiertheit und Organisierbarkeit von Interessen(freiheit) - Der Fall der managerialen Governance akademischer Lehrtätigkeit. Dissertation. Dortmund: Technische Universität Dortmund/Fakultät für Erziehungswissenschaften, Psychologie und Soziologie.

Schmidt, Christiane (2004): The Analysis of Semi-structured Interviews. In: Flick, U./von Kardoff, E./Steinke, I. (Hrsg.): A companion to qualitative research. London, Thousand Oaks, New Delhi: Sage Publications, S. 253–258.

Schreier, Margrit (2014): Qualitative content analysis. In: Flick, U. (Hrsg.): The SAGE handbook of qualitative data analysis. London, Thousand Oaks, Singapore: SAGE, S. 170–183.

Schriewer, Jürgen (2007): "Bologna" - ein neu-europäischer "Mythos"? In: Zeitschrift für Pädagogik 53, 2, S. 182–199.

Schuetze, Hans G./Slowey, Maria (2002): Participation and exclusion: A comparative analysis of non-traditional students and lifelong learners in higher education. In: Higher Education 44, S. 309–327.

Schulmeister, Rolf/Metzger, Christiane/Martens, Thomas (2012): Heterogenität und Studienerfolg. Lehrmethoden für Lerner mit unterschiedlichem Lernverhalten. Paderborner Universitätsreden: Universität Paderborn.
Schulz, André (2009): Strategisches Diversitätsmanagement. Unternehmensführung im Zeitalter der kulturellen Vielfalt. Beiträge zum Diversity-Management. Wiesbaden: Gabler Verlag / GWV Fachverlage GmbH.
Schütz, Alfred (1971): Wissenschaftliche Interpretation und Alltagsverständnis menschlichen Handelns. In: Schütz, A. (Hrsg.): Gesammelte Aufsätze Band 1: Das Problem der sozialen Wirklichkeit. Den Haag: Springer, S. 3–54.
Scott, W. Richard (2004): Reflections on a Half-Century of Organizational Sociology. In: Annual Review of Sociology 30, 1, S. 1–21.
Scott, W. Richard (2010): Reflections: The past and future of research on institutions and institutional change. In: Journal of Change Management 10, 1, S. 5–21.
Scott, W. Richard (2013): Organization Theory and Higher Education. https://cepa.stanford.edu/sites/default/files/Org%20Theory%20and%20Higher%20Ed%2013%20.pdf [Zugriff: 24.04.2016].
Seidel, Susen (2014): Defizitär oder produktiv. Die Heterogenität der Studierenden. In: Die Hochschule 2, 6-21.
Seidel, Susen (2015): Wenn Vielfalt Chance sein soll. Der produktive Umgang mit den Kompetenzen beruflich qualifizierter Studierender in Lehre und Studium. In: Hanft, A./Zawacki-Richter, O./Gierke, W. B. (Hrsg.): Herausforderung Heterogenität beim Übergang in die Hochschule. Münster, New York: Waxmann, S. 69–80.
Seidel, Susen/Wielepp, Franziska (2014): Heterogenität im Hochschulalltag. In: Die Hochschule 2, 156-171.
Senge, Peter M. (1990): The fifth discipline. The art and practice of the learning organization. New York: Currency Doubleday.
Shore, Cris/Wright, Susan (2000): Coercive accountability: The rise of audit culture in higher education. In: Strathern, M. (Hrsg.): Audit cultures. Anthropological studies in accountability, ethics, and the academy. European Association of Social Anthropologists. London, New York: Routledge.
Spanke, Gregor (2017): Europeanization of higher education in Germany. A case study of alternative access routes to higher education in the Free Hanseatic City of Bremen. Master Thesis. Enschede, Münster: University of Twente; Westfälische-Wilhelm-Universität zu Münster.
Spiegler, Thomas/Bednarek, Antje (2013): First-generation students. What we ask, what we know and what it means: an international review of the state of research. In: International Studies in Sociology of Education 23, 4, S. 318–337.
Steinke, Ines (2004): Quality criteria in qualitative research. In: Flick, U./von Kardoff, E./Steinke, I. (Hrsg.): A companion to qualitative research. London, Thousand Oaks, New Delhi: Sage Publications, S. 184–190.
Stensaker, Bjørn (2007): Quality as fashion: Exploring the translation of a management idea into higher education. In: Westerheijden, D. F. (Hrsg.): Quality assurance in higher education. Trends in regulation, translation and transformation. Higher Education Dynamics, Band 20. Dordrecht: Springer, S. 99–118.

Stifterverband (2020): Diversity audit. https://www.stifterverband.org/diversity-audit [Zugriff: 31.01.2021].

Stöter, Joachim (2012): Öffnung der Hochschulen für neue Zielgruppen. In: Hanft, A./Brinkmann, K. (Hrsg.): Offene Hochschulen. Die Neuausrichtung der Hochschulen auf Lebenslanges Lernen. Münster: Waxmann, S. 53–96.

Strauss, Anselm (1998): Grundlagen qualitativer Sozialforschung: Datenanalyse und Theoriebildung in der empirischen soziologischen Forschung. 2. Auflage. Stuttgart: UTB.

Suddaby, Roy/Greenwood, Royston (2005): Rhetorical strategies of legitimacy. In: Administrative Science Quarterly 50, S. 35–67.

Teichler, Ulrich (2003): The future of higher education and the future of higher education research. In: Tertiary Education and Management 9, 3, S. 171–185.

Teichler, Ulrich/Wolter, Andrä (2004): Zugangswege und Studienangebote für nicht-traditionelle Studierende. In: Die Hochschule 2, S. 64–80.

Thomas, David A./Ely, Robin J. (1996): Making differences matter. A new paradigm for managing diversity. In: Harvard Business Review 74, 5, S. 79–90.

Thornton, Patricia H./Ocasio, William (1999): Institutional logics and the historical contingency of power in organizations: Executive succession in the higher education publishing industry, 1958-1990. In: American Journal of Sociology 105, 3, S. 801–843.

Thornton, Patricia H./Ocasio, William (2008): Institutional logics. In: Greenwood, R. et al. (Hrsg.): The SAGE handbook of organizational institutionalism. Los Angeles, London: SAGE, 99-129.

Tierney, William (1988): Organizational culture in higher education: Defining the essentials. In: The Journal of Higher Education 59, 1, S. 2–21.

Tinto, Vincent (2009): Taking student retention seriously: Rethinking the first year of university. Keynote. FYE Curriculum Design Symposium 2009. Brisbane, Australia.

Tolbert, Pamela S./Zucker, Lynne G. (1983): Institutional sources of change in the formal structure of organizations: The diffusion of civil service reform, 1880-1935. In: Administrative Science Quarterly 28, 1, S. 22–39.

Trow, Martin (2005): Reflections on the transition from elite to mass to universal access: Forms and phases of higher education in modern societies since WWII. In: Forest, J. J. F./Altbach, P. G. (Hrsg.): International handbook of higher education. Part one: Global themes and contemporary challenges. Wiesbaden: Springer.

University of Hamburg (2017a): Nachhaltigkeit. Universität der Nachhaltigkeit. https://www.uni-hamburg.de/uhh/profil/leitbild/nachhaltigkeit.html.

University of Hamburg (2017b): Teaching Quality Pact. Bridges to the University - Pathways to Academia. https://www.uni-hamburg.de/en/uhh/profil/leitbild/qualitaetspakt-lehre.html.

Vaara, E./Tienari, J. (2008): A discursive perspective on legitimation strategies in multinational corporations. In: Academy of Management Review 33, 4, S. 985–993.

van Leeuwen, Theo/Wodak, Ruth (1999): Legitimizing immigration control: A discourse-historical analysis. In: Discourse Studies 1, 1, S. 83–118.

VDMA (2021): Der VDMA-Hochschulpreis. https://www.vdma.org/v2viewer/-/v2article/render/18737903 [Zugriff: 31.01.2021].

ver.di (2016): First law amending the law on fixed-term employment contracts in the science and research sector. Joint opinion issued by the National Working Groups on University, Students, and Research, of the Executive Board of the National Sector of Education, Science and Research in the United Services Trade Union, ver.di, on the. Fachbereichsinformationen.

Viebahn, Peter (2009): Lernerverschiedenheit im Studium. Ein Konzept zu einer großen didaktischen Herausforderung. In: Das Hochschulwesen, 2, 38-44.

Vollstedt, Maike/Rezat, Sebastian (2019): An introduction to grounded theory with a special focus on axial coding and the coding paradigm. In: Kaiser, G./Presmeg, N. C. (Hrsg.): Compendium for early career researchers in mathematics education. ICME-13 Monographs. Cham, Switzerland: Springer, S. 81–100.

Waeraas, Arild/Nielsen, Agger (2016): Translation theory 'translated': Three perspectives on translation in organizational research. In: International Journal of Management Reviews 18, 3, S. 236–270.

Wæraas, Arild/Sataøen, Hogne L. (2014): Trapped in conformity? Translating reputation management into practice. In: Scandinavian Journal of Management 30, 2, S. 242–253.

Walgenbach, Katharina (2014): Heterogenität. Bedeutungsdimensionen eines Begriffs. In: Koller, H.-C./Casale, R./Ricken, N. (Hrsg.): Heterogenität. Zur Konjunktur eines pädagogischen Konzepts. Paderborn: Ferdinand Schöningh, S. 19–44.

Wanka, Johanna (2013): Vorwort. In: Aufstieg durch Bildung. Bilanz und Perspektiven für Deutschland, S. 5.

Watson, David (2006): How to think about widening participation in UK higher education. Discussion paper for HEFCE. Seminar Series on Mass Higher Education in UK and International Contexts.

Weick, Karl E. (1976): Educational organizations as loosely coupled systems. In: Administrative Science Quarterly 21, S. 1–19.

Weick, Karl E. (1979): The social psychology of organizing. Reading, MA: Addison Wesley.

Weick, Karl E. (1993): The collapse of sensemaking in organizations: The Mann Gulch disaster. In: Administrative Science Quarterly 38, 4, S. 628–652.

Weick, Karl E. (1995): Sensemaking in organizations. Thousand Oaks, London, New Delhi: Sage Publications.

Weick, Karl E./Sutcliffe, Kathleen M./Obstfeld, David (2005): Organizing and the process of sensemaking. In: Organization Science 16, 4, S. 409–421.

Wendt, Peter-Ulrich (2009): Grounded Theory. Working paper.

Wiegand, Martin (1996): Prozesse Organisationalen Lernens. Neue betriebswirtschaftliche Forschung, Band 174. Wiesbaden: Gabler.

Wielepp, Franziska (2013): Heterogenität. Herausforderung der Hochschulbildung im demografischen Wandel. In: Pasternack, P. (Hrsg.): Jenseits der Metropolen. Hochschulen in demografisch herausgeforderten Regionen. Leipzig: Akademische Verlagsanstalt, S. 363–386.

Wild, Elke/Esdar, Wiebke (2014): Eine heterogenitätsorientierte Lehr-/Lernkultur für eine Hochschule der Zukunft. Fachgutachten im Auftrag des Projektes nexus der Hochschulrektorenkonferenz.

Wildt, Johannes (1985): Zum Umgang mit Heterogenität: Didaktische Modelle für den Studienanfang. In: Welzel, A. (Hrsg.): Heterogenität oder Elite: Hochschuldidaktische Perspektiven für den Übergang Schule - Hochschule. Weinheim, Basel: BELTZ, S. 91–115.

Wilkesmann, Uwe et al. (2012): Abweichungen vom Bild der Normalstudierenden – Was erwarten Studierende? In: Kerres, M. et al. (Hrsg.): Studium 2020. Positionen und Perspektiven zum Lebenslangen lernen an Hochschulen. Münster, New York, München, Berlin: Waxmann Verlag, S. 59–81.

Wilkesmann, Uwe (2016a): Methoden und Daten zur Erforschung spezieller Organisationen: Hochschulen. In: Liebig, S./Matiaske, W./Rosenbohm, S. (Hrsg.): Handbuch Empirische Organisationsforschung: Springer Reference Wirtschaft, S. 1–24.

Wilkesmann, Uwe (2016b): Teaching matters, too: different ways of governing a disregarded institution. In: Leisyte, L./Wilkesmann, U. (Hrsg.): Organizing academic work in higher education. Teaching, learning, and identities. London, New York: Routledge, S. 33–54.

Wilkesmann, Uwe (2019): Methoden der Hochschulforschung. Eine methodische, erkenntnis- und organisationstheoretische Einführung. Weinheim: Beltz Juventa.

Wilkesmann, Uwe/Schmid, Christian J. (2012): Vorwort. In: Wilkesmann, U./Schmid, C. J. (Hrsg.): Hochschule als Organisation. Wiesbaden: VS Verlag für Sozialwissenschaften, S. 7–14.

Wilkesmann, Uwe/Würmseer, Grit (2009): Lässt sich Lehre an Hochschulen steuern? Auswirkungen von Governance-Strukturen auf die Hochschullehre. In: Die Hochschule 2, S. 33–46.

Wilson, Thomas P. (1970): Conceptions of interaction and forms of sociological explanation. In: American Sociological Review 35, 4, S. 697–710.

Wirtschaftslexikon (2018): Revision von Web 2.0. https://wirtschaftslexikon.gabler.de/definition/web-20-51842/version-274993.

Wissenschaftsrat (2006): Empfehlungen zur künftigen Rolle der Universitäten im Wissenschaftssystem.

Wissenschaftsrat (2010): Empfehlungen zur Differenzierung der Hochschulen. Lübeck.

Wissenschaftsrat (2013): Perspektiven des deutschen Wissenschaftssystems. Braunschweig.

Wissenschaftsrat (2021): Über uns. https://www.wissenschaftsrat.de/DE/Ueber-uns/Wissenschaftsrat/wissenschaftsrat_node.html.

Wolter, Andrä (2011): Hochschulzugang und soziale Ungleichheit in Deutschland. In: Öffnung der Hochschule. Chancengerechtigkeit, Diversität, Integration. Dossier, S. 9–15.

Wolter, Andrä (2012): Die Öffnung für Berufstätige als Beitrag zur Diversität der Hochschule. In: journal hochschuldidaktik 23, 1-2, S. 23–25.

Wolter, Andrä (2013a): Gleichrangigkeit beruflicher Bildung beim Hochschulzugang? Neue Wege der Durchlässigkeit zwischen beruflicher Bildung und Hochschule. In: Severing, E./Teichler, U. (Hrsg.): Akademisierung der Berufswelt? Bonn: Bundesinstitut für Berufsbildung, S. 191–212.

Wolter, Andrä (2013b): Massification and diversity: Has the expansion of higher education led to a changing composition of the student body? European and German experiences. In: Zgaga, P. et al. (Hrsg.): Higher education reform: Looking back - looking forward. Higher Education Research and Policy. Frankfurt am Main: Peter Lang, S. 149–172.

Wolter, Andrä et al. (2014): Durchlässigkeit zwischen beruflicher und akademischer Bildung als mehrstufiges Konzept: Bilanz und Perspektiven. In: Beiträge zur Hochschulforschung 36, 4, S. 8–38.

Wolter, Andrä/Banscherus, Ulf/Kamm, Caroline (Hrsg.) (2016): Zielgruppen Lebenslangen Lernens an Hochschulen. Münster, New York: Waxmann.

Würmseer, Grit (2010): Auf dem Weg zu neuen Hochschultypen. Wiesbaden: VS Verlag für Sozialwissenschaften.

Yin, Robert K. (2003): Case study research. Design and methods. Third Edition. Thousand Oaks: Sage Publications.

Zacher, Hannes (2018): Keine Pauschalurteile über Studierende. In: Forschung & Lehre 25, 8.

Zucker, Lynne G. (1977): The role of institutionalization in cultural persistence. In: American Sociological Review 42, 5, S. 726–743.

Index

C
case study design 109-112
Czarniawska 21, 56, 68, 70ff, 101-104, 108-109, 114,159, 173, 221, 227
coding paradigm 123-125,189, 223

D
discourse 24, 35ff, 44ff, 215-218, 226, 229, 236
diversity paradigms 94ff, 178-179, 183-184, 187-188, 217, 222

E
editing rules 73-74, 160ff, 220-221, 227

Q
quality criteria 22, 125ff, 132

S
Sahlin-Andersson 46, 64, 73-74, 76, 103, 112, 128, 159ff, 227-228, 235
Scandinavian institutionalism, 70ff, 76ff, 112, 159, 227-228, 231-235

T
travel of ideas 71ff, 128

W
Weick, 13, 16, 21, 60, 64, 71-72, 75-76, 108-109, 220

www.ingramcontent.com/pod-product-compliance
Lightning Source LLC
Jackson TN
JSHW011344070125
76711JS00013B/129